THE VOICE OF THE IRISH

THE VOICE OF
THE IRISH

by Blanche Mary Kelly

Professor of English
College of Mt. St. Vincent

SHEED & WARD · NEW YORK · 1952

*Manufactured in the United States of America
by The Haddon Craftsmen, Inc., Scranton, Pa.*

"I TOOK ROOT IN AN HONOURABLE PEOPLE"

FOREWORD

This book has been written with the two-fold purpose of assembling the essential facts of Irish literary history within the compass of a single volume, in order to present the characteristic qualities of Irish literature properly so called, and of showing in its proper relief and perspective one phase of the literary history commonly associated with Ireland, the so-called Irish Renaissance.

The very term *renaissance* implies a cultural restoration, but to many people, even some of Irish descent, the phrase *Irish Rennaissance* must constitute a contradiction in terms, since to the best of their knowledge, Ireland never had a culture worth restoring, and is only accorded a place among the cultured peoples of the world by grace of the achievements of a group of modern writers whose medium is English, not Irish. A superficial acquaintance with the movement which they represent serves only to confirm this impression, since such an acquaintance takes no thought of the implications of the word *Irish*, nor inquires to what extent it is applicable to their work.

Closer scrutiny, however, reveals certain facts, most of them indisputable, but many of them so generally unrecognized as to warrant the presentation which I have undertaken in this book. These facts are:

(1) that Ireland once possessed a culture of ancient origin and of an exceptionally high order;

(2) that that culture bore upon it certain racially characteristic marks, in virtue of which it was warrantably called Celtic or Irish, and as a consequence of which it is only reasonable to expect that the same marks should be discernible in any culture that professes to reproduce the ancient pattern;

(3) that that ancient culture was deliberately and systematically destroyed, together with the order of things by which it was produced;

(4) that despite that destruction, the Irish love of the things of the mind was never uprooted, but persisted under the most adverse conditions until such time as it might again bear fruit;

(5) that under favorable circumstances it has borne fruit, so that for more than a hundred years there has been going forward in Ireland a renewal of intellectual and literary activity, stamped with the age-old racial marks;

(6) that the so-called Renaissance, far from bearing these marks, is for the most part stamped with those of the alien force which destroyed Irish civilization and sought to destroy the race itself, and hence is not in any true sense either Irish or a real renaissance.

With these facts in mind I have sought in this book, although the attempt is necessarily inadequate, to describe and analyze the native Irish culture, to account for its disappearance, to chronicle its restoration, and to examine the extent to which the Renaissance may warrantably be included in that restoration.

I have endeavoured, perhaps at the risk of defeating my chief purpose, to refrain from entering into the details of Irish history, especially Irish political history, although a knowledge of the subject is necessary to an understanding of Irish literary history, not only because the literature has been shaped and coloured by those facts, but also because most so-called Irish historical writing is a distortion or a misrepresentation of them. In the course of the following pages I have attempted to show where the truth is to be found.

For help in the preparation of this book I am indebted to many persons. In expressing that indebtedness I must mention first my Irish forebears, who brought from enslaved Ireland a burning love for freedom, so that an ardent love for the country they had left, remembrance of her matchless beauty and her heroic spirit became an integral part of their staunch Americanism. Next on the list of benefactors comes the late Rev. Thomas J. Campbell, S. J.,

who many years ago kindled the imagination of a young girl
from the fire of the bardic stories and thus opened up a world of
which she forthwith became a denizen.

It would be impossible to evaluate what I owe to the late
Monsignor William J. Livingstone, distinguished Irish scholar, the
bequest of whose books to the college of whose faculty I was by
that time a member, provided me, to him unknown, with a wealth
of resources to which otherwise I could scarcely have had access.
In writing this book I cannot but feel that I have done, although
poorly, what he must have intended to do, because in using his
books I have found myself walking in his intellectual footsteps,
and I know I have not betrayed my guide.

There is personal affection as well as gratitude in my acknowl-
edgements to the Sister librarians of the college since their
unfailing kindness has not only provided me with additional
books, but caused the Irish Room to be recognized and respected
as the place of my habitual abode.

To the late Rev. John J. Wynne, S.J., to my colleague and
friend Gabriel Liegey, to Dr. Katherine McSweeney I am indebted for the gift of necessary books; to the President of the
Irish Historical Society for permission to make use of the Society's
fine library; to the staff of the Irish Industries Bureau in New
York, especially Miss Eileen O'Sullivan, for their zeal and cour-
tesy in procuring wanted items.

Only the resources of the Gaelic language could adequately
express my gratitude to my chief benefactor, the distinguished
scholar, Rev. James A. Geary, Associate Professor of Celtic Languages and Comparative Linguistics at the Catholic University
of America, who in the midst of his own truly colossal labours
has so carefully read the book in Ms. By his luminous and constructive criticism it has, I trust, profited. If it has not, the fault
is mine.

Stamford, N. Y.
September, 1951   *Blanche Mary Kelly*

Grateful acknowledgement is made to the following publishers for permission to quote from the books listed:

Clonmore & Reynolds, Ltd., *The Life and Legend of St. Patrick*, by Ludwig Bieler

Columbia University Press, *Sources of the Early History of Ireland*, by James F. Kenney

E. P. Dutton & Co., *Call for a Miracle*, by Benedict Kiely

W. H. Gill & Sons, *The Hidden Ireland*, by Daniel Corkery

Messrs. Victor Gollancz, Ltd., *Insurrection*, by Liam O'Flaherty

Harper & Brothers, *The Well of English*, by Blanche Mary Kelly

Henry Holt & Co., *The Wandering Scholars*, by Helen Waddell

Longmans, Green & Co., *The Flowering Dusk*, by Ella Young

Macmillan Co., *Collected Poems*, by W. B. Yeats, *The Three Brothers*, by Michael McLaverty

Oxford University Press, *The Real Charlotte*, by Somerville and Ross; *The Western Island*, by Robin Flower

Random House, *Famine*, by Liam O'Flaherty

Charles Scribner's Sons, *Axel's Castle*, by Edmund Wilson

Sheed & Ward, *Poor Scholar*, by Benedict Kiely; *Candle for the Proud*, by Francis MacManus

Talbot Press, *The Hedge Schools*, by P. J. Dowling

CONTENTS

Chapter I.[1] *INISFAIL*

There is honey in the trees where her misty vales expand,
And her forest paths in summer are by falling waters fanned,
There is dew at high noontide there and springs in the yellow sand,
   On the fair hills of holy Ireland.
               From the Irish, tr. FERGUSON

A DELIGHTFUL MIDDLE ENGLISH lyric extends an "invitation to
the dance" in the following words:

> I am of Irlaunde,
> And of the holy lande
>   Of Irlande.
> Good sir, pray I thee,
> For of saint charity
> Come and daunce with me
>   In Irlande.

The holy land of Ireland! The phrase, it is worth noting, occurs
in a fourteenth-century English MS, and not in an Irish source.
Perhaps there is nothing strange about this evidence of English
use of the phrase in the Middle Ages, when Ireland's reputation
for sanctity was so generally recognized, but it is remarkable

[1] Since this chapter was written, its contents have been almost entirely
discredited by the conclusions of Thomas F. O'Rahilly, Director of the
Dublin Institute for Advanced Studies, as set forth in his monumental work
Early Irish History and Mythology, published in Dublin in 1946. Since the
chapter as it stands rests upon the opinion of scholars to whom Professor
O'Rahilly accords respect, even though he takes issue with them, and since
it represents what most Irish writers accepted as the facts of Irish history
and legend which became the chief source of modern creative writing and
the cultural revival generally, it has seemed best to leave this chapter untouched, and to present Professor O'Rahilly's findings in the form of a Postscript to the chapter.

that the earliest recorded reference to the country, dating from a period more than three hundred years before Christ, should call it the sacred island of the Hibernians, without, however, explaining in what its sacredness consisted.

Hibernia, obviously a form of *Irin* or *Ierna,* names by which Ireland was commonly known to the ancients, was said to signify a Western land, although it has also been interpreted as a derivation of Heber, one of the sons of Milesius, just as *Irlandia* or the Plain of Ir has been traced to Ir, another son of the reputed founder of the Gaelic race. Still another son of Milesius, Amergin the druid, is credited with acceding to the requests of the Danann queens, Eriu, Banba and Fotla, that he bestow their names upon the country.[2] Down to the eleventh century of our era it was called Scotia, the Irish Gaels having been the original Scots, a name variously explained as of Scythian origin and as commemorating Scota, wife of a legendary Gaelic hero. A reference to the country's historical antiquity is found in Homer's *Ogygia,* meaning *very ancient.*

But the most significant of all Ireland's early appellations is Inisfail, Island of Destiny, a title based on the existence at Tara of the Lia Fail or Stone of Destiny, upon which the king stood during the coronation ceremonies. Whatever its origin, the term was unquestionably charged with prophetic import, for the fortunes of Ireland have been unique in human history, so singular, so fraught with mystery, that there is no understanding them except in terms of destiny amounting to predilection.

What is now generally recognized as legendary in Irish history was for centuries accepted as authentic fact, largely because among the ancient Irish the preservation of historical, especially genealogical, records, was regarded as an almost sacred duty, but these matters are now approached in a more scientific spirit. The results of the approach, however, do not amount to any wholesale discrediting of the records, but rather to a new understanding of them and in some instances even to a clearer realization of their historical accuracy.

[2] Henri d'Arbois de Jubainville, *The Irish Mythological Cycle and Celtic Mythology,* p. 143.

The history of Ireland, therefore, resembles the history of other countries in the legendary and even mythical character of its earliest chapters, which naturally enough are concerned with the country's first inhabitants. According to these accounts, Ireland was successively invaded at a remote and indeterminate period of time by several races, of whom the fifth, and, as matters turned out, the most important, was the Gaelic[3] or Irish race. Since these invasions are not only the subject of a voluminous collection of writings,[4] but also the occasion of many literary allusions, they have an obvious bearing on Irish literature in general.

According to legend, the first invasion was led by one Partholan, whose descendants, after a period of 300 years, at which time they numbered 2000, died of a pestilence within the space of a single week, leaving one of their number, Tuan mac Caraill, to survive in many forms until the time of St. Patrick. This was obviously a device of the narrator for the purpose of bringing the Partholanian invasion within the range of recorded history. Another legend lists first the abortive invasion of Cessair, granddaughter of Noah, who, for her attempt to escape the Deluge, the prediction of which she had at first flouted, was overtaken by it, and drowned off the Irish coast with all her company, except her husband, Fintan. He, like Tuan, lived on to tell the story to later generations.

Next, that is second in the series of invaders, came a group under the leadership of Nemedius. After establishing themselves in the country, the Nemedians had to withstand the attacks of a race of pirates called Fomorians, a savagely cruel people, who exterminated most of the Nemedians and drove the survivors out of the country. These survivors went to Greece, where they became a subject people, to whom was given the name Firbolgs (men of the bags), from their custom of carrying earth in bags for the enrichment of the barren Grecian soil to which they had been relegated.

After a period of some 300 years the Firbolgs returned to

[3] I have not used the term *Milesian* for reasons explained below. See Postscript to this chapter.
[4] Cf. O'Curry, *Ancient MSS Materials*.

Ireland, whose possession they contested with their ancient enemy, the Fomorians, eventually driving them from the country, so that they were forced to take up their abode on Tory Island, off the coast of Galway. From this stronghold the Fomorians repeatedly made incursions on the mainland, especially for the purpose of harrying and exacting tribute from the Tuatha De Danann when that race had succeeded the Firbolgs in the domination of the country. The Tuatha De Danann have sometimes been identified with another branch of the Nemedian race who were driven out of Ireland at the same time as the Firbolgs, with whom they returned to do battle for the domination of the country and to defeat them in the battle of Moytura. The Firbolgs, however, were not annihilated in this battle, since a remnant lived on side by side with the De Dananns, to whose superiority they were so completely deferential as to have been instrumental in building up the Danann reputation for the possession of preternatural qualities.[5]

Finally, at a period usually set at about 1000 years before Christ, came the Milesians, sons and kindred of Golamh (the Hero, Latinized *Milesius*), whose arrival even legend seeks to endow with historical certainty by linking it with Christian chronology. The Milesian leaders, Heremon, Heber and Ir, first worsted the Danann in a contest of magical arts and then defeated them at Tailtenn in a contest of arms. In consequence of this victory the Milesians assumed possession and domination of the country, bestowing upon it through the agency of another son of Milesius, the druid, Amergin, the several names by which it was known in ancient times and by which it is still known to the poets, Eriu (whence Eire), Fotla and Banba,[6] and assigning to the defeated Dananns their "half" of Ireland, namely all that lay underground, especially in the interior of the hills. For this reason the Danann came to be known as people of the hills, or *Sidhe* (Gaelic for hill, pronounced *shee*), and by a long process of deterioration to be identified with the fairies. The Milesian share in this transaction was the "half" that lay above ground.

[5] Cf. de Jubainville, op. cit.
[6] Ibid.

That there were pre-Celtic dwellers in Ireland is a well-established fact. To the Continental Celts they were known as Crui-thni,[7] who have been identified as Picts, a people whose racial origin is shrouded in mystery, but whose social institutions were to some extent absorbed by the Celts.

Much of the legendary lore which concerns the Dananns constituted the religious belief of the pagan Irish and as such will be dealt with below. Modern scholarship dismisses as baseless most of what is related of the early invaders, though it must be said that legend itself, even fairy legend, has provided many modern scholars with an occasion for serious, even scientific study, and inspired many a learned treatise. The story of Cessair is dismissed as an invention of Christian scribes, and historians likewise cast doubt on the very existence of the Fomorians, who, it is contended, if they ruled over the country for 300 years, should have left upon it some enduring mark, whereas the only material phenomenon with which their name is associated is the Giants' Causeway, whose 40,000 curiously shaped columns of basalt rock are explained by our scientific age in terms of geological shrinkage.

Modern historians, however, do not include the Fomori and the Tuatha De Danann among the invaders, because they do not regard them as mortals, but as beings possessed of supernatural powers, nature gods taken over by the Gaels from older races. According to this theory the Fomorians were "gods of Death, of Night and of Storm, the elder of the two divine groups that share the veneration of the Celtic race."[8] They were, according to another authority, gods of baleful darkness out of the chill North or the gloom of Tory Island, "demon bringers of pestilence, gods of monstrosity, of death and night and storm."[9] The Dananns, on the other hand, were "gods of Life, of Day, of Sunshine,"[10] "good folk of light and comeliness and benevolence,"[11] who came to Ireland without boats, bringing with them

[7] See Postscript.
[8] de Jubainville, op. cit., p. 59.
[9] A. S. Green, *History of the Irish State to 1014*, p. 15.
[10] de Jubainville, op. cit.
[11] Green, op. cit.

wonderful treasures for the enrichment and happiness of the
Milesian race, among them the Lia Fail, or Stone of Destiny, the
Cauldron of Plenty and Spear of Victory.[12]

Many theories are advanced by historians concerning the origin
of the Milesians. Certainly every effort has been made by modern
writers to strip away from their story every vestige of legend in
order to reach a kernel of truth, with the result that little is left
beyond the incontestable fact of their existence. Professor Eoin
MacNeill, a dependable because so learned and so dispassionate
a guide, pares even that statement down to the assertion that
there is no such thing as a Milesian race,[13] and that all that can
safely be maintained of the men who at some remote period of
time colonized Ireland and stamped their racial personality
ineffaceably upon it is that they were Celts, the term *Celtic*
signifying not so much race as language, in this instance the
Gaelic.

So insistent is Professor MacNeill on this point that he maintains that there is not today in Ireland or elsewhere any Celtic
race in the sense of inherited physical characteristics. But that
Professor Edmund Curtis does not share Dr. MacNeill's objection to the term *Milesian* is evident from the fact that he found
it possible to write in 1936: "To be of the old Milesian strain is
an honourable distinction."[14] For that matter, it is only to the
pedantry which he detects in the word *Milesian* that Dr. Mac-
Neill objects, for of the race which the word is commonly used
to describe he says: "In ancient Ireland alone we find the autobiography of a people of European white men who come into
history not moulded into the mould of the complex East nor
forced to accept the law of imperial Rome; Christian indeed
when that record first comes to be written down, yet accepting
Christianity freely with all the freedom that is possible to men."[15]

Christian they were in the period to which Dr. MacNeill refers,

[12] Ella Young, *Celtic Wonder Tales.*
[13] "The term *Milesian* ought to be discarded as a mere pedantic substitute
for Gaelic" (*Celtic Ireland*, p. 3, n.).
[14] *History of Ireland.*
[15] *Celtic Ireland*, p. 11.

the period in which they began to set down in writing the historical records which had hitherto been preserved by tradition, but even as pagans they had developed a civilization which does not suffer too much even in comparison with that of Greece, to which it is in some particulars even superior. That civilization was characterized by the development of institutions, the possession of even a few of which has warranted in many another race the boast of cultural maturity.

To begin with, the ancient Irish had a political organization. There was once, as Professor Curtis points out, such a thing as an old Gaelic state, and, for good or ill, it was wholly Irish. The government of that state was monarchical, but there was no supreme or absolute ruler, even after the establishment of the high kingship. The provinces of Ulster, Connaught, Munster, and North and South Leinster constituted a Pentarchy of kingdoms (the Five Fifths), each of which was divided into sub-kingdoms or *Tuaths*, which eventually numbered about 1000. According to Dr. O'Rahilly, "the earliest division of Ireland was a quadruple one, Uisnech being regarded as the central point of Ireland and the meeting place of the four divisions or provinces. As a result of the Goidelic invasion of the Eastern Midlands another province was added; and henceforth the country was divided into five provinces, each called a *coiced* ('fifth part'). This division (Ulster, Connacht, Munster, Leinster, together with the Midland province), continued down to modern times, though naturally the provincial boundaries were liable to alteration with the passage of time."[16]

Since Ireland never formed part of the Roman Empire, her political framework did not resemble that of the feudal system. Mrs. Alice Stopford Green,[17] in this following earlier historians, makes the differences to consist in the existence in Ireland of a tribal or clan system, a theory with which Dr. MacNeill takes sharp issue. Not only, he insists, did the clan system never exist in Ireland, but neither was there, as has sometimes been asserted,

[16] *Op. cit.*, p. 181.
[17] *Irish Nationality.*

anything resembling communal tenure of land. The social organization of ancient Ireland was at once simple and complex,
simple because the various classes into which the people were
divided were definite enough, complex because the terms applied
to groups or classes were of variable meaning, the word *tuath*,
for example, meaning sometimes a state, sometimes a territory,
sometimes the rural population as contrasted with that of towns
(there were no cities in ancient Ireland).

In the Irish social system the unit was first of all the family
and then the commune, formed of a group of families. It held its
goods in common, but it was not an outgrowth of either the
feudal system, with its principle of primogeniture, to which the
ancient Irish attached no great importance, nor of a tribal system
involving communism. A family, according to Irish theory, consisted of five persons,—a man and his two sons and a son of each
of his sons, a family commune being made up of "four generations alive together."[18] Since the family property would be
re-allotted as its younger members came of age, the system, far
from being communistic, was, as MacNeill maintains, an extreme
form of private ownership.

Kingship was not hereditary in the feudal sense, but eligibility
to the kingship was hereditary in the sense that the choice was
limited to certain families from whom kings had already been
chosen. The charge that at the time of the Norman invasion of
Ireland the Irish had not progressed beyond the "tribal state"
is especially resented by Professor MacNeill, who realizes only
too clearly what a picture of aboriginal savagery the phrase
conjures up, while at the same time it conceals the reality of a
proud and cultivated aristocracy such as was maintained by the
lordly and victorious Celts. Besides, as Dr. MacNeill points out,
civilization and barbarism are relative terms. "Men," he writes,
"are barbarians in the degree to which they are dominated by
their non-human natural surroundings, and are civilised in the
degree to which they succeed in dominating these, including
among these all that lower nature within themselves that men

[18] MacNeill, *Celtic Ireland*, p. 159.

have in common with animals."[19] With such a definition in mind, it becomes obvious that the ancient Irish were far removed from barbarism.

In a subordinate position, ranging from that of wealthy free-men to landless laborers and slaves, were the members of the older subject races,[20] but in the course of time and especially under the influence of Christianity when it came, there developed a tendency to break down the barrier of race and class and to sink all such distinctions in a deep sense of national unity. Even the Christian Irish, however, it must be admitted, were char-acterized by a fierce racial pride, to which Professor MacNeill attributes the eventual downfall of their order: "The Irish nobility were perhaps the most intensely proud race of men that ever existed. This pride was bred in their bones. It came to them out of an immemorial past. . . . Two thousand years of unbroken sway may suffice to set pride above prudence in the tradition of any class."

It was a foolish, even a disastrous pride; from the Christian standpoint it was unquestionably culpable, but that even in the pagan Gaels it was not ignoble, is evident from the things in which they gloried when, after Tara had been established as the seat of the high kingship, an event which marked the end of the Pentarchy, the noble kindreds flocked thither in their splendour to attend the annual Feis. "This was the state in which fairs and assemblies were attended by the men of Erin in this time: Every king was clad in his royal robes, and with his golden helmet on his head, for they did not put on their royal crowns but on the field of battle only."[21] Now the purpose for which the high king, the provincial monarchs and the noble kindreds came together was a legislative assembly in which not only men of law but poets and scholars participated, and in which not only laws were enacted and reformed, but historical records rectified and at which there was great telling of epic tales and much making of

---

[19] *Early Irish Law and Institutions*, p. 49.
[20] Green, *Irish State to 1014*.
[21] This is quoted by O'Curry from a description in the *Book of Ballymote*.

music on the pipes, the harp and the flute, and much poetic production.

For if the class distinctions to which reference has been made seem like a petty form of pride, even snobbery, it must be borne in mind that in ancient Ireland the highest class of all was honoured not for birth or power or material possessions, but for learning and artistry. Cormac, greatest of the legendary pagan kings, was the more highly esteemed for his wisdom and his learning, for the books he wrote and the schools he endowed, his respect for men of learning being expressed in the fact that it was he who decreed that all future kings should be constantly accompanied by certain representatives of the learned class.

Various functions later divided among a number of persons who together constituted this class were at first merged in the druid, the official representative of a system called druidism, although precisely what it consisted in seems impossible to say with any degree of clearness or certainty. Long described as a religion of which the druid was the priest, it is no longer so regarded by the best authorities. "The druid was not a priest," declares Professor MacNeill.

That the pagan Irish had some kind of religious belief is indisputable. Apparently it was a form of nature worship which involved ceremonial rites, including sacrifice (but not human sacrifice), although the ancient Irish seem to have had no temples. The druid is sometimes referred to as participating in that sacrifice, but never as offering it. St. Patrick is described as having overthrown only one idol, Crom Cruach, and the group of lesser images by which it was surrounded, but there is no indication of the manner in which Crom Cruach, apparently a sinister and terrible deity, was worshipped. The real gods of the ancient Irish were the Dananns, "shaped by men who never worshipped them."

The great Celtic scholar, Zimmer, was of the opinion that the Irish pantheon was as highly organized as the Germanic, a theory which is scarcely tenable, although it is possible to draw a parallel, as de Jubainville has done, between certain members of the Danann race and the deities of other races, the Greeks, for example. Without entering into the details of a theory that for all its interest and importance is not relevant to the present subject, it seems in order to mention a few of the Gaelic gods or half-gods. First of all there was Dana herself, from whom the De Dananns derived their name as people of the goddess Dana (or Ana), the mother of the gods. The Dagda, meaning the great god, was "an Irish Jupiter."[22] His son, Aengus, called the Young, was a god of youth and love; his daughter Brigit, the goddess of poetry; while Mannanan was a combination of Proteus and Neptune, without any of their more fearsome aspects. Other important beings were Diancecht, the god of healing, Lugh, a kind of sun-god, whose father was Cian, son of Diancecht, and his mother Ethlin, daughter of the Fomorian king, Balor of the Evil Eye.

In addition to these more or less benevolent deities (and of course these names are far from exhausting the list), the Gaels also paid the tribute of fear and horror to certain beings, such as the war goddesses, Anann, Bodb (the Morrigan or Crow of Battle), and Macha, beings at least as dread of aspect and terrible of portent as the Furies or the Valkyrie. The Gaelic belief contrived to hold the De Dananns in awe as a superior race and at the same time to conceive of them as a conquered race, condemned in virtue of what amounted to a bit of sharp practice on the part of Amergin to reside henceforth in the interior of the hills, generally invisible, but occasionally manifesting themselves in visible form, usually with kindly intent, to certain of the Irish. To some men, indeed, one or other of the elder race stood almost in the character of guardian or protector, as Aengus to Diarmuid. In the process of becoming identified with the fairies the old gods lost their superhuman stature and beauty and shrank to a size which permits them to be called "the little people." They are also known as "the good people," but this is by way of placating their well-known power of working mischief and their will to do so, which would seem to indicate that in the process they have also lost their original character of benevolence and acquired some of the traits of their enemies, the Fomorians, but on a smaller scale.

[22] Douglas Hyde, *Literary History of Ireland*, p. 48.

The De Dananns had dwelling places other than Ireland and its hills, another plane of existence which made them independent of the earthly and the mortal, happy countries which are called by various names such as Tir-na-noge (Land of the Young, of Everlasting Youth, of the Ever-Living Living Ones), Tir-na-mbeo (Land of the Ever Living), Moy Mell (Plain of Pleasure), Tir-fa-tonn (Land under Wave), and Hy-Brasil, the Island of the Blessed, a dim far country, discernible every seven years shining jewel-like upon the surface of the sea. Such as they are, these ideas do not compare unfavourably with other pagan conceptions of immortality, with the dark regions over which Pluto presided or the Elysian Fields amid which Aeneas sought his father. "They [the Irish]," writes Dr. Hyde, "certainly believed in a happy Other-World, peopled by a happy race, whither people were sometimes carried while still alive."[23] The most famous instance of such a sojourn in that world is that to which Oisin was persuaded by Niamh, but others who visited the Land of Youth were Connla of the Golden Hair and, under different circumstances, his father, Conn of the Hundred Battles.

To what extent such beliefs were incorporated in druidism is impossible to say, but they must have been at least implicit in it. Druidism itself, however, seems to have been not a religion but a culture, whose official representatives, the druids, were at first the sole members of the learned class, "the exclusive possessors of whatever learning was then known,"[24] combining in themselves the offices of judge, poet, historian and musician. When the druids sank to the level of wizards, the scholarly functions they had discharged were apportioned among a number of persons who thenceforth constituted the learned class (*fili*), and until the fall of the Gaelic order in 1603 the members of this class were the hereditary keepers of ancient lore and learning (Curtis), and so highly regarded that it is recorded that in Erin only three sorts of persons were permitted to speak in public, a chronicler, a bard and a brehon.

It was the duty of the brehon or judge to explain and interpret

[23] Op. cit., p. 96.
[24] Joyce, *Social History of Ancient Ireland*, I, p. 222.

the laws and to act as the king's advisor in these matters. For one of the distinctive marks of the ancient Gaelic state, even while it was pagan, was that it was governed by law. The original Irish jurists were the druids, the origin of the science of jurisprudence having been credited to the druid, Amergin.

The so-called Brehon Laws do not constitute what is called a Code, in the modern sense, but they were none the less a national system of law, applicable throughout the country, but carried into effect by each state separately. They were not issued by any individual or body possessed of legislative powers or authority. The *Senchus Mor*, which is attributed to St. Patrick, is a compilation of already existing laws, including "every law which prevailed among the men of Erin, through the law of nature, and the law of the seers, and in the judgments of the island of Erin, and in the poets."[25] The Law was therefore a Digest rather than a Code, the knowledge and interpretation of which was the prerogative of the brehons. But the fact that the laws were not promulgated by a legislative body with power to command and to enforce sanctions does not mean that they were not binding. They were what is called customary law, by which even the kings were bound.

The early brehon had of necessity to carry these laws in his memory, and since his pronouncements were couched in language which grew increasingly archaic, as legal terminology has a tendency to do, it will be readily understood that he came to have a mysterious character, partly it is true, inherited from the druids, and to be regarded as divinely inspired.[26]

Not only did ancient Ireland possess an hereditary caste of men thus skilled in the law, but schools of law were maintained for the training and preservation of that caste, so that when Irish law came to be written it was the product of such schools and of immemorial tradition. In the description of the contents of the *Senchus Mor*, it will have been noted that poets are included

[25] *Ancient Laws of Erin*, Introduction to *Senchus Mor*, Pt. III.
[26] *Book of Rights*, ed. O'Donovan, 1847. Cf. MacNeill, *Celtic Ireland*, p. 73; Idem, *Early Irish Laws and Institutions*, passim; Idem, *Phases of Irish History*, p. 274; Sophie Bryant, *Liberty, Order and Law under Ancient Irish Rule*, passim.

among the sources of the laws thus brought together, a fact which will occasion no surprise to anyone who is at all acquainted with the characteristics of that ancient culture, in which it was customary to cast the most learned treatises into poetic form (the whole of the *Book of Rights,* for example, is in verse). Moreover, the poet or bard shared the semi-sacred and privileged character of the druid or the brehon, of whom he sometimes took precedence.

The existence of the Brehon Law is alone sufficient evidence of the Irish effort to dominate the lower aspects of human nature, and a proof that even in ancient times the Irish were a civilized people.

POSTSCRIPT TO CHAPTER I.

Professor O'Rahilly's purpose in writing his monumental work, *Early Irish History and Mythology,* was to correct a generally erroneous idea of early Irish historical writings by refuting the pseudo-historical statements of the *Lebor Gábala* (*Lebor Gabdla Erenn,* the Book of the Conquests of Ireland). This is a compilation dating from the eighth century onwards, containing what purports to be the history of pre-Christian Ireland, including an account of the successive invasions of the country from a point preceding the Deluge, and a list of the Kings of Ireland from the time of the Firbolgs to the introduction of Christianity.

Professor O'Rahilly calls this compilation "a deliberate work of fiction," whose purpose was to exalt the Goidelic racial strain by pushing the Goidelic invasion into the remote past, by describing the earlier invasions as non-Goidelic and designating them as those of Partholan, Nemed and the Domnainn. Its compilers, adds O'Rahilly, even "invented another invasion, that of the Tuatha de Danann, with the deliberate intention of reducing the faded deities of pagan Ireland to the status of mere mortals."[27] Their object was "to provide a fictitious antiquity for the Goidels and a fictitious Goidelic descent for the Irish generally."[28]

The Goidelic invasion they placed under the leadership of the

[27] Op. cit., p. 194.
[28] Ibid., p. 267.

sons of Mil, Eber and Eremon, whose place of origin was said to be Spain, the same "learned" theorizing deriving the name Hibernia from Iberia. The number of Mil's sons was increased to four by borrowing from Irish mythology the figure of Donn, who, under the name of Eber Donn, is occasionally confused with Eber, and Amergin.

In his presentation of the facts, which is made not by mere assertion but by an almost overwhelming array of scholarly evidence based on philological and ethnological research, Professor O'Rahilly recognizes four authentic invasions of Ireland, all of them Celtic. Dismissing that of Partholan as "a learned invention," he lists these invasions, as follows:

1. The Cruthin, who under the name of *Pretani* or *Pritani* were known to early Greek geographers. (The Cruthin of Scotland, where they were much more prominent, were commonly known as Picts.)

2. The Builg (recognized by O'Rahilly as an offshoot of the Belgae), commonly known as Fir Bolg and also as Erainn. This group he shows clearly to have had historical existence, dismissing as "childishly fantastic" the various theories regarding their origin and their name, which have been accepted by some of the most distinguished of Irish scholars. His explanation is that they took their name from a deity called Bolg, who was also venerated as their ancestor, a being whom O'Rahilly easily identifies with both the lightning and the sun, both of which phenomena were accorded divine honours.

This invasion of the Fir Bolg or Erainn, which O'Rahilly identifies with that of Nemed, listed as second by the *Lebor Gábala*, he assigns to the sixth-fourth centuries B.C.

3. The Laginian invasion, which included, besides the Lagin themselves, who gave their name to the province of Leinster, the Domnainn and the Galioin. All of these O'Rahilly regards as one people, although of slightly different origin, whose arrival in Ireland he sets at the third century B.C., and who, after their arrival, settled in different parts of Ireland, as the Domnainn, largely in Connacht.

4. The Goidels, who in O'Rahilly's opinion came to Ireland

from Gaul within the years 150-50 B.C. Not only does he reject the
story of the Milesian invasion, but he also dismisses as unhis-
torical most of the royal pedigrees, declaring that Loegaire is
"the first King of Ireland of whom we know with reasonable
accuracy the dates of both his accession . . . and his death."[29]

He shows further how much of legend and myth is mixed with
what has been accepted as history even by modern scholars,
explaining the fabulous character of much of Irish history as
euhemerism, that is, "treating divine beings as if they were men
of a far-off age." On this basis he rejects any claim to historicity
on behalf of either the Ulster or the Fenian cycle of tales. In
some ways the chapters devoted to the mythological ideas which
are the basis of that literature are the most interesting in the
book, because for the most part their legendary character has
been pretty generally recognized, a fact which does not in the
least impair their literary importance nor detract from their
significance as a source of literary inspiration.

From the data established by O'Rahilly it follows, not only
that much of what so long passed for history and genealogy is not
only unreliable but false, and that most of what has hitherto been
believed concerning the diffusion of races in Ireland, as well
as the organization of its pre-Christian social and political fabric,
cannot be accepted. At the same time he affirms the reliability of
the Irish records which begin immediately after the introduction
of Christianity. These, he affirms, "give us fact." Furthermore,
with regard to the *Lebor Gábala* itself, he takes issue with such
a view as that of d'Arbois de Jubainville, who treated it as a kind
of Irish theogony. "It is no more a mythological treatise than it is
a historical one."

This attempt to give in a few brief paragraphs the substance
of so scholarly and epoch-making a book borders on impertinence.
I could scarcely have ventured it except that it would have been
a worse impertinence not to have called attention to the extent
to which the contents of this chapter have been affected by its
publication. Merely to have deleted the chapter would, it seemed
to me, have been further to falsify the picture.

[29] Ibid., p. 209.

Chapter II. *THE GAY AND GALLANT GAEL*

When the gay and gallant Gael were alive in the land,
The lays were lightning flashes, the lore a blazing brand;
Brave and bright-eyed princes met bards with honour grand—
When the gay and gallant Gael were alive in the land.

From the Irish, tr. SIGERSON

THE MENTION OF the poet with whom the chronicler or historian was not only closely associated but often identified, brings us to the subject of literature proper. St. Patrick was long credited with the introduction of script into the country, so that it was consequently maintained that the pagan Irish had no written literature, the Ogham alphabet, with whose existence scholars were familiar, being considered suitable only for inscriptions. However, it is now contended[1] that the pagan Irish did have books, and that they may even have had a knowledge of classical literature.

Their native learning, as is clear from what has been said about the law, was transmitted by oral tradition, since the Ogham alphabet (so called because supposedly the invention of the god Ogma) was a system of dots and lines incised along the edge of wooden or stone shafts, and hence used chiefly for inscriptions. This restriction is credited to the druids' unwillingness that their doctrines should become widely diffused.

Whether or not St. Patrick introduced the art of writing, and the present evidence seems to be against that theory, it is nevertheless true that the form in which the literature of Irish pagan-

[1] Cf. especially Graham, *Early Irish Monastic Schools*, p. 9.

17

ism has come down to us was given to it by Christian scribes, and
that in the beautiful Gaelic script which has become so renowned.
In that script there was recorded and preserved a body of literature which describes the life of the pagan Gaels, which assuredly
originated in the pre-Christian era, and of which some knowledge
is absolutely essential to an understanding of subsequent literary
history.

Of primary importance is the fact that this literature was
written in Gaelic, the language of the Celts, which centuries
later Carleton was to describe as possessed of "the finest and most
copious vocabulary in the world for the expression of sorrow or
love," subjects which became part of this literary heritage from
the earliest times. As already noted, this language was the distinctive form of the Indo-European tongue spoken by the Celts.

It was, therefore, this cultivated and already ancient language
that was used by Christian scribes for the preservation of the
literature originally composed by pagan bards and *ollamhs*, and
hitherto preserved orally, a literature which despite a number
of inevitable Christian allusions, naturally depicts a pagan way
of life, lived against the background of that civilization of which
the preceding pages have attempted to convey some slight idea.

One of the most important characteristics of that civilization
was the existence, indeed, the maintenance, of a learned class,
whose members acquired their skill in various branches of
knowledge by a long and arduous process of training. The education of the druids, which was the basis of the ancient Irish
educational system, has been set by some authorities at as much
as twenty years. The bards, who generally acted as both poets
and chroniclers (their distinctive name was *ollamhs*), also,
especially after their poetic duties were separated from those of
the historians, underwent a long period of training at bardic
schools. In this case the course lasted twelve years, and involved
the mastery of the intricate and wholly Irish system of prosody,
as well as the knowledge of that great collection of romances and
chronicles, of which what has survived is, in the words of Dr.
Hyde, "an almost inappreciable fragment," although the whole

is "vastly more ancient and more numerous than anything that the rest of Europe has to show."[2]

This is not to say that this literary achievement, immense though it is, deserves to rank with that of Greece, for instance, for as Dr. Dunn[3] points out, these Tales never found their Homer. They rather correspond to that mine of literary ore which Homer wrought into enduring art, although even in its unworked condition the Irish is far in advance of *Beowulf* or the Scandinavian sagas. The Irish tales may not have found a Homer, but they did find generations of men to hand them on to the Christian scribes.

For although the form in which they have come down to us is the work of Christian writers, inasmuch as their subject is essentially pagan it will be briefly outlined here, in order that the essentially Christian literature of the later period may be separately appraised. It will be noted that in this connection the term *pre-Christian* refers not to the period before the birth of Christ, but to that prior to the conversion of Ireland.

This pagan literature is divided roughly into two periods, each marked by a characteristic cycle of Tales: the Ulster period, set chronologically at about the time of Christ, and depicted in the Red Branch or Ulidian cycle, and the Leinster period, set at about the middle of the fourth century, during the reign of King Cormac mac Art, and depicted in the Fenian cycle. Obviously what was handed on in these Tales was the substance and not the form. Those who wrote them, therefore, were not even as close to the conditions they depict as Homer was to the Trojan War, although Professor MacNeill is of the opinion that the Ulster cycle was committed to writing very early in the Christian period, while he dates most of the Fenian Tales from the ninth century of our era.[4]

Some idea of the extent of the training to which the ancient bards were subjected may be gleaned from the fact that they were required to be familiar with more than three hundred tales,

[2] *Literary History*, p. 263.
[3] Preface to his edition of the *Tain*.
[4] *Celtic Ireland*. Cf. his edition of *Duanaire Finn*.

foremost among which were the so-called Three Sorrows of Story-telling or the Three Sorrowful Tales of Erin. Of these the first two pertain to members of the De Danann race. These are the *Fate of the Children of Lir,* which relates the poignantly beautiful story of Fionnuala and her three brothers who were changed into swans by the evil wizardry of their stepmother, and in that guise obliged to spend three hundred years on each of three inland seas, until the sound of the Mass bell broke the evil spell, obviously a Christian interpolation; and the *Fate of the Children of Turann,* which describes the terrible penalty or eric-fine which Lugh exacted of Turann's sons for their slaying of his father, Cian. The third story, the *Fate of the Children of Usnach,* is one of the most memorable in the whole of this literature because it is primarily the story of Deirdre, to whom a great injustice is done when she is called, as she has been, the Irish Helen. It is true that she was dowered with great beauty of which it had been foretold that it would bring disaster to men, true also that her flight with Usnach's son, Naisi, precipitated that disaster, as Helen's flight with Paris caused the Trojan War and the destruction of Ilium, but the man with whom Deirdre fled was her husband and not a paramour, and it was by the treachery of King Conchobar, who unlawfully desired her, that she and her husband and his chivalrous brothers were brought at last to their doom.

These tales are the most important of the great Red Branch cycle of Tales, which center about the court of King Conchobar Mac Nessa, who was said to have reigned from the stronghold of Emain Macha in Ulster at about the time of the birth of Christ. The cycle derives its name from the Red Branch hall or structure in which Conchobar's courtiers, who in so many respects resemble the knights of Camelot, kept their armour and their weapons. Foremost among these warriors or champions, all of whom were said to have been of the race of Rury (supposedly a descendant of Miled's son Ir), was the great hero, Cuchulain, to whom was attributed a semi-divine paternity in the person of Lugh, his mother having been Conchobar's sister,

Dechtire, and his putative father, Setanta. Cuchulain is the very embodiment of the old Gaelic spirit, with his towering stature, attaining superhuman proportions under force of the "battle frenzy," his physical comeliness and splendour of countenance, his superb courage, his prowess in battle, his success in love and his high chivalry.

And Cuchulain is only one, although the greatest, of the Red Branch heroes, as the *Tain bo Cuailgne* (The Cattle-Raid of Cooley) is only one, although the greatest, of the Ulster cycle of Tales. This narrative, which is called by Dr. MacNeill "the greatest constructive composition in the Irish language," is not only of epic proportions, but numerous lesser Tains stand to it in the relation of introductory or supplementary material. By the reader unacquainted with Gaelic it should be read preferably in the distinguished translation of Dr. Joseph Dunn, who in his Preface describes its form as consisting of prose interspersed with rhymed and alliterated verse, and a third form known as the rosc, which is neither prose nor poetry.[5]

The *Tain* recounts the story of the war against Ulster under-taken by Maeve, the Amazonian queen of Connacht, for the purpose of seizing a priceless bull from one of Conchobar's sub-jects, in order to outmatch her husband's herd. In this she is joined by Fergus, step-father of Conchobar, out of chagrin for having been made instrumental in the betrayal of Deirdre and the sons of Usnach, and also by the champion, Ferdiad, who incidentally was of Firbolg stock, and in his youth had been the friend and companion in arms of Cuchulain. On the side of Ulster, alone for the most part, owing to certain circumstances too lengthy for narration here, fought Cuchulain, who at one stage of the conflict, although much against his will, engages Ferdiad in single combat. This is the famous Fight at the Ford, than which there is nothing more poignant in all literature, inasmuch as

[5] Besides Dr. Dunn's translation, the reader is referred to Miss Hutton's and Miss Hull's, to Lady Gregory's *Cuchulain of Muirthemne*, and to the poetical treatment of the theme by such different writers as Aubrey De Vere, *The Foray of Queen Meave*, and Mr. Austin Clarke, *The Cattledrive in Connaught*.

Ferdiad dies at the hands of Cuchulain, who thereupon lifts up his voice, not in exultation over a defeated foe, but in true Gaelic lamentation for the death of his friend.

Voluminous as the Red Branch cycle is (and it contains besides the great saga of the *Tain* and its attendant stories, a number of Tales which have no connection with Meave's Foray), it was itself only part of a more voluminous collection known as the Historic Tales, which were handed down by tradition among the *ollamhs* until the time when it became possible to record them in writing. These are the Tales which O'Curry, basing his classification on the evidence of the twelfth-century *Book of Leinster*, lists under the headings of Destructions, Cow-Spoils (*Tains*), Courtships or Wooings, Navigations, Tragedies or Deaths, Feasts, Sieges, Adventures, Elopements and Slaughters. Even allowing for the fact that many of the works listed by O'Curry have been lost, there is obvious warrant for the claim that the amount of ancient Irish literature still in existence is far in excess of that of Greece and Rome.

Of later development than the Ulster cycle is the Leinster or Fenian cycle, which is not only less extensive but wholly different in character. In its present form it apparently dates from the ninth century of our era onwards, one of the most important tales being assigned to the eighteenth century. Of course, it cannot too often be remarked, these dates refer only to the writing, not to the time of origin of the Fenian stories, of which the central figure is Fionn mac Cumal, "Fionn of the Generous Hand," leader of a band of mercenaries maintained by the high king, Cormac mac Art.

Even under such circumstances of subjugation a caste developed, in this case a warrior caste, living by the chase and plunder, and known as Fianna. "The fiana," says Dr. MacNeill, "are prehistoric; but that such a class could have been invented for literary purposes is inconceivable. Their existence is a fact preserved by a genuine and vivid if somewhat idealised tradition."[6] It is noteworthy that it was preserved not by the learned

[6] Preface to *Duanaire Finn*, 1908.

class of the dominant race, that is the Gaelic, but in the popular imagination of the subject races. In the course of time the Fenian cycle became the possession of the whole people of Ireland, which is one of the marks that distinguish it from the Ulster cycle, which was a literary classic and never widely popular.

For all his mythological origin (and in the earliest account of him, the so-called *Boy-Deeds*, Fionn is described as the grandson of a god and a De Danann god at that), Fionn develops into an exceedingly human, even familiar hero, degenerating in the course of time into a somewhat ludicrous figure of gigantic proportions capable of performing fantastic physical feats. But there is nothing fantastic or absurd about the Fionn of the early stories, the Fionn whose brave and chivalrous company included his son, Oisin the poet, the gentle and swift-footed Caoilte, the sharp-tongued Conan, and Diarmuid of the Love-spot,—Fionn the hero who was not only valiant but wise, since he possessed a tooth of knowledge, but who for all his wisdom and valour could not hold as his own either the pledged hand of Grainne or the sworn friendship of Diarmuid. This failure is the subject of the most important of the Fenian tales, *The Pursuit of Diarmuid and Grainne*, which relates how the elderly Fionn sought the hand of the high king's daughter in marriage, and how at the betrothal feast the lovely and none too gratified princess cast her glance among the feasting guests until it rested upon the comely features of Diarmuid. His identity she forthwith sought to learn, since she knew at once that it was he and not the aging Fionn who must be her husband. Having dropped a sleeping potion into the drink which she served to all save Diarmuid, she persuaded him against his honour, and at first even his will, to flee with her from her father's court to the woods and hills and a life of danger. For on arousing from their drug-induced slumber both Cormac and Fionn set out in pursuit of the lovers, a quarry from whose hunting Fionn at least never desisted until Diarmuid lay dead, slain by a wild boar, in accordance with a prophecy, it is true, but betrayed to his death by Fionn.

Besides such Tales as that of the *Fairy Palace of the Quicken*

Trees and the *Pursuit of the Gilla Dacker*, this cycle contains an extraordinary feature, which by what Dr. Hyde calls a supreme stroke of genius, brings the pagan world into contact with the Christian period. This is the story of Oisin's journey to Tir-na-noge with the fairy, Niamdh, over whose protest he returns to Ireland in the belief that he has been but a short time away, only to find on his arrival that the old pagan order has disappeared, since in his absence St. Patrick has won Ireland to Christianity. This provides the occasion for a series of spirited and sometimes amusing disputes between St. Patrick and the old pagan, in which the saint is ultimately victorious, so that Oisin submits to baptism, although with rather poor grace.

Connected with the Fenian cycle, though not directly with Fionn, are a number of stories relating to Cormac mac Art, so-called High King of Ireland, who inspired considerable legendary lore, and is himself the reputed author not only of numerous poems, but of the important *Book of Acaill*. The circumstances under which this is said to have been written, as they are set forth in the introduction to the *Book* itself, illustrate the extent to which the traditions of the ancient order endured. For the *Book of Acaill* is an important law-tract, so-called because Cormac was at Acaill when he wrote it, and the reason why he was there rather than at Tara was because he had been obliged to relinquish the kingship in consequence of having been accidentally blinded by a spear-thrust aimed at his son, since the Brehon Law declared any man with a physical blemish or incapacity ineligible for the kingship.

Another offshoot of the Fenian cycle is the Poem Book of Finn (*Duanaire Finn*), which Professor MacNeill in the edition of it which he made for the Irish Texts Society (1904), attributes to the Middle Irish period. If it seems strange that a rugged warrior like Fionn should be credited with the authorship of any poetry at all, it must be remembered that according to tradition the development of the poetic faculty was almost as requisite for membership in the Fianna as prowess in arms, but as a matter of fact most of the poems in the *Duanaire* are attributed to Oisin, who was as it were the laureate of the Fianna and who, it is scarcely necessary to mention, is identical with the "Ossian" to whom Macpherson ascribed the authorship of his so-called translations, the originals of which he never produced. As Professor MacNeill points out, one of the clearest evidences of the fact that Macpherson did not draw upon authentic sources is the extent to which he confuses the Ulster and the Leinster cycles of tales.

Regardless of the period at which these matters were first set down in writing, they unquestionably existed in some form or other long before that was done. A knowledge of the Historic Tales, as they were called, was one of the requirements in the training of the *file* or poet, who reached a still higher stage of proficiency when he himself demonstrated his ability to compose poetry on these traditional themes. This sort of composition or improvisation goes back to the pagan druids, a fact which partly accounts for the highly cryptical, because technical, language of which they made use, as well as for much of the consequent bardic obscurity. The Tales themselves were composed in prose interspersed with "lays," but Fionn's Book consists entirely of verse.

The reading of this chapter should be supplemented by the perusal—better, the intensive study—of two fine books by Dr. Myles Dillon, *Early Irish Literature* (1948) and *Cycles of the Kings* (1946). Although published later, the *Literature* should be read first, because it deals with an earlier period. It sets forth in more detail than would be possible in the present work the principal stories in the Ulster, the Fenian and the Mythological Cycles, as well as material grouped under the headings *Adventures, Voyages* and *Visions*. Much of the so-called historical material, it will be borne in mind, is just as mythical as anything in the mythological cycle, an observation which applies with equal force to the material collected in the *Cycles of the Kings*, for although this material deals with ostensibly historical events and persons and although Dr. Dillon maintains that these tales are "not negligible as a source of Irish history," they are for the most part the inventions of the resourceful *file*. Dr. Dillon supplies a helpful hint concerning the "historical" or chronological sequence of the contents of his two books. He further states that while the amount of history contained in these stories is a matter for investigation and the findings of some investigators have led them to pronounce them mere fiction, Dr. Dillon's opinion, based on prolonged study, is that "there is a great deal of history in them."[7]

The term *improvisation* as used above should not be understood to imply any lack of finish or artistry, for the Irish poet had to improvise in accordance with exceedingly intricate and difficult metrical rules, which have been studied in great detail by Professor Kuno Meyer in his *Primer of Irish Metrics*. Professor Meyer recognizes three successive periods in the history of Irish versification, of which the first (Early Irish) corresponds to the period now under discussion. Of this age only a few specimens are extant and they are scattered through some of the oldest sagas. This poetry is characterized by unrhythmical alliterative verse, typified by the *rosc*, which Dr. Dunn describes as neither prose nor poetry, since it consists of short exclamatory sentences, in which, however, there is an abundance of assonance and alliteration. As time went on, Irish metrics became increasingly difficult, making almost incredible demands on the poetic faculty. That those demands were met, however, is evident from the fact that Professor Meyer's and other works on the subject are based on the study of actual achievements, which warrant Meyer's claim that "the vernacular literature of ancient Ireland is the most primitive and original among the literatures of Western Europe. . . . [whose] importance as the earliest voice from the dawn of West European civilisation cannot be denied."[8] Meyer's familiarity with this subject leads to a profound critical observation which can always be used as a touchstone in testing the racial quality of a writer's work. "The Celts," he says, "were always quick to take an artistic hint; they avoid the obvious and the commonplace; the half-said thing to them is dearest."

Dr. Dillon has vastly increased the value of his work on *Early*

[7] *Cycle of the Kings*, p. 118.
[8] Introduction to his *Selections from Ancient Irish Poetry* (1911).

Irish Literature by his chapter on Irish poetry, in which he not only outlines its historical development, but analyses the Irish metrical system, basing his observations, it is true, to a great extent on Kuno Meyer (see above), but adding enormously to the importance and charm of his study by drawing on his own knowledge, not only of Irish literature, but of literature generally.

Irish civilization, therefore, was attested by a high degree of artistic appreciation which led to the accumulation of vast stores of literary material and the development of a characteristic and difficult literary technic; by a regard for the things of the mind which resulted in the organization of an educational system and the maintenance of a learned class whose exponents were treated with a deference unparalleled elsewhere.

Chapter III. *THE DEER'S CRY*

May Christ on my way
To Tara today
Shield me from prison,
Shield me from fire,
Drowning or wounding
By enemy's ire,
So that mighty fruition
May follow my mission.
From the Irish, tr. A. P. GRAVES

IN THE YEAR 432 the old pagan order, insofar as it was pagan, came to an end, but insofar as it was an order, that is, a culture, it entered upon a new and fuller life, became a higher civilization. For in that year the former swineherd, Patrick, returned to the land of his captivity and took it captive for Christ. Throughout the years of his freedom, as exiles hear the voice of home and kindred, he had heard "the voice of the Irish," pleading with him to return and walk once more amongst them. To his apostolic soul that meant a plea that he would bring them to walk in the presence of God, and when finally, after overcoming many obstacles emanating both from himself and from his ecclesiastical superiors, he undertook that task, it was in the full realization of its stupendous proportions. For it meant bringing the gospel of meekness to a proud and mettlesome people, secure in their political institutions, confident in their cultural, and arrogant in their religious, beliefs.

Patrick was born in Britain, then under Roman domination, about 385. His father, Calpurnius, was a decurion, and therefore a person of rank and wealth, so that Patrick's youth, until the time of his capture, was one of ease. The language of his home was probably Latin, but he must have been acquainted with the Celtic that was spoken in Britain, and he must have had some classical education. When he was about sixteen (401), he was taken captive by invading Irish and carried to Ireland, where he became a slave, his duties as such obliging him to tend flocks of swine and sheep.

This period of slavery lasted six years, during which he must have acquired a certain affection for his captors. The interval also afforded him the opportunity to acquire the Irish form of Celtic, the knowledge of which became an indispensable instrument in his missionary labours. The period came to an end when, by divine direction, he fled his captivity, set out on a long journey afoot and was taken aboard a ship carrying a cargo of Irish wolfhounds to the Continent.

After numerous vicissitudes, he returned to his home in Britain, only to be beset by "the voice of the Irish," beseeching him to "come and walk again among us," but it was some time before he was able to heed their call. Meanwhile he visited various monasteries in Gaul, in almost any one of which he would have been glad to remain, since each was a haven of peace in the midst of the chaos into which the barbarian, especially the recent Vandal, invasions had plunged the world. Meanwhile he was ordained and offered himself for the Irish mission, but was not at once accepted, the tradition being that Palladius, another missionary, was consecrated and despatched to Ireland, but died before he could begin his work, whereupon Patrick was consecrated a bishop and given the desire of his heart by being sent to the people who thenceforth were to be his people.[1]

His coming was not wholly unexpected, for when he lit the paschal fire on the hill of Slane opposite Tara, in the "very nostrils

---

[1] The place of Patrick's consecration having always been a matter of uncertainty, it was with something like excitement that I recently heard from an Italian friend that the cathedral of Ivrea cherishes the tradition that it was there the Apostle of Ireland was made a bishop.

of King Laoghaire," then reigning as high king, at a season when
it was forbidden in Ireland to light any save the sacred druid
flame, there were those who recognized it as the sign the druids
had foretold, not without foreboding. As might have been expected, therefore, the Christian missionary met with some opposition at first, but on the other hand there were qualities
in druidism and in the whole of the native culture that amounted
to a kind of preparation for the Gospel, so that Christianity was
introduced into Ireland without encountering anything like organized persecution. For the primitive Irish Church there was no
age of the catacombs, nor any relapse into paganism, such as
there had been in other countries.

In fact the conversion of the Irish was so rapid and so complete
that the Apostle himself was astonished, or would have been
except for his recognition of the miraculous power of grace.
And that power was exerted in Ireland to such effect that within
St. Patrick's lifetime the country became not only Christian but
holy, a land of saints. Then indeed was verified the prophetic
title bestowed by the ancients, "holy island." Churches were
founded, priests in their thousands were ordained, bishops were
consecrated, and most amazing of all, the young people, mere
lads and girls, ran literally hot-foot to God, to the convent, to
the cloister, to the hermit's cell, in joy and exultation for the
sparse diet and the rocky bed, so that in a remarkably short time
the country was dotted with monastic houses, every one of them
a nursery of heroic holiness, and nearly every one of them a
school.

There is nothing like it in the history of sanctity, for sanctity
was achieved on so grandiose a scale, that it becomes almost
commonplace, and yet nowhere was it so highly personalized
and individual. Of this type of holiness Patrick himself sounded
the keynote by his way of life, which was essentially Irish. For
he went about his apostolic business with a "company" resembling
that of an Irish chieftain, which included not only clerics and
those charged with ecclesiastical tasks, but craftsmen of various
kinds and even a brewer. He was not Irish, but he made himself

Irish for Christ's sake, or he could not have moulded the soul of a whole people as he did, according to a pattern which has never since been broken, much less destroyed.

The design of that pattern is recognizable not only on Irish Christianity as a whole, but on the individual soul of the Irish Christian, from that young prince of Munster who made no sign when, during the baptismal ceremonies, the saint unwittingly thrust the point of his crosier through his foot, since the neophyte regarded the pain as part of the price every Christian was expected to pay for the privilege of admission into the Church, through Brigid and Columcille and Malachy and all those thousands of "candles of the Gael" down to Matt Talbot and Father "Willie" Doyle in our own time. It is the mark which shines resplendently from the soul of the entire race through the long centuries of the persecution which came at last from without.

I have written the foregoing in full awareness of Professor O'Rahilly's theory, set forth in *The Two Patricks* (1942), that two Christian missionaries named Patrick worked in Ireland in the early fourth century, their acts having become, in the words of the latest writer on the subject, "inextricably confused." This writer is Professor Ludwig Bieler, one of the most eminent scholars of our time. Beginning his career as a Classicist, he became interested in Celtic, in which field he has worked for some time, devoting special attention to the legends of the Irish saints. His recently published *The Life and Legend of St. Patrick* (1949) is a masterpiece of its kind, for the way in which it combines broad scholarship, moderation of tone, and conciseness of style.

Of Professor O'Rahilly's theory he says that if his arguments "cannot be easily dismissed, they cannot, on the other hand, be easily accepted." In his own treatment of the subject he goes, of course, directly to sources, but leaves his final word on the question to an article on which he is now engaged. Commenting on St. Patrick's scant and "rusty" literary remains, he says that "behind the words we feel a great personality," and yet, he insists, "It is not the man that counts, however striking was his personality, but the faith he brought, a faith that is interpreted by the Irish of our time in the same stern and yet integral manner as it was by the Irish of the fourth century."

It is on the basis of such facts that I have ventured to write as I have of St. Patrick, because throughout the centuries the Irish people, knowing nothing of academic theories and caring less, have cherished in their hearts and minds, in the dark hours of their suffering as in the bright ages of their glory, the figure of a great and living personality, a saint of God, to the Irish always the supreme hero, *their* saint, Patrick.

And surely there is a sense in which the seal of the Irish is stamped on that personality, on Patrick himself, or at least on the profession of the faith which the Irish received from him, for into it they poured all the fierce ardour, all the passionate devotion, which glows in the bardic tales, in the heroism of Cuchulain, the generosity of Deirdre, the courage of Fionnuala, the chivalry of Ferdiad. Patrick courageously destroyed the few idols which he found, he withstood such of the druids as opposed him, but for the most part his task consisted in pointing out to generous souls the only Hero worthy of their devotion, "Christ of the graces." It consisted in turning druids into Christian priests, in instructing brehons in the law of God, in raising up a new generation of scholars and poets versed in heavenly lore, whose conaclons and roscs, such as the *Deer's Cry*, were instruments for the praise of God and heavenly things.

For the highest Gaelic culture dates from the time of Patrick, which marks the beginning of that long tradition according to which every monastery became a school and every saint a scholar or at least a patron of scholarship. Obviously this was a continuation of the old pagan custom of maintaining a learned class, whose functions were at first merged in the druids and afterwards so separated that the practitioners of each constituted a class in themselves. Under the Christian dispensation not one of these functions was repudiated or discredited. Instead St. Patrick elevated each of them immeasurably and encouraged its use for purposes of which the pagan Irish could have had no conception.

It may not be true that St. Patrick introduced into the country the Roman alphabet and the use of script, but he did promote their use, he did exert himself to procure the multiplication of books, copies of the Scriptures and liturgical books. This meant that scribes had to be trained in an art which became not only one of the glories of Irish culture, but one of the glories of Christian art. He himself was bilingual, speaking Latin, which he confessed was a bit "rustic," and the Gaelic, which he had learned during the six years of his captivity. By his encouragement and practical assistance, Patrick inaugurated that long and glorious history of Irish manuscript literature in which are combined the two arts of letters and illumination, in a fashion which is still in many respects the wonder of the world.

The extent to which it was the saint's policy to adapt rather than destroy the ancient native institutions is instanced in the *Senchus Mor*, which Dr. Healy calls "the greatest monument in existence of the learning and civilization of the Gaedhlic race in Erin,"[2] and which according to ancient tradition contains all of the law of the brehons that did not clash with the law of God.[3] It does not greatly matter whether anything so specific as a Christian redaction of the ancient text was undertaken and that by a commission appointed at the saint's suggestion. In his book on St. Patrick Dr. MacNeill casts doubt on the idea, but in this same book there is ample substantiation of the claim that the saint's attitude towards the native institutions was consistently constructive.

It is quite in keeping with that consistency, therefore, that Patrick should be credited with the inauguration of the new literature, first by the authorship of the first Christian poem in Gaelic, his so-called *Lorica* or *Breastplate*, also known as *The Deer's Cry*. This is a prayer which the saint uttered on the occasion of his first approach to Tara, a prayer to be protected against the power and the malice of the druids, to whose

[2] *Christian Schools and Scholars*, p. 55.
[3] Bryant, *Liberty, Order and Law in the Ancient Irish State*.

watchers, in consequence, he and his companion appeared like a
deer with her fawn.

> I invoke upon my path
> To the King of Ireland's rath
>   The Almighty Power of the Trinity;
> Through belief in the Threeness,
> Through confession of the Oneness
>   Of the Maker's Eternal Divinity.
>
> I invoke on my journey arising,
> The power of Christ's Birth and Baptizing,
> The powers of the hours of His dread Crucifixion,
>   Of His Death and Abode in the Tomb,
> The power of the hour of His glorious Resurrection
>   From out the Gehenna of gloom
> The power of the hour when to Heaven He ascended,
> And the power of the hour when by angels attended
> He returns for the judgment of Doom!
>   On my perilous way
>   To Tara to-day
>   I, Patrick, God's servant,
>   Invoke from above
>   The Cherubim's love![4]

In subsequent stanzas he summons to his assistance the company of patriarchs, prophets, apostles, confessors and virgins,
and in a magnificent gesture wrests out of the power of the
heathen the natural world which they had made their own,
summoning the glory of the sun, the radiance of the moon, the
splendour of fire, the swiftness of the wind, the sea's depth and
"the rock's austerity," to the side of Christ in the battle against
"druid counsel dark, the black craft of Pagandom."

Patrick's second claim to be regarded as the founder of the new
Christian literature lies in the fact that he was the subject of the
first Latin poem written in Ireland, the hymn in his praise which
is attributed to his nephew, St. Sechnall (Secundinus). It was
written in Latin, but in Irish characters. Patrick himself is re-

---

[4] Tr. Graves. See also Kenney, op. cit., below, pp. 272-274.

vealed as the author of the *Confessions*,[5] not only by the "rustic"
Latinity of his style, but also by the note of simplicity which is so
incontestably his. He is the subject of two other important early
works, his *Life*, "written in pure and perfect Gaelic," by St. Fiacc
of Sletty, whom legend identifies as the nephew of King Laoghaire's brehon, and the famous *Tripartite Life*, assigned to dates
ranging between the sixth and the eleventh centuries.[6]

These works are not only the foundation stones in what was to
become an incomparable literary edifice, the record of Irish
sanctity, but they serve as a reminder of the extent to which
throughout its history that sanctity was allied with learning and
the promotion of learning. For the centuries from the fifth to the
seventh constituted the golden age of Irish culture, when the
Irish Church produced saints who established a new cultural
order in which every Irish aptitude flourished under the auspices
of religion.[7] As already intimated, the foremost factor in this,
under God, was Patrick's personality, operating upon a race
already inclined to individuality, with the result that the saints
who followed in his footsteps, in numbers beyond calculation,
contrived at the same time to reproduce the pattern and to leave
upon Irish culture the mark of their own vivid personalities.

It is not strange, therefore, that so many of them should have
established schools, seats of learning where attention was directed,
primarily, it is true, to the study of the sacred Scriptures, but
where the most humane aspects of secular learning were recognized and preserved, since it was to the great volumes compiled by
monastic scribes that the scholars of later generations had to go,
not only for religious literature, but for secular history, the heroic
romances and poetry.

[5] Dr. Bieler quotes this in full (ch. iii, *The Saint's Testimony about Himself*), and Dr. Kenney (see below) naturally makes it the subject of some
of his most interesting observations (op. cit., pp. 165-168).

[6] See Kenney, op. cit., below, pp. 342-345.

[7] What these skills were and how highly they were regarded is shown
in countless pages of Irish history, but perhaps they are most characteristically summed up in the fact that the ancient sun-god Lugh was called
Lamhfada, because he was the master of every craft.

Some idea of the prodigious literary activity of these Christian centuries may be obtained from the perusal (better still, the intensive study) of Dr. James F. Kenney's *Sources for the Early History of Ireland*, Vol. I, Ecclesiastical (New York, 1929). Besides an introductory chapter on History in Ireland, which is a survey of Ireland's cultural history to practically the date of the book's publication, the volume contains sections dealing with Ireland in the ancient world; the Irish Church in the "Celtic" period; the Monastic Churches, in three chapters, dealing with the subject from the Primitive Foundations to the ninth century; the expansion of Christianity from the seventh to the twelfth centuries; Religious Literature and Ecclesiastical Culture, seventh to twelfth centuries (subdivided under the headings: Biblical and Intellectual, Liturgical and Devotional; Homiletical, Apocryphal and Imaginative); the Reform movement of the twelfth century.

Under each of these headings is given an historical account and a bibliographical analysis of the documents, 659 in all, pertaining to the periods surveyed, from the MS of the Carthaginian mariner, Himilco, of the sixth or fifth century before our era (which is described as "the first written source of Irish history" and whose allusion to the "Sacred Island" was long interpreted as referring to Ireland), to the year A.D. 1170. There is a certain fitness in the fact that the list of works annotated by Dr. Kenney should terminate with a Life of St. Lawrence O'Toole, a fitness explained by the tradition that as a child he was held as a hostage by Dermot Macmurrough and that as Archbishop of Dublin it became his duty to cope with the results of the invasion which resulted from Dermot's appeal to Henry II, becoming, as Dr. Kenney remarks, "deeply involved in all the difficulties and horrors resulting therefrom."

Of special significance is the following comment by Dr. Kenney: "Ireland was the only Celtic land where the Roman eagles never flew. She alone carried down into the Christian middle ages the political, social and cultural traditions of western Europe unbroken by the impact of the Mediterranean civilisation."[8] That

[8] Op. cit., p. 129.

for Ireland this did not constitute a cultural isolation, much less anything even remotely resembling barbarism, this book alone bears abundant witness. Its most inspiring chapters are of course those dealing with the Celtic period, not only because of the number and interest of the documents studied, but because Dr. Kenney's wide literary and historical knowledge emphasizes their humanistic significance.

So closely are the illustrious personalities of the Irish saints associated with the schools they founded and maintained that it is difficult to say from which aspect the subject were best considered, that of the founder or that of the school. Certainly the great names answer to one another plangently, like a chime of deep-toned bells, as in the case of the School of Armagh, founded by St. Benignus, to whom are attributed the *Book of Rights* and a share in the *Senchus Mor*; that of Kildare, over which presided St. Brigid, "the Queen of the South, the Mary of the Gael," with which school are connected two important manuscript books, the lost Book of Kildare and the great Book of Leinster; the school on rocky Aran Mor, transformed by St. Enda, of royal Gaelic stock, into Aran of the Saints, which maintained among its awesome Firbolg ruins a monastic foundation to which resorted many famous saints (synonymous with scholars), among them the youthful Columcille. Others were the School of Clonard, which developed into a renowned national college where its founder, St. Finian, taught at one time as many as 3000 students; the noble establishment of Clonfert, founded by St. Brendan the Voyager, who is sometimes credited with the pre-Columban discovery of America; Moville, established by another Finian, where the youthful and not yet sanctified Columcille got himself into difficulties by secretly making a copy of the Vulgate from the copy which St. Finian had brought from Rome, an achievement which incidentally led to a legal decision against Columcille's ownership of the copy he had made, which decision (To every cow her calf; to every book its copy) contains in germ the principle of the law of copyright.

At Clonmacnoise were situated "the greatest school and the

greatest monastery in Ireland." Founded by St. Ciaran, it produced distinguished scholars beyond number, among them Alcuin. Among those educated at Clonenagh was Aengus the Culdee (d. 824), so-called from his great love of prayer. The fame of his austerities drew such throngs to his hermitage that he had to abandon his solitary life and withdraw to the monastery of Tallaght, where he wrote in prose a martyrology of that monastery and in 805 completed his famous *Felire* or Festology of the Irish saints in verse. A translation of this poem by Whitley Stokes was published in 1880 by the Royal Irish Academy. Dr. Stokes disputed Aengus's authorship of the poem, which still continues to be attributed to him.

Among the most famous of these Irish schools were those founded by Columcille before his departure for Iona, among them Derry, "where angels crowded every leaf on the oak trees," Durrow, whose famous Book[9] he is said to have written with his own hands, and Kells, whose glorious history was enhanced by the possession of what is still admittedly the most beautiful MS in the world. Some authorities credit Columba with the actual workmanship of this marvelous Book, but it is now generally considered to have been the work of more than one scribe.

Illustrious among the scholar saints was the great Adamnan, disciple and biographer of Columcille and his successor at Iona. Adamnan was born at Drumhone, Co. Donegal, about 624 and educated there. He entered the monastery of Iona in 650 and became its head in 679. During one of the several visits which he paid to Ireland during his term of office, which lasted until his death in 704, he succeeded in introducing the Roman observance of Easter, and during another was instrumental in bringing about the adoption of the famous Canon or Law of Adamnan, which secured for women and children protection from the evils of war.

His *Life* of Columba has been called by the antiquary, William Pinkerton (1809-1871), "the most complete piece of biography that all Europe can boast of, not only at so early a period, but

[9] This masterpiece, which ranks next in beauty to those of Kells and Lindisfarne, is now in the possession of Trinity College.

even through the whole Middle Ages." The work is typical of the literary treasure which Colgan (see p. 74) strove to salvage, for it was first printed by him, but the best edition is that of Dr. Reeves (see p. 174).

These names are far from exhausting the list, either of the monastic founders or of the institutions of holiness and learning which they established; still less does it do more than faintly suggest the achievement for which these names stand, so that something of the poignancy with which Dr. Healy laments the destruction of Clonmacnoise attaches to all those vanished glories: "How solitary now she sits beside the great river, that once thronged city. Her gates are broken and her streets are silent. Yet in olden times she was a queen, and the children of many lands came to do her homage. She was the nursing mother of saints and the teacher of our highest learning for a long six hundred years. . . . View it as you may, Clonmacnoise was the greatest of our schools in the past as it is the most interesting of our ruins in the present."

Several points are worth making in connection with the monastic schools. One is that they were in the direct line of development from the ancient druidic and bardic schools; another is that they constituted the basis of the Irish educational system while it continued to subsist as such.

Contrary to a common impression, the course of studies in the monastic schools included secular as well as religious subjects, although the emphasis was naturally on the religious. Instruction was imparted in both Latin and Irish, and some attention was paid to the native literature as well as to the classics. A most important feature of the monastery was the scriptorium, where text-books, liturgical books, such as Missals, Graduals, Vesperals, Breviaries, and copies of the Scriptures were produced, besides works of general interest for the library.

Furthermore, it was characteristic of the Irish system that it encouraged scholarship in laymen as well as in clerics, so that besides the monastic schools the Irish, in this, the golden age of culture, maintained secular institutions, represented chiefly by the bardic schools. Each province had its principal bardic college, with a lesser one for each district. Each of these was presided over by an *ollamh* or man of profound learning whose social prestige entitled him to a seat beside the king at court functions.

In addition to these schools the Irish educational system recognized a form called fosterage, usually reserved for the children of the wealthy, who were placed in the home and under the direct tutelage of a man whose duties, clearly defined by the Brehon Law, required him to prepare his charges for the position they were to fill in life.

It was typical of Irish scholarship that it was diffusive, a characteristic that was due in part to the missionary spirit that was so strong in the Irish Church, whence it followed that the cliffs of Iona bear witness to the zeal of the "first exile," Columba, "light of all the Celtic West," as Bobbio[10] in Italy and St. Gall in Switzerland preserve the memory of that other wanderer for God, Columbanus, of whom Dom Louis Gougaud says that in order to follow the progress of monasticism in Gaul in the seventh century it is only necessary to follow in that saint's footsteps.[11] John Scotus Eriugena (810-877) has been called the greatest Irishman abroad during the ninth century, and certainly his learning was immense, but some of his theological doctrines were condemned as pantheistic. He spent most of his life teaching in France, enjoyed the patronage of Charles the Bald, and is known chiefly for his translation of Pseudo-Dionysius. Professor Kenney, who calls him "the most important individual that Ireland gave to continental Europe in the middle ages,"[12] devotes an entire chapter to him.

In describing Irish medieval learning, whose renown drew so

[10] The town of Bobbio is said to have a large population of families with unmistakably Irish names. The Italian gentleman who informed me of this fact was plainly puzzled by it, but that was because he was unaware of the Irish origin of the town itself, and so could not surmise how naturally many of the Wild Geese would have winged their way to a haven which was already known to them as in part Irish.

[11] Gougaud, *Gaelic Pioneers of Christianity* (tr. 1923).

[12] Op. cit., p. 571.

many students from the Continent to Ireland, Gougaud says:
"There was held to be but one science, that of the Sacred Scriptures. It was that science people came chiefly to seek from the
Irish doctors." He then comments on the two arts of calligraphy
and illumination which were brought to such perfection in
Ireland, chiefly in the service of the Scriptures, but also devoted
to the embellishment and multiplication of other religious works,
such as liturgical books and the writings of the Fathers.

It is, of course, a matter of common knowledge that the Irish
developed the art of writing to an incomparable degree of beauty,
so that the Irish scribe became famous throughout the world.
The extent to which MSS were multiplied, considering how long
and arduous was the scribe's task, staggers the imagination. One
has only to glance through such compilations as O'Curry's *Manuscript Materials of Ancient Irish History* and the two volumes of
O'Grady's *Silva Gadelica*, to form, from such incomplete lists,
some notion of what the magnitude of the whole must have been.
That many medieval MSS have been irretrievably lost is evident
from the fact that some of the greatest works extant date from
a much later period, when conditions were less conducive to
their production.

Meanwhile the course of Irish life proceeded according to
ancient custom. The monarchy became centralized, never in a
feudal sense, but in a manner whereby the heads of the "noble
kindreds" acquired a status between that of provincial kings and
great landed proprietors. The law of the brehons, now adapted
to Christian principles, was the law of the land, regulating the
various social grades and classes and held to be binding on all
from the king down. The influence of religion manifested itself
in the matter of rank and honour, since in the Church lowly
birth was no hindrance to high ecclesiastical position.

Among scholars, the functions of the bard tended to become
distinct from those of the *ollamh* or historian, while the *ollamh*
inclined to devote himself more and more exclusively to the task
of tracing the genealogies of noble families and "synchronizing"
the events of history. This ability to synchronize had from

ancient times been one of the most important features of academic training, but by the fresh emphasis now placed upon it,
the Annals of Ireland, as the early histories are called, acquired
an almost fabulous character that will be dealt with below.

The esteem in which the learned class was held has already
been referred to. In the case of the bards this attitude led to
a deplorable state of affairs, for they grew exceedingly arrogant
and so exacting in their demands that it was finally determined
to suppress them as an order. For this purpose a synod was con-
vened in 575 at Drumceat, before which St. Columba appeared
and pleaded their cause so vehemently that the sentence was re-
voked, but only on promise of reform. From this dates the re-
organization of the bardic order and the rehabilitation of their
schools.

One of the unquestionable results of this reform was the
fuller development of that system of metrics which Kuno Meyer
reduces to such succinct terms in his *Primer*, in which he shows
that besides the alliterative rhythmical verse already alluded
to, the Irish wrote a great quantity of unrhythmical syllabic
poetry, characterized by the use of a fixed number of syllables
in each line, with the additional metrical devices of end rhyme
or consonance, internal rhyme and alliteration. The mass of
poetry from the eighth to the eleventh century was written in
syllabic verse, which required (1) a fixed number of syllables
in each line, and (2) either rhyme or consonance at the end.

Rhyme, which the Irish are often credited with inventing,
began with the stressed vowel of a word, while consonance fell
on the stressed vowels of monosyllables, and in polysyllables
began with the first unstressed syllable. An extremely complicated
form of syllabic verse called Debide regulated both rhyme and
the number of syllables. Internal rhyme occurred between a word
or words in the first and second line of a stanza and a word or
words in the third and fourth lines of a stanza. The concluding
word in every poem had to repeat either the whole or a part
of the first word. The chief varieties of Irish metre were stanzas
with rhyming couplets; Debide; stanzas with rhyming couplets

containing a variety of syllabic verse ends; and stanzas of varied structure.

An interesting literary form of which Meyer made an intensive study is the triad, a sententious epigram of which Meyer believes the model to have been Hebrew poetry. Collections of triads have reached us in nine MS collections which are nearly identical in content. The following is a typical example: "Three fewnesses that are better than plenty: of fine words; of cows in grass; of friends around good ale."[13]

From what has been said concerning the importance accorded to learning in the scheme of Irish life, especially under the influence of religion, it must not be supposed that the Irish were an impractical race, given over exclusively to the cultivation of the things of the soul and the mind, to the neglect of practical affairs. As a matter of fact, they were to a very large extent given over to the cultivation of the soil, since they were a highly successful agricultural, and by the same token, an industrial people, whose ancient fairs were centres of trade and industry. Legend traced the origin of many of the ancient roads to the gods, but the monks had a hand in their making, "pilgrim's ways," as they were, running between monastery and monastery, from shrine to shrine. They served also for practical purposes of traffic, nor were such activities restricted to the Irish roads, since a brisk trade was carried on with France, Spain and the Low Countries, a trade in which wine was the chief and the oldest import. At home there were stone quarries to be worked, as well as the prosperous business of linen and woollen weaving, and leather working to be conducted. The ancient art of the metal worker, so ancient that specimens dating from pre-Christian times have been recovered by modern antiquaries, was devoted not only to the making of weapons and armour, but to the service of the Church, so that from the exquisite workmanship of the Ardagh Chalice, supreme in this field as the Book of Kells is in that of illumination, it is possible to surmise what masterpieces have been lost,

[13] Meyer, *The Triads of Ireland* (R. I. A. Todd Lecture series, 1906).

snatched away as booty, perhaps, or ground under the marauding feet of the Danes.

For another race of invaders, the fifth, had landed in Ireland. From the ninth century the Scandinavians, called collectively Danes, and by the Irish Galls, had been coming in great waves, and endeavouring to establish themselves on Irish, as they had on English, soil, but although they did gain a foothold in certain port towns, such as Dublin, where they established a "kingdom," they never made any permanent settlements inland. Throughout this period the Irish waged unrelenting war against the invaders, who in turn wrought terrible havoc, especially upon churches and religious houses. It was they who reduced Clonmacnoise to the condition deplored by Dr. Healy, and who destroyed or carried off most of the great MS books, masterpieces of the scribe's art, so that we could form little idea of their value save for the examples which survive on the Continent. Which fact is a reminder that the Danish invasions were beneficial to European culture generally, however disastrous they may have been to Ireland, since it was the destruction of their monasteries that sent many monks to the Continent, thus promoting the spread of religion and learning among other races, and this apart from the number of those who had gone when there was no reason for them to leave Ireland save their desire to spread the kingdom of God.

This period was terminated by the battle of Clontarf (1014), in which the great Brian Boru lost his life in the course of inflicting a crushing defeat on the "Strangers." An important piece of literature which grew directly out of this event was the historical tract, *Cogadh Gaedhil re Gallaibh* (*The War of the Gaedhil with the Gaill*), of undetermined authorship, but generally attributed to a contemporary of the events it records, one who is usually identified with Muircheartach MacLiag, Brian's chief poet, author of the *Lament for Kincora*.

In the renewal of culture which followed the Danish wars, Irish culture not only continued to flourish, but rose to new heights of glory, a glory in which the Galls thenceforth shared, since they gradually became assimilated with the Gaels and were therefore the first of the foreigners of whom it could be said that by their adoption of Irish ways they became "more Irish than the Irish themselves." The Irish in turn had learned of the Gall, who were great traders, to extend their commerce and build up their industry.

To judge by the remains of the literary activity of that time it seems to have been almost feverish, as though a whole people felt themselves under the urgency of the command to work while it was day, since the night was at hand when no man could work. Certainly it was a day of dazzling brightness, wherein the old seats of learning, except such as had been utterly destroyed, like Kells and Clonmacnoise, grew and flourished and won fresh prestige; when poets not only sang the glories of the ancient heroes in the form in which the great cycles have come down to us (crediting the "recovery" of the *Tain* to the summoning of Fergus mac Roy from the grave by the chief poet of Ireland), but turning certain of the classics, including the *Iliad* and the *Aeneid*, into Irish verse, and singing with special exuberance and love the natural loveliness of the country itself. It was certainly a poet of this time who found poetic speech for Columba's heartsick remembrance among the rocks and the waves and the ravens of Iona, of Derry's gentler aspect, her "snowy-blossomed sloes," her blackbirds and her "groves of angels." And they were also of this time, the poets who framed some of the earliest dirges, thus inaugurating that long tradition of the keen and the lament, which gave warrant to the saying "All mourners of the world weep Irish."

The Irish faculty for expressing sorrow seems to have been almost prophetic, for certainly they possessed it long before their own unparalleled sorrows provided them with such abundant occasion for the expression of grief. "The life of the Gaels," says Dr. Douglas Hyde, "is so pitiable, so dark and sad and sorrowful, and they are so broken, bruised and beaten in their own land and country that their talents and ingenuity find no place for themselves, and no way to let themselves out but in excessive foolish mirth, or in keening and lamentation."[14] Surely there is no other race with whom it is instinctive in the midst of bereave-

[14] *Love Songs of Connacht*, p. 2.

ment to "proceed from ordinary weeping to singing weeping," and of whom it can be said that "when in that state they sometimes improvise both words and music."

This characteristic is especially evident in their music, perhaps the most ancient of their arts, since the *Goltraighe* or music of sorrow was one of the three sorts of musical composition whose mastery was required of the bards or doctors of music, the other two being the *Suantraighe* or slumber music and the *Geantraighe* or music of joy. The cultivation of these three types and the use of the pentatonic scale produced a national music that is peculiarly and essentially Irish and warrants "the undoubted claim of ancient Erin to the possession of the loveliest airs in the world." As part of their general tendency to make art long by adding to its difficulties, the bards invented a type of singing called the *Cronan*, that is crooning, which is described by Grattan Flood as a kind of purring, but certainly the performance described in The Proceedings of the Great Bardic Association[15] could never be called that. For there it is related that when Marvan, as part of his attempt to reduce the intolerably proud spirit of the bards, challenged them to a performance of the Cronan, refusing to be put off with any other feat, no matter how marvelous, group after group of them failed, until finally Seanchan, the chief bard himself, undertook the task. Marvan had already rejected the "regular" Cronan, in the pious hope that the more difficult bass variety would prove the death of the performers. Of Seanchan he demanded the even more difficult guttural, with the result that Seanchan so strained himself that one of his eyes "gushed out on his cheek."

The incidental result of this failure was that Marvan required of the one who boasted that he was the best story-teller in the bardic institute that he recite to him the *Tain*. It developed that not only he but the whole bardic company had to confess their inability to do so, whereupon Marvan placed them under *geasa* not to desist from the search until they had recovered it. This, after long seeking and many adventures, they did, by enlisting

[15] Ed. Connellan (Ossianic Society 1860).

the help of Marvan himself to summon Fergus mac Roy from the
tomb. A goodly company, including numerous saints, sat about
while the hero related the story in which he had been a par-
ticipant, his recital being taken down by St. Ciaran of Clonmacnoise, surely a literary device similar in form and spirit to that
other which won the admiration of Dr. Hyde,—the preservation
of Oisin to have speech with St. Patrick, thus bringing the old
pagan culture into contact with the Christian imagination.

The subject of Irish music is one on which that eccentric
genius, the late Rev. Dr. Henebry, whose opinions, it is true, are
not unreservedly accepted by musical authorities, makes some
observations that at least serve to demonstrate the unique character of this music. It is, he maintains, by way of distinguishing
it from what he calls modern music (by which he means instrumental music), human, that is natural music based on the human
voice. This does not mean that it is simple in the sense of remaining elementary or primitive, nor that it cannot be produced
by instrumentation, but it does mean that it cannot be perfectly
expressed or written in terms of the modern scale. "An Irish
tune," according to Dr. Henebry, "may be learned either from the
mouth or instrument of one who has it, or from the phonograph,
and positively there is no other means."

According to this same writer, it was an "unbroken Keltic
tradition that the office of the instrument was to imitate the
human voice," and there are, he contends, some tunes that cannot be touched by any instrument whatsoever. It is well also
to bear in mind, although I do not think the fact is mentioned by
Dr. Henebry, that the airs were originally composed for Gaelic
words and cannot be perfectly rendered when set to those of
any other language.

Anyone who has heard Irish music under circumstances in
which these conditions are happily met, or who is even aware
of them as the ideal, will have little difficulty in agreeing with Dr.
Henebry on at least one point, which is that this music is the
perfect medium for expressing the higher states of feeling,
"though it be the wail of a heart that is past breaking, or the

dark and seething torrent that burst the floodgates of overcharged emotion, or the blood-tingling rally of a great reel, or the song of woe that cleansed the passion of love in tears and raised it to a dignity with the highest of human attributes, an achievement that no other nation has even thought it worth while to attempt."

Whatever the tradition concerning the relation of instrument to voice, the ancient Irish undoubtedly possessed a wide variety of instruments, the most characteristic of which were the harp, the flute and the bagpipe. The Irish harp or *cruit* was originally a small lyre, carried by the harper, the large harp having been known as the *clairseach*. The flute was really a recorder. The bagpipes are mentioned as early as the fifth century, but came into general use only in the eleventh, after which they provided the characteristic music of the Irish kerns. The development of this music was not halted even by the Danish invasions; in fact, it would seem to have been augmented by them, since the stirring *Brian Boru's March* and the convivial air of the *Cruiskeen Lan* have been credited to a Scandinavian origin, a theory which Dr. Grattan Flood rejects.

Throughout the period with which we are dealing the *ollamhs*, like other Irish scholars and artists, were labouring assiduously at their task of synchronizing, thus enlarging the voluminous historical literature whose commencement some of them traced to Cormac mac Art, to whom is attributed the authorship of the so-called *Saltair* of Tara. Of unquestionable authenticity are the synchronisms of the eleventh-century Flann of Monasterboice and those of Tighernach (Teer-nah) of Clonmacnoise, of which monastery he was abbot when he produced his famous *Annals*.[16] Their writings are typical of Irish historical literature not only in their own age, but through several subsequent centuries, especially in the labour expended on the tracing of genealogies and the synchronizing of historical events, as a result of which Irish history was synchronized not only with itself but with the history of the world. To those who would cast doubt on the

---

[16] The annals of Clonmacnoise have been lost.

accuracy of such records O'Curry replies that even before the coming of St. Patrick such pedigrees and genealogies had been collected into a single book, which means that they must already have been in existence, "doubtless in the various tribe-books,"[17] and even Dr. Hyde considers them worthy of credence, for he writes: "There are many considerations which lead me to believe that Irish genealogical books were kept from the earliest introduction to the art of writing, and kept with greater accuracy perhaps than any other records of the past whatsoever."

But to Dr. MacNeill both the synchronisms and the genealogies are "synthetic history," partly mythological in origin and therefore unreliable.[18] That he would be the last, however, to dissent from the comment made by Thomas Moore to Dr. Petrie in the hearing of O'Curry, "These huge tomes could not have been written by fools nor for any foolish purpose," is evident from his own memorable words on the ancient MSS: "We can still use the scrapings of our vellum as a cure for the foreign snake-bite." It would be absurd to expect anything like what is called critical history during the eleventh century or for some centuries later, in Ireland or anywhere else, but to a truly critical historian like Dr. MacNeill the writings of the Irish Annalists have values of their own, values which he in part enumerates, in part exemplifies.

It is not strange that Christianity, which everywhere recognized in the greatness of pagan thought an expression of spiritual aspiration which it satisfied and exalted, should have found in the Irish, who even in their pagan condition had exhibited exceptional spiritual aptitudes, a race peculiarly eager for the truth which satisfies the world's perennial hunger. Neither is it strange that the satisfaction of that hunger should have promoted the development of all their native love for the things of the mind and impelled them not so much to the creation of a new culture, as to the immeasurable elevation of all their ancient powers. The result was a civilization and a culture that are char-

---

[17] *MSS Materials*, 206.
[18] This is even more specifically and emphatically the opinion of Prof. T. J. O'Rahilly.

acterized to an exceptional degree by a recognition of spiritual values. It is not merely that this culture recognizes the existence of these values, but that it asserts their pre-eminence and unique importance, in the light of which the things of this world, the lust of the eye and the pride of life, have no significance whatever. It is a mere matter of fact to say that Irish culture is stamped with the image of God to an extent that does not characterize the literature of any other race. That is its distinctive racial quality, a fact which must be borne in mind when the occasion arises for the appraisal of any cultural phenomenon that professes to be Irish.

Chapter IV. THE DOWNFALL OF THE GAEL

> We starve by the board,
> And we thirst amid wassail—
> For the guest is the lord,
> And the host is the vassal!
>
> Through the woods let us roam,
> Through the wastes wild and barren;
> We are strangers at home,
> We are exiles in Erin!
>> From the Irish, tr. FERGUSON

THE COMING OF Strongbow in 1169 introduced into Ireland a new type of foreigner, the Saxon or *Sassenach,* who succeeded in remaining a stranger for seven hundred years, and this despite the fact that many Saxons displayed what seemed to their countrymen an almost indecent haste to put off that quality in order to become assimilated with the Irish. As a matter of fact, of course, the earliest members of this invasion were not Saxons, but Anglo-Normans, sent by King Henry II in response to the appeal of Dermot Macmurrough, King of Leinster, for assistance in his quarrel with the high king, Turlough O'Connor. This conflict had grown out of an earlier one with Tighernach O'Ruark, Prince of Breffny, whose wife, Dervorgilla, Dermot had abducted.

There has been a tendency to regard Dervorgilla as one of those *femmes fatales* of legend, such as Helen of Sparta, Guinevere and Iseult, whose beauty was disastrous not only to themselves but to their country, but the facts concerning her do not substantiate that idea. She was forty-four years old and, according to some accounts, already living apart from her husband, when, willingly or not, she went to Leinster with Dermot, who was twenty years her senior, and whom in a year's time she left, either to return to her husband or to go to her family in Meath, of which kingdom she was a princess. Macmurrough seems to have been in most respects no worse than his adversaries; in some he was even better, for he was known for his benefactions to monasteries, the great *Book of Leinster,* one of the noblest cultural monuments of the period, having been compiled for him. In fact, one of the entries in the Book bewails his deposition and exile. He is none the less the villain of the piece, for it was his flight to Wales and his plea to Henry II that precipitated the catastrophe.

It is no part of the purpose of this book to recount the details of the struggle which followed, but until the Reformation, with the consequent introduction of the religious element, it was, as it never ceased to be, primarily a conflict of cultures, the traditional Irish culture on the one hand and the new feudal order on the other. Feudalism had its unquestionable merits, but they were so essentially different from everything the Irish had lived by for countless generations, from everything which on that account they held sacred, that conflict was inevitable. And conflict bloody and prolonged there was, with the Normans striving to occupy and plunder Ireland and the Irish seeking by every means in their power, and they were many, to thwart them. The difference is indicated by the fact that when in the early stages of the struggle O'Connor relinquished the high kingship to Henry II the act held no significance for the provincial kings, who recognized only the Brehon Law, which did not accord to the high king the power to do anything of the sort. ("Whatever Henry's theory might be, the taking of Dublin was not the taking of an Irish capital.")[1]

In spite of the inevitable and prolonged conflict, one of the ultimate results was the absorption by the Irish race of such vast numbers of foreigners as to produce a new racial strain, the Norman-Irish. Thenceforth might be witnessed the spectacle of Norman families adopting Irish ways, wearing the Irish dress, speaking Irish rather than English, and living so completely

[1] Green, *Irish Nationality,* p. 99.

according to the Irish pattern that many of them came to be included with the O'Neills and the O'Donnells amongst the great Irish families.

Foremost among these new Irish were the Fitzgeralds, Earls of Kildare, the first of whom had sailed from Wales with Strongbow, and among whose earlier members was one of whom some of its later scions, especially the dashing Silken Thomas, would not have been quick to boast. This was Gerald de Barri, Gerald of Wales (*Cambrensis*), who accompanied Prince John on his expedition in 1185, and who inaugurated a long and voluminous literature of slander. Incidentally, he was connected in a somewhat left-handed way with the Plantagenets themselves, whose apologist he constituted himself in his erroneously entitled *Hibernia Expugnata*, for before her marriage his grandmother had been the mistress of Henry I. His grandfather, her husband, however, was a Geraldine, member of a family which traced its origin to Florence, their seventeenth-century chronicler, Father Dominic O'Daly, maintaining in practically the same breath in which he disputes Henry's conquest of Ireland that his great heroes, the Fitzgeralds, by that time full-fledged Irishmen, were "transplanted from the desolated plains of Troy," by way of the Italian city.

Between Cambrensis, the first vilifier, to the Geraldines, who are praised by O'Daly for their "Irishry," not only did much history supervene, but such a change occurred as to warrant Dr. Hyde's claim that "Dane and Norman, drawn to the kindly Irish breast, issued forth in a generation or two fully Irishised."[2] To this extent, therefore, the Norman conquest of Ireland was a failure, and its panegyric by Cambrensis was, to say the least, premature. The failure is attributed by Dr. MacNeill, with characteristic irony, to "the perversity of the Irish mind, afflicted with a double dose of original sin, refusing to recognize either physical superiority in the arts of war or moral superiority in the arts of peace."[3]

As far as the arts of peace were concerned the Irish had as yet

[2] Cf. *The Revival of Irish Literature* (1894).
[3] MacNeill, *Phases of Irish History*, p. 324.

but slight occasion for misgiving, for in the midst of continuous warfare they beheld their native institutions not only surviving but taking on new life, flourishing even to the extent of being accepted by the Strangers. It is true that there was some beginning of anti-Irish legislation, including the establishment of the Pale, a palisaded section in the vicinity of Dublin, within which the English interests were entrenched and, according to Campion, "whereout they durst not peepe."[4] But beyond that everything Irish throve, particularly Irish culture. The monastic schools still nurtured the things of the mind, raising up scholars to keep alight the torch of native learning, and sending them forth to kindle new fires on the Continent by founding colleges (really universities), where the fame of such scholars was so firmly established that it still lingers on, as in Paris and certain parts of Italy. Scribes worked sedulously at the compilation of beautiful MSS, among those dating from this period, besides the *Book of Leinster* already referred to, being the *Annals of Innisfallen,* the *Annals of Boyle,* compiled at a monastery whose foundation preceded the Invasion by about eight years, the *Annals of Ulster,* begun by Cathal Maguire, an illustrious priest, philosopher and historian, the concluding portion of the *Annals of Loch Ce,* and the exceptionally interesting *Annals of Connaught.*

In addition to the compilers of these works, numerous scholars won renown for their writings not only on the subject of history, but also on philosophy and law. One of them was the founder of the family of hereditary historians named MacFirbis, whose most illustrious member was Duald (see p. 77). The bardic schools likewise continued to function, and from them poets emerged to devote their gifts to one or other of the old families, as in the past poets had so served kings. The most notable of these constituted the hereditary poetic family of O'Daly, whose most distinguished member was Donnchadh (Donogha Mor, d. 1244), whom Dr. Douglas Hyde calls "the

[4] *History,* p. 6.

greatest and best religious poet that perhaps Erin ever had."[5]
He is said to have been abbot of the great abbey of Boyle and is
credited with the authorship of more than thirty devotional
poems, some of them of considerable length, and many of them,
even in translation, testifying to the profound religious faith and
high poetic skill of the author, who, as a matter of fact, on
account of the smoothness of his verse, was called the Irish Ovid.

A branch of the family, called the O'Dalys of Meath to distinguish them from their kindred of Clare, included Muiredach
(fl. 1215), called *Albanach*, because he was forced to flee to
Scotland for having slain the steward of the O'Donnell. This
chieftain, in a manner characteristic of his race and his age,
permitted the fugitive to return on the strength of a plea he had
addressed to him in poetic form.

Carroll Mor O'Daly, who lived in the fourteenth century and
was the author (1390) of the famous song *Eileen Aroon*, was an
accomplished gentleman, whose desire to marry Eileen Kavanagh
was opposed by her friends, so that he was forced to flee. He
returned, however, on the eve of her marriage and in the disguise of a harper poured out this song, in consequence of which
she eloped with him that night. He seems not to have been a
member of either branch of the family mentioned above, whose
work testifies so strongly to the persistence of the Gaelic cultural system, despite the intrusion of the foreigners. When the
O'Dalys wrote and for some time after, the poets who wrote in
Irish exhibited supreme mastery over the traditional forms of
Irish prosody, which included besides the ancient *rosc* and *con-
aclon* such later developments as the Great Ranneacht, consisting
of lines of seven syllables, each line ending in a monosyllable.[6]

A new school of poets had arisen to take the place of the
departed bardic order, and the new metres which they introduced, based more upon stress than upon number of syllables,
continued to be used by the Gaelic poets of the following centuries. Besides such purely devotional poetry as that written by

---

[5] *Religious Songs of Connaught.*
[6] Hyde, *Religious Songs.*

Donough Mor O'Daly, a plentiful crop of controversial verse was begotten of the persecutions and the religious wars, some of it more scathing than anything uttered by the most satirical of the pagan bards.

The extent to which the newcomers became culturally assimilated by the Irish is exemplified by the Geraldine Earl of Desmond, who, although Lord Justice of Ireland (1367) and therefore a Palesman, was also a poet, writing mostly in Irish, though he also used Norman-French. In the *Annals of Clonmacnoise* he is described as "a nobleman of wonderful bounty, mirth, cheerfulness in conversation, charitable in his deeds, easy of access, a witty and ingenious composer of Irish poetry, and a learned and profound chronicler, and in fine one of the English nobility that had Irish learning and professors thereof in greatest reverence."[7]

Unquestionably, despite the continuous tumult by which the country was rocked, despite the innumerable legislative attempts to discriminate against the native population in favour of the English, Irish literary art was still vigorous, still powerful not only to sustain itself, but to communicate something of its vitality. Gaelic was still so much a living tongue that, as we have seen, it was spoken even by some of the residents of the Pale, and beyond that boundary English was not spoken at all. The process of assimilation described by Spenser in the sixteenth century was well begun in the fourteenth: "'What is this that you say?'" exclaims Eudoxius, "'of so many as remain English of them? Why? Are not they that were once English English still?'" To which Eudoxius replies, "'No, for some of them are degenerated and grown almost mere Irish, yea, and more malitious to the English than the Irish themselves.'"[8]

The Irish neglect of English, as Mrs. Green points out, must not be attributed, as it has been, to indifference to learning or self-improvement, for the Irish had never yet been shut out from knowledge by lack of knowledge or lack of the desire for it. Their own language and Latin or even Greek had hitherto served their need, when, as they so often did, they sought learning at Con-

[7] Quoted by Sigerson, *Bards of the Gael and the Gall*, p. 419.
[8] *State of Ireland.*

tinental sources, although as often as not it was the Irish traveller who carried learning abroad. It is true that the country was practically untouched by the Renaissance, and there are scholars (such as Corkery, *The Hidden Ireland*) who in their understanding of the true character of the Renaissance do not regard this immunity as a calamity.

Such in any case was the situation when Henry VIII asserted his claim to the kingship of Ireland, a situation which warrants the statement that up to that time the English kings were never lords of the country in anything but name. Thenceforth matters were considerably simplified, if not improved, for with the title of King, Henry likewise assumed the title of Head of the Church in Ireland, a role which he interpreted, as he had in England, in terms of pillage. But in Ireland Henry encountered, as he had not in England, an obstacle to his conception of supreme lordship in Church and State, and that was the Irish race.

Dr. Kenney gives it as his opinion that nothing was less desired than the conversion of the Irish people to Protestantism, the real design being to "deprive the Irish race of all power which might come from the possession of property, educational rights, social or official position, even special industrial skill—to reduce them to a helpless, hopeless mass of ignorant agricultural helots."[9] Be that as it may, there remains, of course, the simple fact that the basis of this deprivation was the refusal to apostatise, and that most of those who accepted the conditions were not "reduced." In any case, there forthwith began a campaign against the race itself, compared with which the sporadic barbarities of the Plantagenets resembled acts of benevolence. Clearly, since the campaign was undertaken in the name of enlightenment and religion, it was directed primarily against the Irish Church and Irish culture, regardless of the incidental acquisition of vast tracts of Irish land and ecclesiastical properties. Irish commerce and industries were assailed continuously and systematically, the Irish Fairs, once such incentives to trade, were abolished, English speculators were introduced with the object of exploiting the country's vast material resources, and the Irish were driven out

[9] Op. cit., pp. 48-49.

of the crafts they had developed to such an admirable degree of excellence, so that they might be taken over by English workmen. The direct purpose of these measures was the enrichment of the English; indirectly it provided the occasion to accuse of thriftlessness and profligacy a people reduced by poverty to enforced idleness. They were permitted to work only at the most servile occupations, particularly the members of the old families who had been lords of the land. Irish customs were attacked, usually in the most humiliating way, as when the women of Galway were forbidden to wear their native cloaks and the Irish fashion of wearing the hair was prohibited.

But it went deeper than that. The long effort to extirpate the Irish language, to wipe out every vestige of the Irish spirit, was begun by Henry VIII, of course in the name of enlightenment, and a time came when a Gaelic grammar was compiled for the use of Queen Elizabeth, so that she could study a language whose use was forbidden to the Irish-born, at least those of them who were Catholic, as most of them were, and an Irish harper was engaged to entertain the Queen with music that was banned in the country which produced it. Large numbers of Irish harps had been destroyed under Henry VIII, and great treasures of MSS, including valuable historical documents, were systematically done away with. After the final pillage of Clonmacnoise it was recorded that there was not left a bell of any size, an image, or an altar, or a book, or a gem, or even glass in a window. As part of this same cultural iconoclasm the schools were ruined and the students scattered, largely as a result of the rifling of the monasteries.

Thenceforth for upwards of two hundred years the Irish Catholic was debarred from seeking any education whatever, reduced to such a condition of poverty and illiteracy as apparently to warrant the constantly reiterated but obviously unfounded charge of barbarism and degeneracy. Subsequent to the Norman invasion, Irish students seeking a career at law were wont to resort to Oxford, there to study the English feudal code, although as early as the reign of Henry V they were driven from its precincts. But after the Reformation no Irish Catholic could open any sort of public school, nor could any Catholic send his children to the Continent to study. Needless to say, the bardic schools were closed and the poets silenced, although Spenser was aware of "a certain kind of people called bards who are to them instead of poets."

And yet the thirst for knowledge and the means of satisfying it persisted, for the Queen's deputy reported to her with some exasperation that the number of Irishmen's sons sent to Continental universities was trebled, and in a later report there is a note of something resembling desperation in his recommendation that all brehons, bards, rhymers, friars, monks, Jesuits, pardoners and nuns should be executed by martial law. Trinity College was founded by Elizabeth in Dublin in 1595 for the purpose of attracting scholars who had hitherto sought an education in France, Italy or Spain, but inasmuch as the education there imparted was intended to fit students for the Protestant ministry, it is scarcely to be wondered at that the Irish, who preferred ignorance to loss of faith, should have strengthened the belief in their savagery by supplying few candidates for the privilege.

Whatever its unquestionable merits as a language, especially a literary language, which had now reached its golden zenith, English had come to be regarded by the Irish as an instrument of proselytism, and as such to be looked upon with suspicion, not to say intense antagonism. For some of the proselytising agencies, realizing the importance of the native speech to Irish minds, had turned certain books, such as the Bible, into Gaelic for use in the schools, which were themselves instruments of proselytism. In general, however, throughout Ireland the Irish tongue was beginning to give way and to be superseded by English, to the wider diffusion of which so many inducements were offered. As a consequence Ireland and Irish subjects began to make their appearance in English books and the figure which later came to be known as the stage Irishman was conspicuous on the English stage as early as the late Elizabethan period.

The average Irishman, whether educated or not, would know little of the English books dealing with Ireland which were published at intervals even so early as this period. Although

Professor Russell K. Anspach's recently published *Irish Poetry from the English Invasion to 1798*[10] points out that some of the earliest specimens of such poetry occur in an early fourteenth-century MS deriving from the Franciscan monastery of Kildare, few of them at any period enhanced the literary prestige of either England or Ireland.

Noteworthy among the English books of this period dealing with Ireland were Stanyhurst's *Description of the State of Ireland, The History of Ireland,* by his tutor Edmund Campion (the same who died a martyr for the Catholic faith at Tyburn, where, according to Standish O'Grady, England rewarded him with a degree higher than any he had ever taken at Oxford, where he had had such a distinguished career), both of which were included in Holinshed's *Chronicles* (1577), and Spenser's *View of the State of Ireland* (1596).

Campion's work, which is exceptionally lively, is dedicated with the usual Elizabethan fulsomeness of praise, to the Earl of Leicester, his patron, to whom he accounts for the book's short-comings by stating that "to handle and lay these things together I had not in all the space of ten weeks," too little time, it might be supposed, in which to do justice to his subject.

Despite the fact that with Stanyhurst's *Description,* Spenser's *View,* and the anonymous *Pacata,* it continues in the Cambrensis vein, Campion's book reveals a certain degree of reluctant admiration for the race whom it reviles. This, for instance, is in part the character which he gives the Irish: "Religious, franke, amorous, ireful, sufferable of pains infinite, very glorious, many sorcerers, excellent horsemen, delighted with Warres, great almesgivers, passing in hospitalitie; the lewder sort both Clarkes and Laymen are sensuall and loose to leachery above measure. The same being vertuously bred up or reformed, are such mirrours of holiness and austeritie, that other Nations retain but a shewe or shadow of devotion in comparison of them. . . . They are sharpe-witted, lovers of learning, capable of any studie where-

[10] By "Irish poetry" Professor Anspach means "poetry written in English in Ireland."

unto they bend themselves, constant in travaile, adventurous, intractable, kind-hearted, secret in displeasure."

Campion recognizes Irish "of both sortes, meere and English," and of the "meere" he has clearly every desire to report unfavourably, but, almost, it seems, against his will, he bears witness to their virtues. He repeatedly accuses them of barbarity and "wildness," making no attempt to reconcile such traits with their studiousness and love of learning, not to mention their holiness. Their language he dismisses, not as barbarous, but as too difficult, and yet he is aware that their poets, who write Irish learnedly, are held in high esteem and bountifully rewarded; and that otherwise the language could be used effectively: "The tongue is sharpe and sententious, offereth great occasion to quick apothegmes and proper allusions, wherefore their common Jesters, Bards, and Rhymers, are said to delight passingly those that conceive the grace and propriety of the language." The custom prevalent among the Irish nobility of employing a story-teller does not meet with his approval, nor did their manner of lamenting the dead, although the keen helped him to understand the proverb "to weep Irish." Whether it was his ignorance of the language or because he was a victim of the native propensity to beguile the Stranger, he picked up more than his share of absurdly tall tales, but when he credits their scant clothing and sparse fare ("Shamrotes, Water-cresses, Rootes and other hearbes they feed upon") to their low stage of civilization, it is difficult to decide whether he is actuated by ignorance or by zeal to maintain the Earl of Leicester "in the eye and speciall credit" of Elizabeth. Certainly the sense of humour of which Edmund Campion gave such abundant evidence on the scaffold was absent when he undertook to show "how much Ireland is beholden to God for suffering them to be conquered."

Richard Stanyhurst, the son of James Stanyhurst, sometime speaker of the Irish House of Commons, was born in Dublin in 1547 and received his early education at the famous establishment of Peter White in Kilkenny (see Chapter *Behind the Hedge*). He then proceeded to Oxford, where he made the acquaintance of Campion, and after some legal studies returned to Ireland accompanied by Campion as his tutor. Campion having undertaken to contribute a *History of Ireland* to Holinshed's *Chronicles*, was instrumental in Stanyhurst's writing for the same collection his *Description of Ireland* and a continuation of Campion's *History*, all from the same partisan standpoint.

Stanyhurst married twice, went to reside in the Low Countries, where he became a Catholic, and, after the death of his second wife, a priest. In accordance with Gabriel Harvey's theories of prosody, he made a translation of four books of the *Aeneid*, which has been called "a literary monstrosity." Keating says that he came to regret his unjust treatment of Ireland in his *History*, but this seems doubtful.

The extent to which the Irish were "sufferable of pains infinite" is further exemplified by Spenser in the course of a work in which the Poet's Poet employed the choicest Elizabethan prose to demonstrate how thoroughly the Queen's agents in Ireland were discharging the task committed to them. Unquestionably the author of the following description, which parallels Campion's account of the Irish diet, wrote of what he had seen with his own eyes: "For notwithstanding that the same was a most rich and plentifull countrey, full of corne and cattle, that you would have thought they should have been able to stand long, yet ere one yeere and a halfe they were brought to such wretchednesse, as that any stony heart would have rued the same. Out of every corner of the woods and glynnes, they came creeping forth upon their hands, for their legges would not bear them; they looked like anatomies of death, they spake like ghosts crying out of their graves; they did eat the dead carrions, happy where they could find them, yea, and one another soon after, insomuch as the very carcasse they spare not to scrape out of their graves; and, if they found a plot of watercresses or shamrocks, there they flocked as to a feast for the time, yet not able long to continue therewithall; that in short space there were none almost left and a most populous and plentiful countrey suddenly left voyde of man and beast."

It is at least interesting to recall how often this terrible picture is to recur not only in the history but in the literature of Ireland, how often the methods advocated by Spenser were to fail of their object, that is, the reduction of the Irish to submission. Their bodies might be reduced to anatomies of death, but the indomitable spirit recognized by Campion, who had his own share of it, remained unsubdued. This fact gives an almost ironic significance to the very titles of such works as Cambrensis' *History of the Conquest* and the anonymous *Pacata Hibernia, Ireland Appeased and Reduced* (1633), the authorship of which its editor, S. J. O'Grady, attributes to Thomas Stafford, who professes to be merely the editor of a MS found among the papers of Lord Carew, whose "warres" would naturally have been seen at close range by a man who served as lieutenant under him, as Stafford did. After reading such an account as that of Carew's achievements it must indeed have seemed as though only some sort of moral perversity, something like a "double dose of original sin," could account for the fact that the country remained in a state so little resembling appeasement, that again and again it had to be "reduced."

In one sense of the word these were Irish books, a sense that all too soon was to be the only sense in which the phrase would have any meaning. They were Irish inasmuch as they were written in Ireland and about the Irish, but they were written by men who intellectually were living within the Pale, whereout they had never ventured to "peepe." Furthermore, they were not written for Irish perusal, which, from one point of view, was just as well, since the Irish needed no further cause of exacerbation, but which, from another standpoint, was unfortunate, because they helped to strengthen the delusion that a literature written by foreigners (even of Irish birth) for foreigners, was in any true sense of the word Irish at all.

With the "noble kindreds" divested of power and lands, as they were under Elizabeth and Cromwell and William III, with the native princes either slain, often by poison, or driven into exile, with the defeat of Kinsale (1602) and the Boyne (1690), and Limerick (1691), with the flight of the Earls and the Wild Geese and the plantation of Connaught, with religion proscribed

and scholarship degraded and a whole people stricken again and
again with famine in a land of abundance, it was difficult to see
how they could be anything but "reduced." And yet they were
not. Although it was possible to write with literal truth that "The
wolf and the best rebel lodge in one inn, with one diet and one
kind of bedding," something of the spirit which flamed in them
rings out over and over again in the native verse, which still
continued to be written. Typical of such writers was David
O'Bruadair, a native of Limerick, where he was born not later
than 1630. His parents were evidently in comfortable circumstances, since he was well educated, that is he was trained in the
speaking and writing of Latin, Irish and English, but where or
how the training was acquired is not specified. He was married
and at first prosperous, but he fell into poverty, in part as the
result of his own spendthrift habits, in part owing to the ill
fortune of his patron, Sir John Fitzgerald of Cloughlais. Arrested
for complicity in the Titus Oates plot, Sir John was scarcely in a
position to bestow patronage, although he survived to fight under
Sarsfield. O'Bruadair was reduced to the condition of an agricultural labourer, and wandered about the district, singing his
poems and seeking assistance, his failure to find which, to him
an indication of the degeneracy of the Irish, once so appreciative
of the arts, is the constant theme of his verse.

That he was an artist is evident from the Introduction to the
translation of O'Bruadair made for the Irish Texts Society[11] by
Rev. John MacErlean, S.J., wherein the learned editor makes
O'Bruadair's mastery of form the occasion for an instructive commentary on Irish metrical structure that not only demonstrates
the impossibility of adequate translation, but also the hopelessness
of arriving at any due appreciation of the original on the basis
of translation. "The charm of alliteration," writes Father Mac-
Erlean, "which binds together for the ear every word connected
by sense, and the constant recurrence of vocalic assonance which
arouses the attention of the mind and satisfies its expectations,
combine to give to every stanza of an Irish poem an harmonious

[11] Pt. I (1910).

unity and a gratifying completeness, which defy reproduction and baffle the translator. Again, the extraordinary copiousness of the Irish vocabulary and the equally astonishing freedom in the employment of figurative language, while enabling the poet to reveal every shade of meaning and to dwell without palling upon the same thought in ever varying language, must, of necessity, when turned into a less copious or less figurative language, either weary the reader by continuous repetitions, or displease him by unfamiliar metaphors."[12]

For English ways and English speech, at least as aped by the Irish, O'Bruadair had nothing but scorn:

> Woe to him who cannot simper English.

In vehement terms he upbraids Ireland, his "stately darling," for submission to the invaders:

> It pains my heart to see her fertile sloping mantle
> Trodden, trampled down by droves of fluffy Saxons,

and he bitterly laments the fate which compels him, because of poverty, to live among "gloomy boors." But bitterly as he resents his own hardships, he is even more keenly aware of the sorrows of his countrymen, which he bewails repeatedly. He is stung to fury by the thought of what the Irish have suffered at the hands of Cromwell, especially the reduction of the ancient race to make room for adventurers:

> To take their places then will come the fat-rumped jeerers,
> After crushing them, their culture, and their cities,—
> Laden all with packs and plates and brass and pewter,
> With shaven jaws and English talk and braggart accent.
> Every dowdy, then, will wear a cape of beaver,
> And don a gown of silk from poll of head to ankle;
> All our castles will be held by clownish upstarts,
> Crowded full with veterans of cheese and pottage.

Among the particular objects of his resentment were the Duke of Ormonde, and his protégé and tool, the Franciscan, Peter

[12] Loc. cit. I, xlix.

Walsh, a product of that Irish monastery at Louvain whose history is otherwise so illustrious. What especially aroused O'Bruadair's ire was Walsh's *Loyal Remonstrance,* which failed of its chief purpose, which was to precipitate the Irish Catholics into schism.

But there was no schism. With a price on his head, the priest still said Mass before dawn in the woods and fields, where many a Mass-rock is still pointed out. Denied education at home, since "the ruin of the monasteries and schools begun by Henry was completed by Elizabeth,"[13] the Irish lover of learning betook himself to the Continent, to Spain, perhaps, where at Salamanca Philip II had founded "the Royal College of the Noble Irish," or to Seville, Alcala or Santiago, where there were similar establishments. Or he might join the numerous groups of his countrymen at Louvain, where the Franciscan, John Colgan, toiled to preserve Irish MSS salvaged from destruction in Ireland, as at Rome Luke Wadding laboured to the same end, or he might repair to France, where the Irish were more numerous still, since by the close of the eighteenth century more than two-thirds of those who were studying abroad were doing so in that country.

"The Wild Geese in foreign colleges," says Professor D'Alton, comparing their lot with that of the Irishmen who fled to serve in foreign armies, ". . . had winged their flight only to return. In the class-rooms their places were often first; and when promotion to the priesthood came, they might, had they remained abroad, have attained to the highest positions in the Church. But they were wanted at home to keep the lamp of faith still burning, and once more, disguised as a sailor or concealed in a smuggler's craft, they were borne across the sea. Crowned with the highest academic honours, able to grapple with the deepest questions of philosophy and theology, familiar with the facts and with the lessons of history, these men of culture settled down in the obscurity of an Irish village. But the poverty and obscurity of their position was the least portion of the hardships they endured. Guiltless of crime, they were declared guilty by the law; eager only to min-

[13] D'Alton, *History of Ireland,* II, p. 510.

ister to the souls of their fellow-countrymen, they were at the mercy of the common informer, the bigoted parson, the ferocious magistrate, the drunken squireen. Their liberty was ever in peril, their shelter often the wood and forest; their end in a village cabin or it might be at the end of a hangman's rope."[14]

As the terrible seventeenth century was merged in the still more terrible eighteenth, a voice was uplifted sobbingly in Kerry, uttering words that may well serve to draw this account of that period to a close. The voice was that of the little-known John O'Connell, Bishop of Ardfert, a member of the O'Connell family of Iveragh, and hence a kinsman of the Liberator. Owing to the dark times in which he lived, little was recorded of his life or his episcopate; indeed, the fact of his clerical quality had to be proved by his translator and editor (Martin A. O'Brennan, Dublin, 1855), since such matters were necessarily shrouded in secrecy in order to outwit the priest-hunters. The work which gives him a place in this chronicle is a lengthy poem entitled *Dirge for Ireland*, in which he reviews Irish history down to his own sorrowful times, its concluding lines vindicating both his warrant and his ability "to weep Irish":

> Whither shall we go in future? or what shall we do?
> No shelter for us, hills, woods, mountains.
> There is not our remedy with a physician in Ireland,
> But God to pray, and the saints together.
>
> O God, that brightenest the moon and stars,
> That formedst the earth, heaven and the sphere,
> That wast, and that art, and that will be without decay,
> One God alone thou art, and not three Gods.
>
> Art thou deaf, or whither art thou looking,
> Was it not you who overthrew the monsters with thy nod,
> What little to you the time that you are patient?
> Our faith is gone; there is living but a spark of it.
>
> Is this your promise to Saint Patrick
> Upon Mount Hermon on his coming to Erin?
> Or on the Reek after his fasting?
> Or of the angel Victor the time he agreed with him?

[14] Op. cit., II, p. 513.

Oh! it is not so! You are not false,
No one knows the time thou hast spent of thy existence,
There is not a hole in thy store, though great thy bounty,
It is ourselves deserved everything that is done.

Whereupon he demands the presence and the prompt assistance of Mary, "fair necked, spotless," and of all the saints from whom Ireland has reason and right to look for help, ending with an *Ave Maria,* half in Latin, half Gaelic.

Ireland's noble cultural edifice had thus been destroyed, and these were the means of its destruction: first invasion without warrant or justification; then a prolonged and inexorable war of conquest, a conquest that was never accomplished nor at any instant of seven hundred years acknowledged by the Irish people. It was accompanied by the confiscation of Irish lands and goods and the reduction of their rightful owners to stark and hopeless poverty. It was hopeless because they were prevented from owning a foot of their ancient territory and from securing employment in which they could earn the means of keeping body and soul together, so that they had no choice but an ignoble idleness which was reputed to them for shiftlessness. Deprived of their own laws by abrogation and of any semblance of right in the sight of English law; shut out from education by the destruction of their native schools and denied admission to English schools save at a price which they were never so far subjugated as to be willing to pay; robbed of their written literature and forbidden to speak the language in which it was written, they possessed, however, one great source of culture. To this the Irish clung, for the sake of it they endured the long martyrdom which constitutes their subsequent history, and that was their religion. This inspired their adherence to the proscribed Catholic Church, whose cultural resources they well knew, since under it their native genius had so flourished; it is still the reason why one of the strongest emotions in an Irishman's heart is the love of learning.

Chapter V. *THE EGGS OF EAGLES*

> *The O'Neills are gone into exile now,*
> *And tortured Ireland weeps her fill,*
> *But the eggs of eagles still make eagles,*
> *Wherever they're hatched they are eagles still.*
> From the Irish, tr. DOUGLAS HYDE.

UNDER THE CIRCUMSTANCES, considering the extent to which Irishmen had always been apostles of culture, it was only natural that despite handicaps and penalties, some Irishmen still should have striven to carry on the work of the interdicted scholars, the penalized *ollamhs* and historians, laymen like Philip O'Sullivan Beare, and Roderick O'Flaherty, for instance, or priests like Wadding and Colgan and Ward, for whom scholarship was possible only at the price of exile.

Philip O'Sullivan Beare was a member of an ancient Irish family, to whose principal stronghold in Tipperary even Cormac mac Art had been forced to send tribute from Tara. There the O'Sullivans remained entrenched until 1192, when they began to be gradually dislodged by the Normans and forced to settle elsewhere, at which time the family divided into two branches, that of O'Sullivan Mor in Kerry and that of O'Sullivan Beare in Cork. In view of the subsequent Spanish associations of this branch, it is of interest to note that the name which became their cognomen and the title of their Irish territory was derived from that of Beara, daughter of the King of Castile and wife of the family's almost legendary ancestor.

Philip was born in 1602 at Dursey Island, one of the seventeen children of Dermot, whose cousin as head of the family bore the title of O'Sullivan Beare. Thirteen of Philip's brothers died in the terrible warfare of that time, and after the fall of Dunboy the four surviving children and their parents emigrated to Spain, where Philip was educated by Irish and Spanish professors and where he received a commission in the Spanish Navy. He is the author of numerous Latin writings, two of them of exceptional importance to Irish literature. They are *Decas Patritiana,* a life of St. Patrick, and *Historiae Catholicae Iberniae Compendium,* published at Lisbon in 1621, an English translation of which under the title *Ireland under Elizabeth,* was made by Matthew Byrne and published in Dublin in 1903. The singular importance of this work rests on the fact that it is based on accounts of the conflict which the author heard from his father and uncles, who had actively participated in it. He died at Madrid in 1660.

Luke Wadding, whom Mr. DeBlacam calls "one of the greatest Irishmen of all time," was born at Waterford in 1588, the youngest of fourteen children. At thirteen he was already well grounded in the Classics, and after the early loss of his parents he proceeded to the Irish seminary at Lisbon, later entering the Order of Friars Minor, in which he was ordained a priest in 1613. Later studies were pursued at Salamanca, where he occupied the chair of theology. This circumstance led to his being chosen to act as theologian to the embassy which King Philip III sent to Rome, to participate in discussions concerning the doctrine of the Immaculate Conception. He was especially eminent in the field of philosophy, having been responsible for the monumental edition of Duns Scotus, as well as for the great collection of the Franciscan writers.

But the paramount interest of Luke Wadding's life seems to have been Ireland, its literature and its lamentable history. This led to his undertaking a collection of the *Annals of Ireland,* most of the labour on which was carried on under his supervision by a group of Irish scholars at the Franciscan College of St. Isidore in Rome, which he had founded in 1625. In connection with this project he set on foot a vast effort to collect MSS in Ireland, a task that was attended by so many difficulties that it had at last to be abandoned, not, however, before five thousand select works had been collected for the library, in addition to eight hundred bound volumes of MSS.

Wadding was instrumental, through Cardinal Ludovisi, in the foundation of another Irish college in Rome, this one for the training of secular clergy, to which was given the Cardinal's name. He was chiefly responsible for the inclusion of the feast of St. Patrick in the calendar of the Church and he was the means of supplying both military and financial aid to Ireland in her struggle for freedom. In 1641 he was the bearer to Owen Roe O'Neill of the Pope's blessing and the sword of the great Earl of Tyrone. A man of eminent piety as well as of profound and varied learning, Luke Wadding died at St. Isidore's in 1657.

Among the scholars at St. Isidore's during this period was Rev. Francis Molloy, born early in the seventeenth century at Meath, of a once princely family, one member of which is said to have entertained 960 men in his home during the Christmas holidays in the reign of Elizabeth. After Francis became a Franciscan he was professor of theology at St. Isidore's, and also agent general for the Irish in Rome. Besides a theological treatise, he was the author of *Lucerna fidelium* (1676), which despite its Latin title was published in the Irish language and characters, but his reputation rests chiefly on his *Grammatica Latino-Hibernica* (1677), the first printed Irish-Latin grammar. This work was dedicated to Cardinal Camillo with the explanation that the proscription of the Irish language in Ireland had occasioned irreparable loss and neglect of historical records and endangered the existence of the language itself. A curious article on Dr. Molloy in the *Anthologia Hibernica* for 1793 manifests considerable pride in Dr. Molloy's achievements, but clearly approves of the suppression and quotes the law as its own sufficient defence: "It doth much more confer to the indiction of rude and ignorant people to the knowledge of almighty God for concordance with them that be civil people." Dr. Molloy died in 1684.

While Wadding was at Salamanca there came to the college another Irishman on whom he had a lasting influence. This was Hugh Ward, born in Donegal about 1590. His father was head of the Tirconnell branch of an ancient family who acted as *ollamhs* to the O'Donnells (hence the family name, Mac am Bhaird, in English Ward). Hugh went to Salamanca in 1607, where a few years later he entered the Franciscans. He already had a profound knowledge of Irish antiquities, which led him to found a school of Irish archaeology at the College of St. Anthony at Louvain, where he projected a comprehensive historical series, including the *Lives of the Irish Saints*. This was an undertaking in which he naturally had the sympathy and assistance of Wadding, as well as of a younger man, on whom was laid the task of returning to Ireland in quest of the MSS on which the Louvain scholars were to work. This was Michael O'Clery, the greatest of the so-called Four Masters.

The college of St. Anthony at Louvain, which Ward thus made such a centre of intellectual activity, and whose reputation was enhanced by so many distinguished Irish scholars, was founded in 1616 by one of the most brilliant of them all, Florence Conry (Flaithri O'Mulconry), born in Galway in 1560. His studies were pursued in the Netherlands and Spain. Having become a Franciscan at Salamanca, he was made provincial of his order in Ireland, and in an attempt to reach the scene of his duties he sailed with the Armada. How he escaped the disaster in which that venture ended is not recorded, but he succeeded in reaching Ireland during Tyrone's rebellion, after Kinsale accompanying Hugh Roe O'Donnell to Spain, where he soon assisted at the death bed of the great chieftain.

In 1609 he was consecrated bishop of Tuam, but was never able to take possession of his see, which he governed through vicars general. In 1616 he founded the great college at Louvain, in whose scholarly pursuits he was a leader. As a profound theologian he wrote many books in Latin, but his only Irish book was the translation of a Spanish devotional work. It was published at Louvain, where Conry had established a printing press.

He never lost his interest in Irish affairs, and it was he who presented O'Sullivan Beare's *Relation* to the royal patron, to whom it was dedicated. Conry died at Madrid in 1629.

Conry's career is closely parallelled by that of Hugh MacCaghwell, who was born at Saul, Co. Down, in 1626. His early education was in part received at a famous school on the Isle of Man, after which he became tutor to the sons of the Prince of Tyrone, by whom he was sent to Spain to solicit help for the Irish cause. There he continued his studies and became a Franciscan, and it was largely through his influence at court that funds were available for the foundation of St. Anthony's College at Louvain. As lecturer in the college, of which he was also superior, he numbered Ward, Fleming and Colgan among his students. Called to Rome as lecturer, he assisted Wadding in the foundation of St. Isidore's and the Ludovisi College. He died in 1626, shortly after having been made archbishop of Armagh and primate of All Ireland. His numerous works are mostly in Latin, but in Irish he wrote a treatise on the sacrament of penance.

Conspicuous among the scholars at Louvain during this period was the Irish Franciscan, Father John Colgan, who was born in Donegal in the early part of the seventeenth century. As a member of the Franciscan Order he was able to make his theological studies at St. Anthony's College, and thereafter participated in those Irish researches for which the college became famous. It was he who utilized most of the materials assembled by Ward, especially the MSS which O'Clery collected in Ireland. Colgan's special task was a work dealing with the whole range of Irish ecclesiastical history, of which only a part has been published, but that part includes the important *Acta Sanctorum Hiberniae* (1645) and the *Trias Thaumaturga* (Sts. Patrick, Brigid and Columcille). Although Colgan had a considerable knowledge of Irish, else he could not have availed himself of O'Clery's services, he wrote in Latin. While D'Alton considers him "as credulous as Keating," he was a man of great ability and industry, who was handicapped in his work by frail health, and who died in 1658.

Michael O'Clery (O Cleirigh), chief of the Four Masters, not only acted as scout for the Louvain scholars, he was a great scholar in his own right; "a chronicler by descent and education," in his own phrase in his memorable dedication of the *Annals*, while elsewhere he describes himself as one "whose inheritance

it is from my ancestors to be a chronicler" (*Book of Invasions*).[1]
He is first heard of in 1627 (he was born in Donegal in 1575) in
connection with his visits to Franciscan monasteries in Ireland in
search of ancient MSS to be turned over to the scholars working
at Louvain, where he was already known as an antiquary when
he arrived there as a layman. Having become a Franciscan lay
brother, he was sent back to Ireland in search of the MS Lives
of the saints, "written in the language of my country and very
ancient." After he had laboured at this task for some fifteen
years, he began his own historical work, of which the most
important part is the great collection of the sacred and profane
Annals of Ireland (1632-1636). In this he was joined by Ferfessa
O'Mulconry, a Franciscan, Cucogry O'Clery, a layman who was
also a poet, and Cucogry O'Degnan, the other three Masters.

For this monumental undertaking they secured, according to
ancient custom, the patronage of a native chieftain, Fergal
O'Gara, hereditary lord of Magh-O'Gara, known as Prince of
Coolavin. In his dedication to O'Gara, O'Clery reminds him that
"it seemed to you a cause of pity and regret, grief and sorrow
(for the glory of God and the honour of Ireland) how much the
race of Gaedhil the son of Niul have passed under cloud and
darkness, without a knowledge or record of the death or obit of
saint or virgin, archbishop, bishop, abbot or other noble dignitary
of the Church, of king or of prince or of chieftain or of the
synchronism or connexion of one with the other." It was in the
hope of somewhat dissipating this darkness that O'Clery and his
colleagues undertook the *Annals*, in addition to which work, of
which the modern edition fills seven quarto volumes, running to
4215 pages, the Masters likewise compiled the *Succession of the
Kings of Ireland* now at St. Isidore's, which includes also the
Book of Rights and the *Book of Invasions*.[2]

Michael O'Clery was likewise the sole author of several Lives

[1] Rev. Brendan Jennings, *Michael O Clerigh, Chief of the Four Masters,
and His Associates* (Dublin, 1936).
[2] Of this, the *Lebor Gabála*, they made a new edition under the patronage
of Brian ruodh Maguire, Baron of Ennis Killen (Kenney, op. cit., p. 42).

of the Irish saints, a volume of poems on the O'Donnells of Donegal (to whom the Wards were hereditary *ollamhs*) and a collection of Irish historical poems, included in the same volume with the tract entitled *The War of the Gaedhil with the Gaill* (see p. 45). Underlying all the work of the Masters was the scholarly realization that, "Should the writing of them be neglected at present, they would not again be found to be put on record, even to the end of the world." The Four Masters, as they were called by Colgan, who gave the title by which it is generally known to the work which the Masters themselves called *Annals of the Kingdom of Ireland,* are the embodiment of ancient Irish cultural tradition, not only because the O'Clerys were hereditary scholars, nor because among the MSS books utilized by all four were one that belonged to the O'Mulconry and another to the O'Degnan family, but chiefly because of the spirit of disinterested consecration in which they worked, amid poverty and discomfort, in the bare cells of the almost ruinous convent of Donegal, with the world whose noble traditions they were striving to save from oblivion going down about them in bloodshed and flame and death. Michael O'Clery died at Louvain in 1643.

Geoffrey Keating, who has been called the Herodotus of Ireland, differed from the Masters in many respects, but chiefly in the fact that he toiled alone, without patron or support, at the gigantic task of writing *Foras Feasa ar Eirinn* or *Elements of the History of Ireland,* "the first comprehensive history of Ireland written in the Irish language."[3] Born at Burges, Tipperary, in 1570, he was educated at Bordeaux, where he became a professor and whence he returned to act as parish priest of Tybrid, Tipperary, in which place he died in 1650. Among his writings are a treatise on the Mass, a moral dissertation entitled *The Three Shafts of Death,* edited with glossary and appendix by Robert Atkinson, professor of Sanskrit and philosophy at the University of Dublin, for the Royal Irish Academy in 1890, and his great "semi-bardic" history, with which modern Irish is said to begin. This work was written amid the caves and rocks of Tipperary,

[3] Kenney, op. cit., p. 44.

to which he had been driven as a result of a violent denunciation
of adultery, which aroused the anger of a Catholic woman whose
scandalous life made her only too obviously the object of the
attack.

Keating's was not critical history, but that it was written at all
was sufficiently extraordinary, considering the straits to which
its author was reduced. Educated abroad though he was, he knew
Irish as well as English and Latin, and in his native tongue he
wrote his *History of Ireland from the Earliest Times to the Norman Invasion.* The fact that he was in hiding does not seem to
have tamed his spirit, for he wrote in a vigorous and courageous
style, calling Ireland in her then condition of subjugation "the
harlot of England." Pearse considered him "the greatest of the
nationalist poets."

The next name on this list is that of Duald MacFirbis, sometimes called the last of the *shanachies.* Born at Lackan, Tipperary, in 1585 and, like O'Clery, an hereditary historian of long
descent, he attended the school of Alexander Lynch in Galway,
where he was a fellow-student of Roderick O'Flaherty and the
master's son, John Lynch, afterwards famous as the author of
Cambrensis Eversus. MacFirbis also attended several native
schools of law and history, going thence to the College of St.
Nicholas in Galway, where he compiled his famous book of
Pedigrees, in which, in accordance with old custom, he states that
the time of writing is that of the religious wars between the
Catholics of Ireland and the heretics of Ireland and Scotland.
He came to a tragic end, having been wantonly murdered (1670),
although at an advanced age, the last, as O'Curry calls him, "of
the regularly educated and most accomplished masters of ancient
Erinn." In commenting on the handwriting of an ancient MS
which he calls "the most beautiful I ever met," O'Curry adds that
it strongly resembled that of MacFirbis. He was in direct line of
descent from the compiler of the great *Book of Lecain,* at which
place his family maintained a patrimony from early times until
the Cromwellian period.

Roderick O'Flaherty, who was a schoolfellow of MacFirbis at
Alexander Lynch's school and who later studied literature and

history under MacFirbis himself, was born at Moycullen in 1629. On appeal he recovered some of the property he had lost by the Civil War and in 1685 published in Latin a *History of Ireland* from the earliest times to the year 1684, under the title *Ogygia seu rerum hibernicarum chronologia.* In a dedicatory address directed to James, "Duke of York and Albany," Ireland, "the most ancient nursery of your ancestors," is depicted as prostrating herself in deep mourning, with dishevelled hair and tears trickling down her cheeks, in order to present this book, "in which are written lamentations and mourning and woe." The book itself was the first scholarly presentation of Irish history to English readers. Its author died in 1718, in the poverty to which he had been reduced by the Williamite wars.

John Lynch, born in Galway about 1600, the son of the famous schoolmaster, was of Anglo-Norman stock and a supporter of Ormond. He was nevertheless forced into exile by the Puritan occupation of Galway, and he is said to have died at St. Malo in France in 1673. In France he made an English translation of Keating's *History* and in *Cambrensis Eversus* wrote a refutation of Giraldus, which at least shook, if it did not wholly overthrow, the reputation of that arch-vilifier. In this Lynch completed the work which an earlier writer, Father Stephen White, had left in MSS, adding much from the wealth of his own learning, scholarly integrity and intellectual power. He at least has never been discredited, and if he failed to discredit Cambrensis, it is because in the long run readers believe as they please.

Inasmuch as it was likewise a product of the penal times, mention must be made here of the work of the Abbé James MacGeoghan and Sylvester O'Halloran. Although born in Ireland in 1702, the first-named was educated at the Irish College in Paris, in which city he was afterwards assigned to parochial duties. While serving as chaplain to the Irish troops in the French Armies, he wrote in French a *History of Ireland.* He was obliged to rely chiefly on Lynch and Colgan, but he also had access to the *Book of Lecain,* which was then in Paris. He died in Paris in 1763.

Sylvester O'Halloran was a native of Limerick, where he was

born in 1728 and where he died in 1807. He studied medicine at
Paris and Leyden, specializing in diseases of the eye, for the
treatment of which he founded the Limerick Infirmary. He was
intensely interested in antiquarian studies and, besides *Insula
Sacra* and *Ierne defended*, wrote a general *History of Ireland*
(1774) that was later to play an important part in the revival of
Irish letters (see p. 132).

In a class by themselves but allied at least by sincerity of
purpose with the authors who wrote in the native tradition are
James Ussher, Anglican Archbishop of Armagh, and Sir James
Ware, historian and bibliographer. Ussher was born in Dublin in
1581 and had the distinction of being the second student admitted to TCD (Trinity College, Dublin). He was made bishop
of Meath in 1621, and archbishop of Armagh in 1625. His collected works, published in Dublin in 1848-1864, fill seventeen
volumes. He died in England in 1656, bequeathing his magnificent
library to Trinity College, Dublin. This gift included the super-
latively beautiful *Book of Kells*.

Ware, who was born in Dublin in 1594, was also educated at
TCD, where he was awarded an M.A. in 1616. At an early age
he began a collection of Irish MSS, employing Duald Mac-
Firbis in their transcription and visiting numerous English libraries in the course of his researches. He wrote in Latin a number of
important books, many of them based on ancient *Annals* and
other native records. Although thoroughly British and Protestant
in sympathy, his interest centers to an amazing extent on the
pre-Reformation period of Irish history, especially the monastic
foundations, and he "thinks it not amiss" to transcribe *in toto*
the Bull by which Leo X bestowed upon Henry VIII the title of
Defender of the Faith. He compiled two Books of Irish Writers,
the former of which and the more extensive, contains the
"natives"; the second, those who had any preferment in Ireland,
in which list Stanyhurst's name is the last but one. Ware acknowl-
edges his indebtedness to Archbishop Ussher for the use of MSS.

As a result of his study of ancient Irish history he points out
with delightful inconsistency that, "it will appear that for some

ages after St. Patrick's coming into Ireland this kingdom flourished in Learning, and was deservedly call'd *The Isle of Saints,*
in regard to the great number of holy Men both living here and
travelling hence into foreign Parts for the good of Souls. It will
likewise further appear that by reason of intestine Wars, and the
Commotions raised there by the Danes and Norwegians, Learning lay long time neglected and dead, and by its happy submission unto Henry the Second, King of England, that Learning
revived."[4] In excuse for writing on historical subjects, he remarks
that "to be ignorant of what happened before a Man was born
is always to be a Boy." His works include *Antiquities,* and *Annals*
of Ireland, *Gesta Hibernorum,* Chronology 1603 to 1704; a list
of the *Prelates of Ireland* (1665); *Books of Irish Writers,* and
Historical Relations, or, *A Discovery of the True Causes Why
Ireland was never entirely subdued . . . . until the beginning of
the reign of King James I.*

Although the work on which the fame of William Molyneaux
principally rests was written in English, his resentment of injustice allies him in spirit with the Gaelic writers. He was born
in Dublin in 1656, and died in 1698, shortly after the publication
of his *The Case of Ireland's being bound by Acts of Parliament in
England stated,* which is the first declaration of Irish independence.

Molyneaux had been stirred to action by the sight of many
inequalities of justice, the most immediate of which was the suppression of the Irish linen trade. In his Introduction he considers
the possibility of the book's not being favourably received in
England, but rejects the suggestion with the remark, "We are
miserable indeed if we are not allowed to complain when we feel
we are hurt." The exact degree of misery his complaint might have
incurred, he did not live to experience, for he died before he
could be impeached, as he had every prospect of being. As it

---

[4] The above is quoted from an edition of Ware's writings "now first
published in one volume in English, very useful for all persons who are
desirous of being acquainted with the ancient and present state of the
Kingdom" (Dublin, 1705).

was, the printer was prosecuted and had to submit to being reprimanded on his knees before the Irish House.

Perhaps this chapter could not more appropriately be brought to a close than with a brief mention of one who in another field than history bore witness to the eagle strain in the Irish blood. This was the famous Turlough O'Carolan, known as the Last of the Bards. He was born in Newton, near Nebber, Co. Meath, and became, not a bard, but a composer and minstrel. Blinded at eighteen by an attack of smallpox, he thereafter lived as a wandering harper, although his life fell in one of the most troubled periods of Irish history. Gifted and proud, he refused to play for hire, but after the manner of the ancient bards expected hospitality, in which matter he seems to have fared better than O'Bruadair, for instance. Several of the great Irish families were still in a position to offer him entertainment, and in their honour he composed most of his songs. Some of these, however, including *Bridget Cruise* and *Mild Mabel Kelly*, were inspired by his love affairs, of which he had several. He died in 1738 at Alderford, the home of his patroness, Mrs. McDermott.

Chapter VI. THE HOUSE OF THE ASCENDANT

> Black fortress of Ascendancy
> Beneath whose wasting sway
> Sprang crime and strife, so deadly rife—
> What rests of thee today?
>
> John O'Hagen

WHILE THE DOWNFALL of the Irish, under which head are included
Gael and Gall and those of Norman stock, was thus being accomplished, the Protestant Saxons were gaining the upper hand
to such purpose that they have come to be described by historians as the Ascendancy, which Barrington, who attributes the
origin of the term to the notorious John Gifford, describes as "a
phrase very fatal to the peace of Ireland."[1] The astrological
term, *House of the Ascendant*, by which are designated those

[1] *Personal Sketches of His Own Time*, I, p. 133. Sir Jonah Barrington,
himself a curious specimen of the Ascendancy class. Born in 1760 of a
family descended from Palesmen, he was educated at Trinity, and after
resigning a commission when there was a prospect of "action," he turned
to the law, in which profession he rose rapidly, becoming a judge of the
Admiralty Court in 1798. He had been twice elected to the Irish House
of Commons, the Act of Union having been passed during his second term.
He publicly opposed the Union and was said to have refused several
offers for his vote, but there is reason to believe that he was instrumental
in buying over others. In 1830 he was removed from office for misappro-
priation of funds, whereupon he left England, never to return, dying at
Versailles in 1834. He is the author of *Personal Sketches of His Own Time*
(1827), a book which is well worth reading for its spirited account of the
Dublin of his day and the naive egoism which inspired the unabashed
portrait of himself; *Historic Memoirs of Ireland* (1832); *The Rise and
Fall of the Irish Nation* (1833). He quotes Grattan's denunciation of
Gifford as "the excommunicated of his fellow citizens—the regal rebel—the
unpunished ruffian—the bigoted agitator. In the city a firebrand—in the
streets a bully—in the field a coward."

degrees of the zodiac between which a planet becomes influential, seems a peculiarly appropriate designation in view of the fact that the Protestant Ascendancy in Ireland was so well typified by the so-called Big House, an establishment which embodied the prosperity and security of the Ascendant class in a country whose inhabitants were otherwise so stricken and forlorn. "In such mansions as these," writes Padraic Pearse, referring to the one in which he had established his famous school, "lived those who ruled Ireland; in such mansions as these lived those who sold Ireland."[2]

They who dwelt in the Great Houses were for the most part landed proprietors, enriched by estates confiscated from their Catholic owners, many of them residing in England while an unscrupulous agent racked the tenantry. Many of them were well-bred, well-educated products of Trinity College, Dublin, or of Oxford, but the worst aspects of the Ascendancy were represented by the squireen (also called half-sir and *shoneen*), whose English counterpart was such a one as Squire Western or Tony Lumpkin, but who on Irish soil developed characteristics that made the manners of these worthies resemble an excess of refinement. Since the squireen represented a class peculiar to Ireland at this period, an extension of the Pale beyond which the authentic Ireland cowered, its portraiture may safely be left to the pen of a temperate-minded historian like Rev. E. A. D'Alton, who devotes several graphic paragraphs to its description. "They were," he says, "an unhealthy product of Irish life. They aped the manners of the upper classes, but in no sense were they gentlemen. They had little education; their manners were coarse and rude, to those above them obsequious, to those beneath them harsh and hectoring; they drank, they swore, they gambled, they fought duels; they were idle, dissolute and immoral; they kept packs of hounds; they indulged in horse racing and ran into debt; they exacted free labour from their tenants, horse-whipped them if they were not sufficiently submissive, and loved to insult them by drinking the health of King William and confusion to the Pope."[3]

[2] *The Story of a Success*, p. 58.
[3] *History of Ireland*, II, p. 476.

Curse though absenteeism may have been to Ireland (and curse it undoubtedly was), the phenomenon itself is from one standpoint at least easy enough to understand, for with the country reduced to its then condition of misery, its aspect of utter desolation, the wonder is that anyone who was free to do otherwise should have been willing to live with its appalling sights constantly before his eyes. Certainly it was by no will of his own that Jonathan Swift returned to the land of his birth, and his enforced residence there was probably one of the causes of the rancour that ate at his embittered heart.

Swift is so much a part of the English literary scene that he exemplifies the extent to which the literature of Ireland had already become Anglicized, and yet certain aspects of his work, generally overshadowed by its English aspects, have a definite significance for Ireland. By making himself a part of the great English tradition in letters, he helped to make eighteenth-century literature in Ireland completely English, and yet there is a sense in which his work as a whole can be rightly understood only in the light of his Irish background. If ever a man represented the Ascendancy it was he, although it was his boast that he was not acquainted with a single squire, but after all he was a clergyman of the Established Church, of whose creed it is true he had no great opinion, though he would have been gratified by a larger share of its honours, and it was the Established Church that enforced the Ascendancy. In one sense it did not matter greatly where Swift lived, since he always carried within him a burning sense of justice, a tremendous capacity for anger at the spectacle of injustice and a gift for scathing speech worthy of a Hebrew prophet or a Gaelic bard.

He was born in Dublin in 1667 and died there insane in 1745. He attended TCD, where he received a degree in 1686, was ordained in 1694, became secretary to Sir William Temple, in whose household he met "Stella," returned to Ireland as Vicar of Laracor, eventually becoming Dean of St. Patrick's. But he was no Gael, nor had he any high opinion of the Gaels as such. He considered their language barbarous and advocated the suppression of Irish place names. But during his residence in Ireland he saw about him on every hand scenes which outraged his sense of justice, kept his wrath constantly aflame and stirred him to outpourings of sardonic mockery that should have seared the paper on which they were written. Not that his were the blind thrusts of an insensate rage, for nothing could be more practical than his suggestions for ameliorating the conditions he deplored, and in the case of the *Drapier Letters* the result was the highly practical one of the suppression of Wood's debased half pence. In his *Short View of the State of Ireland* (1727) he draws up under fourteen heads the universally recognized causes of national prosperity and then proceeds to show the extent to which every one of them was violated in Ireland, pointing out, for example, that the abundance of Irish ports is "of no more use to us than a beautiful prospect to a man shut up in a dungeon."

"We are forced to obey laws to which we never consented," he complains, remarking that the profits that come to a country from the visits of foreigners are denied to Ireland, because strangers will not visit a land "where they can expect to see nothing but scenes of misery and desolation."

Commenting in another paper (*Maxims Controlled in Ireland*) on the principle that the riches of a nation are its people, he says: "If we had the African custom of selling our bodies for slaves to foreigners it would be the most useful branch of our trade by ridding us of an insupportable burden and bringing us money in the stead. . . . Above half the souls in this kingdom support themselves by begging and thievery, two-thirds whereof would be able to get their bread in any other country upon earth." These reflections lead him in *A Short View* to an ironic description of the "glorious reports" a body of English commissioners would be able to make after a tour of the country, in the midst of which description he interrupts himself to exclaim, "But my heart is too heavy to continue in this irony longer, for it is manifest that whatever stranger took such a journey would be apt to think himself travelling in Lapland or Ysland rather than in a country so favoured by nature as ours. . . . The miserable dress and diet and dwelling of the people; the old seats of the gentry all in ruins and no new ones in their stead; the families of farmers who pay great rents living in filth and nastiness upon butter, milk and potatoes, without a shoe or stocking to their feet, or a house so convenient as an English hog-sty to receive them."

Further evidence of the practical character of his observations is to be found in his recommendations for the promotion of agriculture, the suppression of rackrenting, the development of Irish industries and the promotion of foreign trade. Recommending the exclusive use of Irish goods by the Irish, he wrote: "Let a firm resolution be taken by male and female never to appear with one single shred that comes from England and let all the people say Amen." He further gave it as his opinion that Ireland would never be happy "till a law were made for burning everything that came from England except their people and their coals," and he adds characteristically, "As to the former I should not be sorry if they would stay at home; and for the latter, I hope in a little time we shall have no occasion for them."

I have dwelt on Swift at this length (and I have had to resist the temptation to do so at greater), for several reasons. One is that he was, when all is said, an Irishman and, in the works quoted, writing on Ireland and Irish affairs and doing so as a confessed Irishman, for he constantly identifies himself with the country and the people, although he did not personally share any of their disabilities. Another reason is that he wrote in English, for not only did he know no Gaelic, but he regarded the abolition of Irish as a "noble achievement," and thus bears witness to the Anglicization of Ireland's literature, an achievement, whether noble or not, in which he not only participated but helped immeasurably to consolidate by himself attaining major rank in the field of English letters.

This is a condition of which the stage provides further evidence, for the Dublin theatre was merely a poor imitation of the London theatre, and this despite the extraordinary number of actors and actresses of Irish blood whose talents so enhanced the glories of the English drama. Ireland's voluminous ancient literature, for all its variety, did not include the drama in any of its kinds.

That ancient Ireland possessed no dramatic literature is clearly shown by Dr. Peter Kavanagh in his voluminous and scholarly work on the Irish theatre,[4] in the Introduction to which he points out that a few isolated references to some form of popular amusement in the ancient period do not imply the existence of a native drama. While it is not possible to accept Dr. Kavanagh's view that any attempt to introduce the form in the Christian era would have been banned by the Church, since elsewhere in Europe it was the Church which directly promoted the rise and development of the form, it is none the less true that the earliest record of a dramatic performance in Ireland dates from a period subsequent to the arrival of the English invaders. Dr. Kavanagh's comments on the Irish mummers afford an amusing instance of the extent to which the importation underwent inevitable and characteristic changes. Thus, in the Irish version of the famous folk-play of St. George, St. Patrick is substituted for the patron of England, while Oliver Cromwell or the Devil takes the place of St. George's opponent, the Bold Slasher.

English plays were first presented in Dublin late in the reign of Queen Elizabeth, but there is no record of an established theatre in the Irish capital until the time of Charles I (1635). The playhouse which had been established in Werburgh Street was removed in 1661 to Smock Alley, where it had an illustrious (wholly English) history, until the collapse of an upper gallery caused an interruption of performances, the theatre remaining closed until the reign of William III, when it was reopened under the management of Joseph Ashbury. Early in the eighteenth century a theatre was established in Fownes Court, at first for acrobatic performances, but later for plays, and it was at this theatre that *The Beggar's Opera* was given for the first time in Ireland. Smock Alley was again redecorated and reopened in

[4] *The Irish Theatre* (1946). Covering the period from the earliest times and accounting in a most interesting manner for Ireland's lack of drama until it was introduced by the Anglo-Normans, the author deals in great detail with the period before the establishment of the Abbey Theater in 1899, prior to which date, as the book abundantly shows, the Irish theatre was merely an offshoot of the English theatre.

1732, and about the same time another theatre was founded in the Liberties, with still another in Aungier Street in 1734, where Mr. Quinn and Mrs. Cibber appeared in Farquharson's *Recruites Officer*. The year 1741 saw the opening of a Music Hall in Fishamble Street, where Handel in person conducted his *Messiah*. Meanwhile in Smock Alley such celebrities as Peg Woffington, Giffard and David Garrick trod the boards. In 1743 *Richard III* was played there anonymously by "Mr. Sheridan," but the following year he left for London and Drury Lane, although he afterwards returned to manage Smock Alley. A series of outrages on the part of the students of TCD led to the enactment (1788) of measures to regulate the Dublin theatre. In 1821 the Theatre Royal was opened, the occasion being marked by a prologue written by George Colman and spoken by Farren, in the course of which "brave Erin's sons and Erin's fair" were besought

To make your Nation's theatre your care.

Throughout the course of its history no attempt was made to disguise the fact that, whether national or not, the Dublin theatre was wholly English. Ireland had unwittingly, however, made a unique contribution to the drama, and that was the character that came to be known as the stage Irishman. In his marvelously documented study of this subject[5] Mr. G. C. Duggan shows that this figure appears in English drama as early as the Elizabethan age. It is not unlikely that the original inspiration was furnished by the squireen away from home, a theory which would account for the hard-drinking, loud-swearing soldier such as Captain O'Blunder or Sir Lucius O'Trigger, or "the Irish gentleman of a wild roving temper," such as Farquhar's Roebuck, of whom Mr. Duggan says that he "only just misses being a complete stage picture of the Rakes of Mallow."

But, as the same author shows, the caricature was extended to include so many Irish types that it finally included the entire race, designated at first by the generic name of *Teague*, and that

[5] *The Stage Irishman*. A History of the Irish Play and Stage Characters from the Earliest Times (1937).

considerably before the name was so used in the political song, *Lilliburlero* ("They are not Irish words," says Swift of its refrain, "but better than Scotch"). The name *Teague* was afterwards exchanged for *Paddy* or *Paudeen*, without relinquishing the connotation of contempt which invariably accompanied every reference to the figure which Charles Gavan Duffy (*Young Ireland*) calls either "a blundering simpleton or a prodigious fire-eater." The result was a burlesque, not so much of the extravagances of the squireen nor even of the Irish racial traits of courage, wit and open-handed generosity, but of the poverty and ignorance to which the Irish had chosen to be reduced rather than abandon their religious beliefs. But the last stage of cultural degeneracy was not reached until the Irish themselves, who had not waited till now to manifest the wisdom which consists in the recognition of one's faults, showed themselves ready to shout with laughter at this travesty of their virtues.

The fact that the two foremost playwrights of the eighteenth century were of Irish birth did not alter the fact that their work was essentially English. The only evidence of Goldsmith's Irish background is the fact that the deserted Auburn may very well have been inspired by an Irish village from which he had seen many a "poor exile" depart:

> E'n now the devastation is begun,
> And half the business of destruction done,
> E'n now, methinks, as pondering here I stand,
> I see the rural virtues leave the land.
> Down where yon anchoring vessel spreads the sail
> That idly resting flaps with every gale,
> Downward they move—a melancholy band,
> Pass from the shore and darken all the strand.

Often enough in his youth must Goldsmith have witnessed such a dismal scene or an even worse, when, as more frequently happened, the evicted villagers were turned houseless onto the roads, lacking even the mournful comfort of exile.

As a playwright, Sheridan did nothing to enhance the prestige of Irish culture, beyond creating in Sir Lucius O'Trigger a rather disarming specimen of the stage Irishman. The only play he wrote on an Irish subject, *St. Patrick's Day*, was the failure it deserved to be. But Sheridan did distinguish himself in a field in which the Irish have displayed what may almost be called a racial aptitude, that is the field of eloquence. Perhaps there is no more necessity for seeking an explanation of this than of any other similar phenomenon, except that the illiteracy for which the Irish eventually became notorious makes such a propensity noteworthy. As a matter of fact, lack of education has rarely made them, the late Mrs. Bernard Shaw to the contrary, inarticulate; on the contrary it sometimes seems as though their very incapacity to deal with the written word had driven them to find an outlet in speech, the Irish peasant's skill in turning a phrase or loosing a spate of language being well exemplified in the Bessie Burgess of O'Casey's *The Plough and the Stars*.

Naturally, however, the greatest Irish orators were members of the privileged and therefore the educated class, of whom Richard Brinsley Sheridan was one. Burke was Sheridan's elder and immeasurably his superior, and Sheridan's own dramatic work has eclipsed his achievement as an orator, which was nevertheless considerable. As a matter of fact both these men are so completely identified with England and English letters that it is easy to overlook the fact they were both born in Dublin, Burke in 1730 and Sheridan in 1751.

After completing his legal studies at TCD, where he had been interested in metaphysics, Burke at first vainly sought a professorship in the metaphysical land of Scotland, and then became private secretary to two lords lieutenant of Ireland. He entered the English Parliament in 1766, where he at once attracted the attention of Pitt, thus inaugurating the career that was so distinguished by probity of character, elevation of mind, and eloquence of tongue. His was not a typically Irish eloquence, as Grattan's was. It was more coldly formal and calmly persuasive, but it could become almost overwhelming in its cogency.

His most famous speeches constitute an enduring contribution to the treasury of English prose, and they naturally deal with matters that were then of the utmost concern to England and the English people, but no Irishman felt more strongly than Edmund Burke the grievances of his native land, especially of that penalized portion of its people, the Catholics. Although he lacked the opportunity to speak publicly on these matters, he wrote of them with a vigor that is not surpassed by his finest speeches. For instance, to an Irish peer who had consulted him with regard to a proposal to alleviate Catholic disabilities, he wrote: "No man on reading the bill could imagine he was reading an act of amnesty and indulgence, following a recital of the good behaviour of those who are the objects of it. . . . This has surely much more the air of a table of proscription than an act of grace. . . . The laws against foreign education are clearly the very worst part of the code. . . . To render humanity fit to be insulted it was right that it should be degraded. . . . I have ever thought the prohibition of the means of improving our rational nature to be the worst species of tyranny that the insolence and perverseness of mankind ever dared to exercise."[6]

This matter of Irish relief was one in which he became interested early in life and to which he devoted so much thought that he projected a book on the subject, of which, however, he wrote only some fragmentary Tracts. Shortly before his death he addressed a letter on the same theme to an English friend which he concluded with words that are an impressive mingling of pathos and fire: "I do not wish to have it concealed that I am of the same opinion to my last breath, which I entertained when my faculties were at the best."

Richard Brinsley Sheridan was not an orator in the sense of being a master of eloquence, but he entered Parliament in 1780, took part in the impeachment proceedings against Warren Hastings, in which connection he delivered a speech of seven hours' duration which Burke himself pronounced "the most astonishing

[6] *Letter to a Peer of Ireland on the Penal Laws against the Irish Catholics,* previous to the late repeal of a part thereof in the session of the Irish Parliament held A. D. 1782.

effort of eloquence, argument and wit united of which there is any record or tradition."

The "first great representative of Irish eloquence,"[7] however, was Henry Grattan (born in Dublin, 1746; educated TCD; died in London, 1820, buried in Westminster Abbey), whose career is almost inseparable from that of another distinguished orator, Henry Flood (born in Co. Kilkenny, 1732, natural son of Chief Justice Flood; educated, TCD; died in 1791). In 1770, five years before Grattan became a member of the Irish Parliament, Flood was recognized as the foremost man in Irish public life, a position for which he was fitted by birth, property, education and talents. But Grattan's gifts, which included that of much personal charm, were apparently superior, and besides he was intensely Irish, whereas Flood was almost as English as Swift. Both Flood and Grattan were acknowledged leaders of Protestant nationalism, but Grattan was also an ardent supporter of the Catholic claims, in defence of which he delivered some of his most memorable addresses. This is unquestionably at least in part the basis of the assertion that he had "invented an eloquence to which the moral temperament of his country responded."

His best efforts, however, were devoted to promoting the cause of Irish Parliamentary independence, a task which he and many another honest man fancied had been accomplished in 1782. Labouring under this delusion, Grattan retired, but emerged from private life to fight the Act of Union which brought the Parliament of Ireland and the eighteenth century to such an inglorious end in 1800. He afterwards served several terms at Westminster, but the effectiveness of his oratory was ended.

John Philpot Curran (born in Cork in 1750), although elected to the Irish Parliament in 1783, was always better fitted for the court room, a type of oratory of which the history of the nineteenth century in Ireland afforded all too many opportunities. Like the others mentioned, Curran was a Protestant, but he spoke out repeatedly in defence of Catholic Emancipation, which by

[7] Daniel Owen Madden, *Speeches of the Rt. Hon. Henry Grattan. With commentary on his career and character* (1861).

this time was being agitated, and as a matter of fact his forensic career began with the defence of a priest who had been brutally beaten by a nobleman.

From a cultural standpoint Ireland was no longer Irish. Her schools were English, her books were written in English, her stage was English, her oratory enhanced the greatness of English speech, and the House of the Ascendant seemed to be justified by these her children.

But that the Ascendancy was not regarded with complete satisfaction even by some of its own members is evident from the numbers of them who participated in the Rebellion of '98, even to the extent of laying down their lives. Writing years later Valentine Lawless, then Lord Cloncurry, bore witness to the extent to which he shared the convictions of Lord Edward Fitzgerald: "Who that has known an Irish squirearch family, has not seen a brother or uncle, a Master Tom or a Master Dick, who, for sixty years of solar time, has been an occupant of the Hall or Castle, yet in the estimation of himself and all around, is still a frolicsome or stupid boy, whom no one would think of entrusting with any duty more important than that of mixing punch or purveying game for the family table? Would these ancient and indiscreet youths have continued their state of feeble nonage, had their severance with the parent stem forced them to exert their energies in the battle of life?"[8]

To Cloncurry these "ancient and indiscreet youths," who certainly did not represent the worst aspects of the Ascendancy, were typical of the state of "feeble nonage" to which the whole Irish nation had been reduced by the Act of Union.

[8] *Personal Recollections of the Life and Times with Extracts from the Correspondence of Valentine Lord Cloncurry* (2nd Edition, 1850), p. 128.

Chapter VII. *BEHIND THE HEDGE*

Beat, beat, ye muffled drums, ye drones and chanters, wail,
With heart-break of the baffled, broken-hearted Gael.
The clay is deep on Ireland's breast:
Her proud and bleeding heart is laid at last to rest.
* To rest, to rest.*

  Campbell, The Mountainy Singer

And the dear voice of learning is proscribed,
And quavers by the hedge and dies away.

  Farren, Apostasy

GAELIC IRELAND was apparently at last reduced to helpless silence, her proud and bleeding heart laid low in ignominious rest. And yet, although that heart still bled, it was far from being subdued. The paths of learning may have been closed to the Irish, but the love of learning was still strong among them. Therefore, despite the laws which forbade any person professing the Popish religion to teach school, there were still many who did so. One of the most famous of Irish schools established after the Reformation was that founded at Kilkenny by the Earl of Ormond (1565) and taught by the Jesuit Father, Peter White, to whose excellence as a teacher, Richard Stanyhurst, who had been one of his pupils, bears witness. But this school was one of those established chiefly for Anglo-Norman students, and as such not yet under the ban of the law.

About the same period, another great teacher, the already-mentioned Alexander Lynch, conducted a school at Galway, which was attended by 1200 students, pursuing Irish and classical studies. Among them, as already noted, were Duald MacFirbis,

Roderick O'Flaherty, and the master's son, John Lynch, afterwards Archdeacon of Tuam. In 1615 the report of a Royal Commission appointed by James I testified concerning Alexander Lynch as follows: "Wee had daily proofe, during our continuance in that citty how well his schollers profited under him. . . . Wee sent for that schoolemaster before us and seriously advised him to conform to the Religion established, and not prevailing with our advices, we enjoyned him to forbeare teaching."[1]

In the course of time, as the penal laws became more severe and failure to conform was tantamount to treason, education, except as provided under the auspices of the Bible Societies or similar agencies, became treasonable too.[2] To deal with it more extensively here would be to go too far afield, but it is worth noting that the failure of the Charter Schools was not due to Irish indifference to educational opportunities. Under these circumstances there came into existence the famous hedge schools of Ireland, in which to the best of his ability and at the risk of his life the heroic master undertook to continue the tradition of the bardic and the monastic schools. Not that he could hope to approximate their excellence. In fact, he fell so far short of it that he has been turned in literature into a figure of fun, apparently deserving only the contempt and derision which have been heaped upon him.

It was the hedge schoolmaster's wont to gather about him, literally in the lee of a hedge or in a smoke-filled cabin, a few children whose parents were eager to have them taught whatever, under such conditions, the master could contrive to impart. Often this was little enough, for instead of the learning for which the old teachers were famous, all he had in most cases was the hereditary Irish love for the things of the mind. This he had in common with the parents of his pupils, who were only too glad to set by out of their penury the few pence that were the price of his services, for as Carleton, who assuredly knew whereof he

[1] P. J. Dowling, *The Hedge Schools of Ireland.*
[2] And on this subject see W. H. Lecky, *History of Ireland in the Eighteenth Century,* I.

wrote, has testified: "There never was a more unfounded calumny than that which would impute to the Irish peasant an indifference to education."[3]

Often, however, the hedge scholar was solidly, if not extensively instructed, which was as much as could be expected, considering the circumstances under which the master himself had acquired his knowledge, circumstances which involved the hardships of the Poor Scholar, which Carleton, who knew them at first hand, has depicted so poignantly. Sometimes the teacher in such schools had flagrant faults of character, such as extreme vanity, habitual intemperance or a cruel temper, but as a class they gave warrant for the assertion that "The Hedge Schools were the most vital force in popular education in Ireland during the eighteenth century."[4]

It is a fact of the utmost importance that the teaching in these schools was in Irish, which, despite the sustained effort to suppress it, was still in general use throughout the country. Such teaching had naturally to be accomplished practically without books. Even the English books provided for the students were a miscellaneous and none too informative assortment, but of course many of the masters could speak English as well as Irish and Latin. A number of them were exceedingly learned in an unobtrusive way and great teachers into the bargain. Several of them were poets, the fire of whose genius was turned inward upon themselves, so that it burns against the murk of Ireland's dark ages with a somewhat lurid flame, conveying a general impression of recklessness and a desperation that was anything but quiet and that has not entirely disappeared from Irish literature even to the present day.

"The Hidden Ireland" is Professor Daniel Corkery's phrase for the Ireland represented by a group known as the Munster Poets, because they existed in that province in sufficient numbers to constitute a school. They are also known as the Poet Schoolmasters and are called by Douglas Hyde "the last of the Milesians."

[3] *Traits and Stories*, II, p. 179.
[4] Dowling, op. cit., p. 21.

The hidden Ireland was an Ireland in which something of the ancient cultural tradition was carried on in the ancient speech, but behind the scenes, since the action of the piece was now in the hands of the Ascendancy, that is, the group which had got the upper hand in the affairs of the country by reason of being for the most part what the Irish were not, Saxon and Protestant. From the Ascendancy standpoint, as Professor Corkery shows, the natives were "a lesser breed," who "if they have had a language and literature it cannot have been a civilized language, cannot have been anything but a *patois* used by the hillmen among themselves; and as for their literature, the less said about it the better."[5]

This being so, what survived in the eighteenth century of that language and literature could scarcely have been anything but hidden, not only because their exponents were driven under-ground by the terrible enactment of the penal laws which marked that century, but because the very contempt with which Irish culture was regarded by the Ascendancy and even by certain of the Irish, who were beginning to recognize it as the better part of valour to share that view, almost gave it a warrant of immunity by treating it as non-existent. "To picture the Gael's way of life in those days," writes Corkery, "is to feel that one has gone away from human lands and wanders in a dream which must presently break. . . . The bells were silenced. The holy wells were deserted, the priests banished, a certain number of them bought by gold. The dead must not be laid with their fathers in the abbey grounds. Mass could be said only in secret rock-clefts, with sen-tries posted on the hill-tops; if said in some secret garret in a town, then a curtain had better be hung between priest and people, so that the flock might afterwards truthfully swear, if put to it, that they did not know who the celebrant was."[6]

Small wonder, with Gaelic Ireland reduced to these straits, that the Ascendancy considered Irish culture, if it considered it at all, to have been completely disposed of. And yet—it moved. In

[5] *The Hidden Ireland*, p. xi.
[6] Corkery, op. cit., pp. 26, 27.

secret, it is true, and no longer with the vigorous freshness of its youth, but with an almost wilful persistency that sometimes resembled not so much life as the refusal to die.

Among the ways in which this persistency manifested itself were the rise of the hedge schools and the continuation of the bardic schools till about the middle of the seventeenth century, when in Munster, at least, they were transformed into the so-called "Courts of Poetry."[7] The Courts of Poetry were assemblies whose proceedings were patterned on those of courts of law, at which the poets of a district met for the purpose of reciting their verses and submitting them to the judgment of their fellow poets. What chiefly concerned them, and this is essentially Irish, was poetic form, in constructing which they did their best to follow the old bardic rules, an endeavour in which for lack of training they inevitably failed. They succeeded, however, not only in keeping alive the ancient cultural tradition, but even in injecting new life into a poetic code that had more than once given evidence of decadence, by becoming so highly technical as either to destroy all spontaneity or to deteriorate into such a secret language as only the bards themselves could understand.

Lacking mastery over the traditional bardic metres, the poets of the Courts of Poetry borrowed, not without protest, the metres of popular poetry, in which their finer poetic ear and greater skill discovered undreamed-of harmonies and which they endowed with haunting musical qualities that must be sought in all subsequent authentic Irish verse. Not only did the Irish poetic faculty show itself capable of devising new forms; it devoted these forms to the treatment of new subjects, foremost among which is the theme that came to be regarded almost as a proof of poetic ability and in consequence was so constantly used that it threatened to deteriorate into the empty convention that the allegory became elsewhere. It was, in fact, an allegory, although painfully stereotyped,—the *Aisling*[8] or Vision poem, in which

[7] Professor Dowling calls this transformation a decline, which of course it was.
[8] Pronounced "Ashling."

the poet, bewailing the sorrows of his country, beholds as in a dream a beautiful grieving woman who identifies herself in figurative and sometimes cryptic language as Ireland. The poets address her by a number of tender and reverent epithets as the object of their adoration, their almost desperate love, whose sorrows render her a thousand times dearer than those who are wooed in prosperity. She is *Ceann Dubh Deelish*, the Dear Dark Head; *Roisin Dubh*, the Little Dark Rose, Dark Rosaleen; she is Houlahan's Daughter or Sheila na Gara or Grania Uaile, the last name signifying that formidable woman, Grace O'Malley, the so-called "Queen of the West," who strode into the presence of Queen Elizabeth and looked her unflinchingly in the eye, intimating, as probably even Elizabeth understood, that she was well aware of "the price of her."

Because of the hope with which Irish eyes so often turned during this era to the Stuart Pretender for the redress of Ireland's wrongs, many of the Aisling poems are at the same time Jacobite songs, though not all Jacobite songs are Aislings. There was also written a large body of verse, the work mostly of the poets about to be named, which does not belong to either of these categories, although the fact that it was recusant, that is rebel, poetry is plainly evident. Because it was mostly in Munster that the Celtic cultural tradition survived with sufficient vigour to produce the Courts of Poetry and a school of poets, they are usually called the Munster Poets, but sometimes also the Jacobite (because of the political hopes that were pinned on the Stuart Pretender as the deliverer of Ireland), or the Hedge Poets. The survival of the poetic order was not confined to Munster, however, since the other provinces could boast of several illustrious names. The Hedge Poets were peasants for the most part, desperately poor, often vagabonds in the tradition of the wandering scholars of the Middle Ages, but lacking their piety, high-spirited and reckless, even scandalous in their lives.

Foremost among the Munster Poets was Egan O'Rahilly (Aodhagen O Rathaille), whom Corkery calls "that tragic figure, the Dante of Munster." He was born in Co. Cork about 1670 and after a life of wandering and bitter sorrow died in 1726. His sorrows were largely the result of his poverty, which sharpened the irony of his great learning, but both were embittered by his realization of his country's degradation, especially in the matter of culture. Hence his poems constitute one prolonged lamentation for Ireland, serving at the same time as a catharsis of his own humiliated and therefore embittered spirit. What at first glance seems to be one of James Clarence Mangan's most successful lyrics, *O Brightness of Brightness*, is really a translation based on a poem by O'Rahilly (*Gile na Gile*), every single phrase of the original, according to Corkery, surpassing "in music, ease and swiftness the corresponding phrase of the translation."

The predominant tone of O'Rahilly's work is one of vehement passion, passion of grief and resentment, of desperate hope. His grief is mostly for his country, for the downfall of his race and the misfortunes of his friends. From time to time he breaks out into bitter satire against the despoilers, and then he is as fierce in his invective as O'Bruadair in denouncing the coarseness and vulgarity of the Cromwellian settlers, under the scathing denomination of Clan Tomáis, the generic name for all Irishmen of low origin, vulgar manners and barbarous life. According to the poet, they were the offspring of one Thomas, a "diabolical tribe," to whom it was impossible to teach the catechism, or otherwise to civilize. Condemned by St. Patrick to continue their half-savage way of life in isolation from other men, they are represented by O'Rahilly as claiming Cromwell as their special patron. In the literature of grief he signally excelled, and several of his longer poems are noble elegies.

> His death took away her laughter from Erin,

is an expression of his sorrow for the passing of an Irish chieftain, while of another he writes,

> The flower of Munstermen stretched in decay,
> The darling of Banba, the friend of strollers.

Incidentally, in these poems in which he laments the passing of the old order, he paints a graphic picture of the open-handed plenty, the refinements of luxury, that were characteristic of ancient Irish households.

On the other hand, the death of one of the oppressors wrings from him words of savage recrimination:

Beneath thy maw, O stout stone, lies a reprobate who came across the Shannon;
A serpent who embezzled the pledges of every poor ruined helpless man;
A wicked upstart who betrayed every graceful maiden who came in his way;

Wicked steward of a barony, who plundered deceitfully the Mac-Carthys,
And the fair seat of the warrior from the Laune, which is called Parthus,
As a reward he got hell of the damned, in the world beyond he has gone there,
With scarce six feet of the Killarney graveyard.

But the quintessence of his bitterness is distilled from the tears of his own sorrow, as expressed in the lines which he addressed to a friend from his deathbed:
I will not cry for help, till I am put in a narrow coffin,
And I swear, if I were to cry, it would be no nearer to me.

. . . .

I will follow the beloved heroes to the grave,
Those princes under whom were my ancesters before the death of Christ.

By way of final appraisal the following passage from the Irish Texts Society's edition of O'Rahilly seems worth quoting: "In estimating O'Rahilly's place in literature it must be remembered that Irish literature continued in a state of almost complete isolation down to its total extinction at the beginning of the nineteenth century. . . . The number of books printed in the Irish language from the middle of the sixteenth to the middle of the nineteenth century would hardly more than fill a schoolboy's box; and of these none were on general literature. . . . It would be un-

critical to judge this poet according to the canons of taste accepted by the nations of Western Europe. He is a survival of the
antique, in metre, in style, in thought, in spirit. His spirit is as
strong, as fresh, as vigorous and olden as the language in which
he wrote, as the race whose oppression he depicted."[9] Canon
O'Leary regards O'Rahilly's poems as "veritable classics" whose
construction "will always stand as true models of the syntax of
the Irish language."

Of Owen Roe O'Sullivan, who was born at Meentogues in Kerry
in 1703 and died there in 1784, it has been said that he "was to
Ireland what Robert Burns at a somewhat later day was to
Scotland."[10] The product of a classical academy, by which according to Corkery is indicated either "a broken down bardic
school or a court of poetry," he was a real scholar, who was forced
by some irregularity in his conduct to abandon the school he
had opened on his own account, as happened on more than one
subsequent occasion in the course of his wandering, dissolute life.
During most of that life, his principal occupation, despite poetic
gifts which caused his contemporaries to call him Owen of the
Sweet Mouth, was that of a wandering potato-digger or *spalpeen*.
He seems also to have spent some time at sea as a member of the
British navy, in which capacity he participated in the famous
engagement of Fort Royal, a subject on which the Gaelic poet
wrote an English poem (he wrote a number of English poems)
in which he gives credit for the victory to "Rodney's guns and
Paddy's sons." Although the reward for which he asked in the
poem, release from the navy, was refused, we next find him
equally wretched as a soldier, until he contrived his discharge
by poisoning his legs with spearmint. After this he returned to
Kerry and a final attempt to keep a school, the versified pros-
pectus for which, submitted in a letter to the parish priest, not
only is a delightful example of what he could do with the English,

[9] *The Poems of Egan O'Reilly*, with Introduction, Translation, Notes and
Indexes. Edited by Rev. Patrick S. Dinneen, M.A., and Tadgh O'Donoghue,
Irish Texts Society, Vol. III.
[10] Walsh, *Relics of Jacobite Poetry*, p. 6.

but sheds an amusing sidelight on what the speakers of a "barbaric tongue" thought of the speech of their conquerors. He commends himself to the priest as

> Well-skill'd in ancient Greek and Roman lore,
> Fame-laden lays since Erin's days of yore,
> And eke the foeman's tongue, upborne by Law,
> Whose phrase uncouth distorts the Gaelic jaw.

A blow on the head sustained in a quarrel, then fever and death, with the pen literally dropping from his fingers,—such was his end. His poems were collected and published for the first time in 1901.

The following stanza is a characteristic expression of his rakishness:

> The life of the Rake, hear ye now its recital
>   By one who, alas! has long known it too well;
> 'Twas a trampling on virtues and duties most vital,
>   A treading the path leading down into hell.
> Like Judas, a kiss was our mode of deceiving
>   The bright-haired young maids, till their hearts were our own,
> Then perjured we left them to weeping and grieving,
>   Tho' the holy priests taught: "Better leave them alone."
>   (Tr. Erionnach, i.e., Sigerson)

Sean Clarach MacDonnell was not only a scholar and a poet, but the leading poet in his section of Munster. He was not a wastrel, for he worked his own farm, but his verses were mostly Jacobite, and he had to flee the country on account of a fierce satire directed against a local member of the Ascendancy.

Among MacDonnell's poems is a "Vision" in which instead of Ireland he beholds a fairy-maiden who lures him away to her kingdom, where she bewails the sorrows of Ireland and the exile of the Stuart prince.

John O'Tuomy, another Latin and Greek scholar, was born in Limerick in 1706. Known for obvious reasons as "the Gay," he was a vintner whose house was a meeting place of the bards. He was so reduced by his own conviviality that he became a servant on what was once his own farm, being eventually cast out

of even that post for quarrelling with the mistress, against whom
he directed a spirited satire entitled *The Dame of the Wattle*.

Perhaps his most typical effusion is his *Drinking Song*, sung
to the air of *The Growling Woman*:

> I sell the best brandy and sherry,
> To make my good customers merry;
>   But at times their finances
>   Run short, as it chances,
> And then I feel very sad, very.
>
> . . . .
>
> Libation I pour on libation,
> I sing the past fame of our nation
>   For valour-won glory,
>   For song and for story,
> This, this is my grand recreation.

A notable and picturesque friendship existed between O'Tuomy
and Andrew MacGrath, known as *An Mangaire Sugach*, the
Merry Pedlar. This friendship may not always be evident in the
lines they addressed to each other, since these were mostly
abusive, one of MacGrath's being an anything but complimentary
reply to the above drinking song, but it was none the less
genuine. MacGrath, too, had been a country schoolmaster, but
intemperance led in his case also to wandering and generally
disreputable habits. In one of his poems to his friend he boasts
that he is "neither Protestant nor Papist," since he had left his
own Church and been ejected by the other. He has been called
(*Poets of Munster*) "the most melodious Gaelic poet of his day,"
which despite his habits was apparently a long one, since he was
still living in 1790.

The greatest of the minor Munster poets was unquestionably
Donnchadh (Denis) Ruadh Mac Conmara (MacNamara), whose
story is the basic theme of Mr. Francis MacManus's distinguished
trilogy of novels. Mac Conmara was born in Co. Clare in 1710,
another addition to the list of gifted men whose souls were
filled with bitterness because the harshness of their lot was

enhanced by the greatness of their talents. He is said to have been sent to Rome to study for the priesthood, but he was dismissed from the seminary and returned to Ireland, where what is known of his life builds up to another picture of recklessness and wasted gifts. It includes, however, several attempts at school-keeping, a voyage to Newfoundland and, for at least a brief period, conformity to the Protestant Church. Through all his vicissitudes he was a poet, as is evident from his great lyric, so well known in Mangan's translation as *The Fair Hills of Eire.*

> Take a blessing from my heart to the land of my birth,
>   And the fair hills of Eire, O!
> And to all that yet survive of Eibhear's tribe on earth,
>   On the fair hills of Eire, O!
> In that land so delightful the wild thrush's lay
> Seems to pour a lament forth for Eire's decay—
> Alas! alas! why pine I a thousand miles away
>   From the fair hills of Eire, O!
> The soil is rich and soft—the air is mild and bland,
>   Of the fair hills of Eire, O!
> Her barest rock is greener to me than this rude land—
>   O! the fair hills of Eire, O!
> Her woods are tall and straight, grove rising over grove;
> Trees flourish in her glens below and on her heights above;
> O, in heart and in soul, I shall ever, ever love
>   The fair hills of Eire, O!
> A fruitful clime is Eire's through valley, meadow, plain
>   And the fair land of Eire, O!
> The very Bread of Life is in the yellow grain
>   On the fair hills of Eire, O!
> Far dearer unto me than the tones the music yields
> Is the lowing of the kine and the calves in her fields
> And the sunlight that shone long ago on the shields
>   Of the Gaels, on the fair hills of Eire, O!

Already in the time of Donnchadh it was an ancient cry, the wail of the Irish exile, having in it the tears of Columcille, the sighs of many a homesick Irish monk in the cloisters of a foreign monastery, the stifled sobs of the Wild Geese, winging their flight far from Ireland. By the time Mangan had found for it English words, that cry had taken on a new poignancy from the thousands of men and women who were then crowding the steerage quarters of the sailing ships.

In the story of Donnchadh's life, which is not necessarily to be accepted as the unvarnished truth, he describes himself as "the slave of adversity."[11] Professor Corkery has translated a number of passages from his longest poem, but the bulk of his work remains untranslated. At the age of eighty the poet apparently broke a long silence with a lament for the death of another poet, a friend of his youth, Tadhg Gaedhealach O'Sullivan, so called because he was wholly ignorant of English. O'Sullivan was born in Kerry and is called by Dr. Hyde[12] "the poet who most and best wrote religious songs in the province of Munster." He died at Waterford in 1800, the volume of religious verse which was published in his life-time having gone into many subsequent editions.

While most of the Munster poets were men of reckless lives, as their songs testify, none of them wrote in quite such a Rabelaisian vein as Brian Merriman. He was born in Co. Clare probably in 1747 and died in Limerick in 1805, at which time he was a teacher of mathematics, but as a young man he was a poet, having written a long, and for an Irishman of his day, a most unusual poem entitled *The Midnight Court*, which Yeats in his introduction to the translation made by Percy Arland Ussher calls a "vital, extravagant, immoral and preposterous poem." It is a variant of the Aisling to the extent that the poet, falling asleep beneath a tree sees, not a radiant young girl, but a hideous hag, who summons him to a court presided over by "Eevell of Craglee, Munster's Queen," on the complaint that the practice of mating has declined in Erin. The case against the men is vigorously put by a girl, her charge culminating in an attack on the celibacy of the clergy. The poem was written

[11] *Adventures of Donnchadh Ruadh Mac Conmara, a Slave of Adversity.* Now for the first time edited from an original manuscript with metrical translation, notes, and a bibliographical sketch of the author by S. Hayes [O'Grady] Dublin, 1853.

[12] *Religious Songs of Connacht*, p. 224.

in 1780, and Patrick Weston Joyce (see below) records having heard a great part of it recited in 1904 by a man who would have given the whole if Joyce had not stopped him.

Michael Comyn was the son of a man whose loss of his ancestral estate during the Cromwellian confiscation was somewhat recompensed by the grant of a farm at Kilcoran, where Michael was born in 1688. There is no intimation that this grant was made on condition of submission to the Protestant Church, but it is none the less a fact that the poet was a Protestant. Special interest attaches to his work by reason of the fact that whereas most of his contemporaries wrote chiefly of Ireland's sorrows or their own, he goes back to the Bardic tales for his now famous *Lay of Oisin*.[13]

As Corkery points out, Comyn's work is strikingly different from that of the peasant poets, because theirs is coloured by their poverty and suffering and their resentment of their country's fate, while he drew upon ancient bardic lore, instead of writing as they did about his own times. He was nevertheless intensely nationalist in spirit and showed great mastery over the intricate metrical forms which he employed, his skill being especially evident in his "woven rhythms" (Corkery). His son was a man of lesser stature, for he was ashamed of his father's use of the Gaelic and burned his MSS, a sufficient indication of the pass to which the language had been brought.

Of minor importance, but still of considerable interest as members of the Munster School, if only for the extent to which they depart from the "wildness" of the pattern, are William English (d. 1778), an Augustinian priest who had been a schoolmaster, and who is the author of the spirited *Cashel of Munster*, or *The Soft Deal Board*, as the title is literally rendered, best known in the translation of Samuel Ferguson, from which the following is quoted:

---

[13] *Oisin in the Land of Youth*, edited with revised text, literal translation, new metrical version and vocabulary by Thomas Flannery. No date, but probably in the nineties, since the editor remarks that he does not know to what extent Yeats's *Wanderings of Oisin* is a translation of Comyn's *Lay*, as he had not seen the then recently published poem.

I'd wed you without herds, without money, or rich array,
And I'd wed you on a dewy morn at day-dawn grey;
My bitter woe it is, love, that we are not far away
In Cashel town, though the bare deal board were our marriage bed
    this day!

The list includes William Dall (the Blind) O'Heffernan, who
flourished early in the eighteenth century, and who lacked both
educational advantages and literary training; Peter O'Dornin (d.
1768), who when unable to secure the education necessary for the
priesthood, fled to the Co. Armagh, where he wrote an historical
poem which attracted the attention of a gentleman who took him
into his household as a tutor and reviser of records. He finally
lost this patronage, married and opened a school, reverting to
the tactics of the ancient bards by writing a satire against a
rival master, Maurice Gorman, in consequence of which Gorman
lost all his pupils and was forced to leave the district.[14] The
verses entitled *Peter O'Dornin's Courtship* were sung to the air,
The Hills of Feilim:

> Maid of the golden hair,
> Will you with me repair
>   To the brow of the Hill of Feilim?
> Whither we go shall know
> Neither a friend nor foe
>   Nor mortal being nor fairy.

The following is a part of the girl's spirited reply:

> O! cajoler from the South,
> 'Tis you have the girl-winning mouth!
>   Momonia's arts are no fable.
> Long, long, I fear, I should rue
> My journey to Munster with you
>   Ere the honeymoon were waning.

Pierce Fitzgerald (or MacGeralt) is a tragic figure, because in
him, by nature quite unfit to cope with them, met all the tragic
cross-currents of his time and place. A man of some though
greatly reduced property, he clung to that last shred of land

---

[14] Dowling, op. cit., p. 95.

for the sake of his children, to save them from destitution and death, but only at the terrible soul-searing price of conformity (apparently only temporary) with the Established and, to him, abominable Church. Much of the anguish of spirit caused by this step finds vent in his poetry, but his first importance lies in the fact that as chief poet (Sheriff) of Munster he presided for nearly fifty years over the assemblies of the bards, handing over his staff of office at his death in 1791 to Edward Flaherty. Fitzgerald is the author of the noble *Munster War Song*, in whose translation Robert Dwyer Joyce reached a poetic stature beyond any that he attained in his own verse.

Cathal Buidhe Mac Elgun (Mac Giolla Ghunna) was an Ulster poet who lived about the middle of the eighteenth century, whose work was hidden by being written in Gaelic, and whose story indicates that the condition of poets in Ulster resembled that of their Munster brothers. Cathal seems to have been so lawless that the priests forbade intercourse with him. He nevertheless repented on his death-bed and the story of how the priest was then brought to him by the Blessed Virgin herself, when no one else could approach him, has been dramatized by Daniel Corkery in his beautiful one-act play, *The Yellow Bittern*. This is the title of one of Cathal's poems, which has been translated by Thomas MacDonagh in part as follows:

> The yellow bittern that never broke out
>   In a drinking bout, might as well have drunk;
> His bones are thrown on a naked stone
>   Where he lived alone like a hermit monk.
> O yellow bittern! I pity your lot,
>   Though they say that a sot like myself is curst
> I was sober a while, but I'll drink and be wise
>   For fear I should die in the end of thirst.

It must be quite evident that the silence into which the heart-break of the Gael was hushed was only apparent. For all the oppressor knew, he uttered no sound, but all the while behind the hedge he remembered and wept and writhed beneath his sense of wrong. At last, just before the century ended, in 1798, he broke out into fierce and desperate insurrection, a rebellion whose suppression is still a memorial of terrified horror. The Rising served the government as the opportune occasion for the suppression of the Irish Parliament, by the enactment of the Union (1800), an event which certainly seemed to spell the final and total annihilation of the Gael.

But that era of blood and tears produced, as such seasons had always produced in the past, new poetic voices, among them that of Michael O'Longain, whose Gaelic poetry sang the praises of the United Irishmen and sorrow for the failure of '98. O'Longain was a native of Co. Limerick, member of a scholarly family, himself a scholar and scribe, who was residing in Co. Cork at the outbreak of the Rebellion, in which he eagerly participated. For, despite the Jacobite sympathies which kept Munster out of the movement, O'Longain was wholeheartedly with it. His *Song of the Dead Insurgent*, from Dr. Sigerson's translation of which the following stanzas are quoted, is a message from the insurgent in his grave in Wexford to his beloved Southern country:

> Take Munster home my greeting,
>   O comrade, kind and good,
> And say we faced the meeting
>   And armies strong withstood.
> Say children now are cheerless,
> That maidens once so peerless,
> With true men, frank and fearless,
>   Are lying in their blood.
> My woe on Munster's slumbers
>   When we rose out to fight,
> And fronted tyrant numbers
>   With weapons keen and bright.
> But now that all is over,
> And fierce foes o'er us hover,
> Tell Leinster true, I love her
>   Who kept the flame alight.

Chapter VIII. RAGS AND GREEN RUSHES

There's nothing but rags and green rushes for me.   John Keegan

I felt as if the Irish had nothing to be proud of except their beggars.
                                                      John Banim

WHEN THE ENGLISH novel, after a slow process of development, finally reached maturity in the late eighteenth century, it was natural that Ireland, now, by no will of her own, culturally identified with England, should reflect that event by producing a crop of novelists. The first of them was Maria Edgeworth, the theme of whose *Castle Rackrent*, according to Mr. Corkery, was "the decline and fall of an Ascendancy Big House." Corkery distinguishes two types of writers as developing under Ascendancy influence, the first of whom, represented by Miss Edgeworth, "never thought of themselves as cut off from English life and letters"; the second type, whom Mr. Corkery calls Colonial, write from the standpoint of travellers in a strange land, for the purpose of exploiting in a foreign market the land and its people, and this often despite an unmistakably sympathetic attitude towards both. Even Irishmen without an Ascendancy background have done this, first because, as Mr. Corkery says, "it pays better," but also because by this time, with Ireland so thoroughly Anglicized, an Irishman who wanted to write at all could scarcely do otherwise.

No merely mercenary motive influenced Maria Edgeworth (1767-1849), who was always actuated by a high moral purpose, even when she was not writing tracts. The daughter of Richard Lovell Edgeworth, author and inventor, and incidentally the niece of the Abbé Edgeworth who attended Louis XVI on the scaffold, she was born in England, but traced her descent to an old Co. Longford family, and through residence in Ireland had acquired an intimate and sympathetic, if decidedly limited, knowledge of its people.

She was, for instance, well aware of their hardships and keenly alive to their grievances. The very titles of her best and most popular books, *Castle Rackrent* (1800) and *The Absentee* (1809), are eloquent of the evils which they were written to describe and to decry, evils which stemmed from the prodigal excesses of the squireen dwellers in the typical Irish Great House.

Miss Edgeworth did not have it in her (her admirer, Gerald Griffin, to the contrary) to become a novelist of the first order, her besetting sin being an excess of moral earnestness, which found much to feed upon in the scenes amid which she lived, and of course, for reasons given at greater length in Mr. Corkery's study of Synge, she was congenitally incapable of becoming a writer in the Irish sense of the word.

The scenes which stirred her to sympathy and a mild indignation had, however, a directly opposite effect on Samuel Lover, who depicted with zest and robust humour the very aspects of Irish life which Miss Edgeworth deplored. Although Lover, who was born in Dublin in 1797, and was an artist and composer as well as a novelist and poet, ranks with the Irish humourists, the humour in his novels is rather heavy-handed, and by his portrayal of Handy Andy, an Irish servant who is anything but handy, he introduced the stage Irishman into the pages of the novel, and thus helped to perpetuate that burlesque figure. He is more successful in this vein in certain of his sketches, such as *The Gridiron* (see his *Legends and Stories of Ireland*). *Rory O'More* (1837) is a novel of the '98 rebellion. He lived for some years in London, was granted a pension, and died on the island of Jersey in 1868.

Lover unquestionably addressed himself to an English rather than an Irish public, as did also the more versatile Charles Lever,

whose Micky Free, a character in *Charles O'Malley,* is likewise
a contribution to the gallery of stage Irishmen. Lever was born
in Dublin in 1806, was educated at TCD and practised medicine
during the cholera epidemic. He wrote more than twenty-five
novels, the complete edition of 1897-1899, illustrated by Cruik-
shank and Phiz, consisting of thirty-seven volumes. Of these the
best are *Harry Lorrequer, Charles O'Malley, Tom Burke of
'Ours',* and *Lord Kilgobbin,* in which last the author, who had
hitherto been a Tory in politics, displays what almost amount to
nationalist sympathies. He died at Trieste in 1872.

It was natural that all the novelists so far mentioned should
have written for an English public. Not that any of them felt any
animosity towards Ireland, but as Protestants they were cut off
from the bulk of its population, whom Miss Edgeworth saw with
commiseration but little understanding, while both Lever and
Lover beheld in the really tragic figure of the average ragged
Irish peasant the most uproariously humorous fellow in the
world, not so much because, like Falstaff, he was witty himself,
as because like Falstaff, he was by reason of his utter absurdity
the cause of wit in other men.

In William Carleton, however, we are in the presence of something vastly different. Born in Co. Tyrone in 1794 (he died in
1869), his own background unlike that of the novelists so far
mentioned, was that of an Irish peasant, for his father was a
tenant farmer well versed in Irish folk-lore, and the family spoke
both Gaelic and English. Carleton's education was received
chiefly at hedge schools, on which experience he has written
some of his most memorable pages. He, therefore, unlike his
predecessors in the field he was to enter, knew the peasant at
first hand, since he was one himself, but as Corkery, among
others, notably Mr. Stopford Brooke, has pointed out, the most
important fact about the Irish peasant is his religious consciousness, "so vast, so deep, even so terrible a thing . . . that one
wonders if it is possible for a writer to deal with any phase
whatever of Irish life without touching upon it."[1]

Now Carleton had left the Catholic Church and to a great

[1] Corkery, *Synge and Anglo-Irish Literature,* pp. 19-20.

extent supported himself by writing against it for various prosely-
tizing agencies. The chief instrument in this apostasy and in the
literary activities through which it found expression was the Rev.
Caesar Otway, a fanatically intolerant member of the Established
Church, but also founder and publisher of the *Christian Examiner*. In the pages of this periodical Carleton published much of
the work in which he so violently attacks the Church and its
institutions as almost ludicrously to overshoot the mark. The
occasional gibes directed by other writers against the Church,
especially its priesthood, are models of tolerance compared to
the virulence of Carleton's attacks, and yet his work has in it
many elements of greatness, for his gifts were greater than those
of any of the novelists thus far considered. What is tragic is
that these elements, except in some instances, never completely
fulfill their promise—that and the impression forced upon the
reader that in his professed anti-Catholicism Carleton is denying
the witness of his own heart, for his work contains many pages
in which that once Catholic heart speaks out in spite of itself,
although, as his most recent biographer observes, "he knew nothing about dogmatic religion at any period of his existence. . . .
no man ever used his reason less in matters of faith."[2] He is therefore in many respects the reverse of the hedge poets, whose desperation took the form of rakishness. In him, deliberately recreant
to his faith, almost to his race, it breaks out in manifestations
of that faith, in hot protests of devotion to that race.

The list of his novels is a lengthy one, the best of them being
Fardarougha the Miser, Willy Reilly and His Dear Colleen Bawn,
and *The Black Baronet,* which depends for its interest on an
exceedingly complicated and somewhat melodramatic plot. But
the real Carleton, the Irish Carleton, descendant of the *shanachies,* is to be sought in the four volumes of his *Traits and Stories
of the Irish Peasantry* (1854). Here, in spite of an occasional
anti-Catholic outburst, speaks the tragic genius who knows his

[2] *The Poor Scholar,* by Benedict Kiely (1948). This is a masterly study
not only of Carleton's life and personality but of the background against
which that life was lived. It is invaluable for its critical appraisal of
Carleton's work.

gifts, but knows himself prevented by poverty and the consequent lack of cultural opportunity from bringing them to their fullest development. Here speaks the Irish peasant who knows that as such he need not be a lout and a boor, that he was not meant to be an ignorant savage (which despite the calumnies uttered against him, he never became), since he has it in him to be a "master," a man of letters and learning.

Nothing could surpass Carleton's appreciation of the hedge school, of which he himself was a product; nothing could exceed the pathos of his sketch of *The Poor Scholar,* whose fortunes he knew by experience only too well. As is well known, his own mother served as the inspiration for the magnificent figure of the miser's wife in *Fardarougha,* and he used to recall her lovely voice, especially her ability to chant the keen. Of the keen itself he says in the *Traits and Stories* that it "breathes the very spirit of wild and natural sorrow." "The effect of music on the Irish heart," he writes elsewhere, identifying himself with his kind, "I ought to know well"; and of the Irish people he declares, "their mirth is not levity nor is their gloom sorrow."

And so when he writes of Irish poverty, especially of Irish faith in the midst of the hardships of poverty, as he does in *The Poor Scholar* and in *Tubber Derg,* he does so with a power that proves that on such occasions he simply looked in the Irish heart and wrote. *Tubber Derg; or the Red Well* tells the heart-breaking story of Owen McCarthy, who, having fallen into arrears with his rent, goes on foot to Dublin in the hope that a personal interview with the landlord will win him some leniency. In this he is disappointed, as he was bound to be, and on his return, which has been delayed by his own sickness, the neighbours have the sad duty of informing him that in his absence his family has been evicted and his youngest child, Alice, has died.

In Carleton's treatment of this episode he reveals the extent to which he shared the Irish heritage of sorrow, for this is his description of the manner in which the already stricken Owen receives the news of his child's death: " 'Gone!—the fair-haired one!—Alley!—Alley! the pride and joy of both our hearts—the sweet, the quiet, the sorrowful child that seldom played wid the

rest, but kept close to mys— Oh, my darlin'! my darlin'! gone from
my eyes for ever! God of glory! won't you support me this night
of sorrow and misery.' With a sudden yet profound sense of
humility he dropped on his knees at the threshold, and as the
tears rolled down his convulsed cheeks exclaimed in a burst of
sublime piety, not at all uncommon amongst our peasantry, 'I
thank you, O my God! and I put myself and my weeny ones, my
pastchee boght, into your hands. I thank you, O God, for what
has happened! Keep me up an' support me—och, I want it. You
loved the weeny one and you took her—she was the light of my
eyes an' the pulse of my broken heart; but you took her, blessed
Father of heaven! an' we can't be angry with you for so doin'.
Still if you had spared her—if—if—O blessed Father, my heart
was in the very one you took—but I thank you, O my God! May
she rest in peace now and for ever, Amin.' "

Could anyone have written such words who did not enter fully
into the racial heritage of his people, who did not understand
the Irish heart and the extent to which it is motivated by faith,
who did not, as a matter of fact, despite all his disavowals, share
that faith?

The quoted passage further exemplifies Carleton's power to
reproduce the Irish idiom, the use of English speech by a race
that still thinks in its ancestral tongue. It is their failure on this
point that makes so much of the dialogue of Lover and Lever the
broadest burlesque. Carleton, too, is farcical often enough, but
even when his intention is malicious he rarely depends for his
effect on an exaggeration of the brogue.

The Banims were novelists of a different type, since, again
to quote Corkery, "they were one with what they wrote of," and
theirs was the first serious attempt to produce novels for Irish
rather than exclusively English consumption. Even they, however, did not wholly succeed in escaping the "colonial" attitude,
since John, the more enterprising of the two, made his home in
London and won recognition first in England.

They were born in Kilkenny, where their father had a shop
which dealt in sportsmen's equipment, Michael in 1796 and John
in 1798. The younger brother seems to have been something of

a prodigy, since at the age of ten he introduced himself to Tom Moore as a fellow-poet. At about the same age he tried to construct wings with which to fly, and in his thirteenth year was sent to Kilkenny College, then under the mastership of Father Andrew O'Callaghan, a man of great learning.

Since the boy displayed considerable artistic talent, he was next sent to Dublin, where he became a student at the Royal Irish Academy, but at twenty in consequence of a violent love affair, the frustration of which resulted in the death of the young woman, his health was broken to an extent from which he never recovered. In fact, as a result of the illness which followed his prostration, he was the victim of intermittent spells of excruciating pain, which eventually became chronic, depriving him of the use of his legs, so that he was reduced to a condition of helpless and somewhat peevish invalidism.

When he first began to write his efforts were directed towards the stage, and his tragedy, *Damon and Pythias*, was played at Covent Garden by Macready and Charles Kemble. He married in 1820 and took up a permanent residence in London, where he was in a position to show great kindness to his countryman and fellow-writer, Gerald Griffin, when his literary aspirations brought him also to London.

In 1823 John Banim sent the MS of a novel to his brother Michael, with the suggestion that Michael should send him one in return, which eventually he did. Michael's literary methods were unusual according to modern standards, but in many respects they were characteristically Irish, for being under the necessity of working all day in his father's shop, it was his wont to develop his story mentally, devoting the night hours to composition. Thenceforth all their works appeared as *Tales of the O'Hara Family*, John being known as *Abel* and Michael as *Barnes*. John's health forced him to take up residence for a time in France, but his mother's death was such a crushing blow that he returned first to London and then to Dublin. It was on this occasion of return after long sojourn in prosperous places that he was struck by the spectacle of Irish poverty, of which he wrote in the words which appear at the head of this chapter. He finally retired to Kilkenny, where his last years were made more comfortable by a pension. Michael became postmaster of Kilkenny.

What little humour the works of the Banims possess emanated from Michael, but they were both in deadly earnest, since like Miss Edgeworth they had a purpose to serve. But the difference between their background and hers not only made that purpose different, but rendered them incapable of the same detached attitude in handling their material. Their purpose, in the words of Michael, was "to insinuate through fiction the causes of Irish discontent, and to insinuate also, that if crime were consequent on discontent, it was no great wonder." Under these circumstances it was natural that their novels should deal for the most part with serious and even tragic aspects of Irish history, and that they should use these materials both powerfully and realistically.

The best of John's books is *The Boyne Water*, a really great novel of the Williamite wars, despite its multiplicity of incident and character and an extreme complexity of plot. Since it is an historical novel it portrays several actual figures such as James II, William III and Sarsfield, but the most memorable is that of the bard Carolan. It would, however, be difficult to surpass for power and intensity certain passages in his other books, such, for example as the description of the keening at the wake of the murdered Doolings in *Crohoore of the Bill-Hook*, or the portrayal in the same book of the horrors of poverty which drove men such as Terence Delaney to Ribbonism and worse.

While Michael Banim never attempted anything of the dimensions of *The Boyne Water*, although it was he who visited the scenes of the story and procured most of the local historical data, he was on the whole more successful from a literary standpoint than his brother. His most interesting works are *The Croppy*, set against the background of the Rebellion of '98, and *Father Connell*, which excels in characterization and dialogue, especially of the humorous sort.

Despite the fact that the Banim novels had been growing increasingly nationalistic in tone, they could not be said to constitute even a part of a national fiction. As a matter of fact, even when they dealt with deep-rooted grievances, their authors sometimes took a timorous and apologetic attitude, as when in his foreword to his brother's *The Last Baron of Crana*, Michael confesses to their misgivings for having written about the penal times after the enactment of Catholic Emancipation. He explains the belated publication of some of their works by saying that after the "late great decision," they not only revised their books, but rewrote them, and adds, "my brother dedicated the first edition to the emancipating minister, the Duke of Wellington," whom John was later to call a mongrel.

In Gerald Griffin Ireland might have had a novelist of the first order, but he died before he reached the maturity of his powers, and two years before he died he abandoned the literary career in which he had had an encouraging measure of success to become a Christian Brother. Besides, he too "under the stress of the literary moulds of his time," wrote for English readers, although his subject was his own people. That, as a matter of fact, he had no other conception of the purpose or practice of the Irish novelist is evident from his tribute to Miss Edgeworth, whom he describes as "the first to put the sickle into the burthened field of Irish manners; in whose footsteps we follow, like Chaucer's gleaner, at a long interval, with fearful and hesitating pace, casting our eyes around to gather in the scattered ears which remain after the richness of her harvest."[3]

Born in Limerick in 1803 and educated there, he went to London at twenty with the MS of a tragedy in his pocket and dreams of success as a playwright in his head. His *Gisippus* was actually produced at Drury Lane by Macready in 1842, but by that time Griffin had been lying for two years in his grave in Cork. Most of his writing was done in London where he was welcomed by John Banim on terms of intimate friendship, in which there were occasional rifts occasioned by Griffin's extreme sensitiveness, and is chiefly represented by *Tales of the Munster Festivals* (1827, 1829, 1832); *The Duke of Monmouth* (1842); and *The Collegians* (1828). This last, which has been called by eminent authorities the greatest of Irish novels, has a theme not

[3] *The Half Sir.*

unlike that of Dreiser's *American Tragedy,* for it is based on an actual murder, in the trial for which the accused was defended by O'Connell and the proceedings of which were reported for the press by Griffin, but "the mould of the times" is strongly impressed upon it.

The work presents a powerful analysis of the character of Hardress Cregan, which is offset by that of his friend, Kyrle Daly, and poor, clinging Eily O'Connor, whom Cregan has lured from home, secretly married and then got rid of. There are other noteworthy characters, such as Lowry Looby, a retainer of the Daly family, Danny Mann, the Cregan servant, who is the actual slayer of Eily, and Danny's sister, Fighting Poll o' the Reeks, an Amazonian figure, who makes Queen Maeve entirely credible, Myles-na-Coppaleen, Eily's true lover, but above all there are unforgettable scenes such as Mrs. Daly's wake, the questioning of the Naughtons, the death of the huntsman to the accompaniment of the riotous drinking and duelling of the squires (this is a bit out of the Ascendancy picture), the terrible moment in which Hardress, with appalling brutality, tells Eily that he has tired of her, a scene which is equalled if not surpassed by that in which Hardress brings his mother to the realization of their common guilt. The dramatic qualities of the book were recognized by Dion Boucicault, who made it the basis of his phenomenally successful play, *The Colleen Bawn.*

The general impression left by this group of novels is that expressed in Keogh's verse quoted at the head of this chapter, the impression that as far as the native Irishman was concerned his lot consisted chiefly of rags and green rushes. Sometimes this was treated as a regrettable fact as by Miss Edgeworth, sometimes, as by Lever and Lover, as an occasion of infinite jest, sometimes, as by Carleton or the Banims, as charged with unspeakable pathos and tragedy. That writers like the Banims and Griffin did not handle their material with greater power was in all probability due less to lack of literary ability than to a fact to which John Keogh gave such forthright expression: "You might recognize a Catholic on the street by his timid gait."

This could not be said of Charles Kickham, who may be called the first Irish novelist in the sense that he wrote from the standpoint of his own people, with no thought of foreign readers, although circumstances compelled him to write in English. His is a completely nationalist point of view, all the more genuine by reason of its lack of self-consciousness, the absence of any propagandist intention. Kickham was so intense a patriot that he was willing and eager to die for Ireland, but he was too instinctive a *shanachie* to dream of making his story a weapon in the cause, particularly since he was addressing himself to an Irish public in whom he assumed a spirit akin to his own.

Charles J. Kickham was born in Mullinahone, Tipperary, in 1825, the son of a prosperous merchant. At the age of sixteen, the explosion of a flask of damp gunpowder which he was drying inflicted permanent injury on both his sight and his hearing. Nevertheless, he began at an early age to take an active part in the various political movements by which his country was then being stirred, becoming particularly interested in the land question and the efforts of the Tenant Right League to stop the flood of emigration. Its failure caused him to lose faith in legal measures, and he became a member of the Fenian party and a contributor to its organ, *The Irish People*. It was these contributions which led to his arrest, together with that of John O'Leary, and in 1866 he was sentenced to fourteen years penal servitude. His health, already greatly impaired, failed so rapidly during his imprisonment in Kilmainham that his term was shortened and in 1869 he was released. He died at Blackrock near Dublin in 1882.

Kickham's earliest writings, mostly verse, were contributed to the *Nation*, the *Celt*, the *Irishman*, the *Irish People*, but he is best remembered as a novelist, chiefly for *Sally Cavanagh, or Untenanted Graves* (1869), inspired by the character of his mother, and *Knocknagow, or the Homes of Tipperary* (1879), by many regarded as the greatest of the earlier Irish novels. It is not perhaps a great novel in any absolute sense of the word. It has many defects of structure and organization, but it does unforgettably what it set out to do, portray the life of the Irish people, the real Irish, peasant and well-to-do tenant, as well as a specimen or two from the Big House, for even Kickham cannot get away from the device of the visiting Stranger, but, although this is precisely one of the defects in the handling of his material, Mr. Henry Lowe soon drops into the background, leaving no one the sorrier.

There are laughter and tears in the book, music and dancing, weddings and funerals. There are characters, such as Matt the Thrasher, Phil Lahy, the tailor who "does not mend, but only makes or repairs," Billy Heffernan, with his shy love of "poor Norah Lahy," which he is capable of uttering only by means of his flute, the coquette, Bessy Morris, Bob Lloyd, the engaging squireen, any one of whom would be worthy of a major novelist, and there are many more. There are bits of genre portrayal such as that of the blind piper, late survivor of the bardic tradition:

"As he uncovered his pipes their splendour quite took Mr. Lowe by surprise. The keys were of silver, and the bag covered with crimson velvet fringed with gold; while the little bellows was quite a work of art, so beautifully was it carved and ornamented with silver and ivory. Having tied an oval-shaped piece of velvet with ribbon attached to each end above his knee, he adjusted his instrument, and after moving his arm, to which the bellows was attached by a ribbon, till the crimson velvet bag was inflated, he touched the keys, and catching up the 'chanter' quickly in both hands began to play. . . . The musician seemed to forget all mere human concerns. He threw back his head as if communing with invisible spirits in the air above him; or bent down over his instruments as if the spirits had suddenly flown into it, and he wanted to catch their whisperings there, too."

There are innumerable scenes and situations, representative of a wide variety of experience, restricted within a small compass and depicted with an economy of words that stamps them on the memory. One of them, which signalizes the fact that "rags and green rushes" were still symbolic of the standard of Irish living, and which is memorable because it is one more contribution to the large gallery of such pictures provided by Irish fiction, is the scene which depicts the visit of the starving Mick Brien to the cabin of the Heffernans.

Above all else, Kickham is a master of English as it is spoken in

Ireland, for which reason the dialogue provides much of the humour in which the book abounds, although it is scarcely necessary to say that there is never the slightest hint of burlesque. Perhaps one of the most delightful passages in the book is that which presents Father Hannigan's sermon, of which the following is an excerpt:

"But though Father Hannigan had delivered his regular discourse after the first gospel, it was his habit to deliver a few homely words to the people at the conclusion of the Mass, upon what we may call local and individual topics. He now turned round, and began, in his deep *big* voice, with:

" 'Now what's this I was going to say to ye?'

"He pressed the forefinger of his left hand against his temple, as if trying to recall something that had escaped his memory. Mr. Lowe thought he was about giving up the attempt in despair, when he suddenly jerked up his head, exclaiming—

" 'Ay! ay! ay! D'ye give up stealing the turf in the name o' God!'

" 'Everyone,' he continued after a pause, 'must steal turf such weather as this that hasn't it of their own. But sure if ye didn't know it was wrong, ye wouldn't be telling it to the priest. And ye think it would be more disgraceful to beg than to steal it. That's a great mistake. No dacent man would refuse a neighbour a hamper of turf such weather as this. And a poor man is not a beggar for asking a hamper of turf such weather as this when he can't get a day's work, and the Easter water bottles bursting. Ye may laugh; but Judy Manogue stopped me on the road yesterday to know what she ought to do. Her bottle of Easter water that she had under her bed was in a lump of ice, and the bottle,—a big, black bottle that often gave some of ye a headache—an' maybe 'twasn't without giving more of you a heartache—before Judy took my advice and gave up that branch of her business: well, the big, black bottle was split in two with the fair dint of the frost—under the poor woman's bed. And the Lord knows no Christian could stand without a spark of fire to keep the life in him—let alone looking at a houseful of children shivering and shaking, and be able and willing to work and not a stroke of work to be got. But ye all know that stealing is bad, and ye ought fitter make your cases known to the priest, and maybe something might be done for ye. *Pride* is a good thing—dacent, manly pride—and 'twill often keep a man from doing a mane act even when he's sorely tempted. *Sperit* is a good thing. But, take my word for it, there's nothing like HONESTY. And poverty, so long as it is not brought on by any fault of his own, need never bring a blush to any man's cheek. So, in the name o' God, d'ye give up stealing the turf.' "

Such were the beginnings of the Irish novel, Irish only in the sense that it undertook to depict the Irish scene, but in reality an enlargement of the field of English fiction. All the novelists thus far mentioned, by reason of their portrayal of various aspects of Irish life, were under the necessity of presenting a picture whose most salient feature is the appalling poverty which had become the lot of the Irish peasant, a condition which could be accurately summed up in the words of one of them as consisting of "rags and green rushes."

Equally inescapable as a feature of that scene is the ignorance by which such poverty was necessarily accompanied. It is only through the works of native writers like Carleton, the Banims, Griffin and Kickham, native despite their use of the foreign tongue, that we become aware of an extraordinary phenomenon, namely that the ignorance to which the Irish had been reduced was in reality a form of culture, since it was such an unequivocal assertion of their ability to put first things first. Only such a clear-eyed recognition of the spiritual order could explain the depths of insight and understanding which they habitually manifested. Translated into terms of living it constitutes a wisdom which puts the academic philosopher to shame by filling life with dignity, valour and even charm. To the extent that early Irish novels demonstrate the truth of these statements they are transcripts of Irish life. This does not condone or justify the conditions of which such wisdom was the fruit. Irish poverty is not picturesque; it is a shameful crime, of which the Irish are not guilty.

Chapter IX. *REBUILDING THE TOWER*

> *Who sings the song rebuilds the tower.*
> Susan Mitchell, The Builders

EVEN BEFORE the Irish sky was reddened by the conflagration of '98, there were manifestations, sometimes within the very House of the Ascendant itself, that denoted the presence of life where death had long been assumed. For the most part these took the form of attempts to preserve various aspects of the fast-disappearing Irish culture—its music, for instance—to halt the decay of Irish speech and to rescue fragments of the literature of which that speech had been the vehicle.

After long years of neglect, something like justice is now being done to the achievement of a woman from whom it is not too fantastic to date the beginning of the so-called Irish Revival. She was Charlotte Brooke, daughter of the novelist, Henry Brooke, author of *The Fool of Quality*, and therefore undeniably of the Ascendancy class and tradition, but it is a matter of simple fact that certain embers of the Irish literary heritage were salvaged by her, to be blown into flame by the stronger lungs of another generation.

Born in Co. Cavan in 1740, she was educated by her father beyond what was then considered necessary or even desirable for one of her sex. Among her linguistic attainments was Irish, which she knew not only from an academic standpoint, but as the living speech of the Cavan peasantry among whom most of her life was spent. She was therefore even better qualified than Dr. Johnson to challenge the authenticity of Macpherson's *Ossian,* which she proceeded to do, not by denouncing it as a forgery, nor, like Dr. Johnson, declaring the Scotchman a liar, but by publishing, at first anonymously and, it must be acknowledged, in somewhat tame English verse, the genuine Ossianic tales as she had heard them from Irish lips.

When in 1789 she published under her own name her *Reliques of Irish Poetry*, containing both translations and originals, which was more than Macpherson was ever able to do, it was, as Mr. Desmond Ryan points out in the chapter which he devotes to her in *The Sword of Light*, an amazing book, which ended the Ossianic controversy. While its literary effect was not so immediate as that of Percy's *Reliques* in England, it is not too much to claim for it a similar ultimate effect.

Among Miss Brooke's contemporaries there were a few who recognized the importance of her work, such a man, for example, as Joseph Cooper Walker, who shared her interest in Irish studies, particularly the Gaelic language and music. Walker, who was born in Dublin in 1761, spent much time in travel, especially in Italy. After his return to Ireland he held a post in the Treasury, but eventually took up his residence at Bray, where, besides a fine library, he assembled a collection of pictures and Irish antiquities. His absorbing interest in music, coupled with his antiquarian studies, led him to publish his *Historical Memoirs of the Irish Bards*. He died in 1810.

Walker shares with Edward Bunting the honour of having been a pioneer in the effort to rescue Irish music from extinction. Born in Armagh in 1773, Bunting was a musical prodigy who taught the art at the age of eleven. Realizing that Ireland's musical treasure was in danger of being lost to human knowledge, he organized in 1792 a great festival to which he invited all the surviving Irish harpers, and on that momentous occasion himself took down the airs which he afterwards published under the title *Ancient Irish Music* (1796).

Bunting afterwards travelled about Ireland, taking down airs from the people, a task in which he was assisted by an Irish scholar and schoolmaster named Patrick Lynch, who was subsequently discredited as an informer. As a result of these labours Bunting issued in 1809 and 1840 two more collections of Irish music.

The mention of Bunting serves as a reminder that it was chiefly to him that Tom Moore owed his knowledge of the airs, many of them of considerable antiquity, to which he wrote most of the verses that became so famous as his *Irish Melodies.* Perhaps nothing is more illustrative of the extent to which Ireland had become Anglicized by the beginning of the nineteenth century than the fact that Thomas Moore was so generally and for so long regarded as the greatest of Irish poets, whereas he knew no Gaelic and had not the slightest sense of the essential spirit of the race to which indeed he belonged, but which he did not truly represent. If there be any warrant for the claim made by his most recent biographer (L. A. G. Strong, *The Minstrel Boy,* 1937), that he put Ireland back on the cultural map of Europe, it is only because Europe and the rest of the world, including large sections of the Irish race, accepted as genuinely Irish what an engaging but misinformed Irishman proffered as such.

Born in Dublin in 1779, at a time when the penalties against Catholics had been eased but not entirely removed, Moore grew up in an atmosphere of general approbation, charming first his own household and then his fellow-students at Trinity, where he was admitted, although, as a Catholic, still in many ways disqualified, forced to be content, as he said himself, with the mere barren credit. Moore early developed a native facility for lisping in numbers. He also possessed a delightful drawing-room voice, the instrument which first rendered and introduced his famous melodies, graceful English verses set to what purported to be traditional Irish airs, and thus launched his career of almost unprecedented personal popularity and stimulated the universal affection in which his songs were cherished.

That Moore was an Irish Catholic who was everywhere received in the best English society was assuredly one of the reasons, although a tragic one, for his vast popularity in his own country, many of whose people were now Anglicized to the point of regarding English approbation as a piece of enviable good fortune, although on the whole they were still strong enough in their faith to be quick to rejoice over any instance of its courageous profession, and an outstanding instance of such boldness they fancied to exist in Moore. But that, of course, was precisely where they were mistaken, for he was never anything but a nominal Catholic and at several periods of his life he was on the verge of becoming a Protestant. His whole philosophy of life seems to boil down to a kind of hedonism, that has little in common with the long martyrdom of his race.

As for his cultural service to Ireland, there are those (notably the late Professor Stockley, *Essays in Irish Biography*, 1933) who couple him with O'Connell, whom he detested, in the de-Gael-icizing of Ireland: "By his popular English words he helped forward in a country then chiefly Gaelic-speaking, the indiffer-ence to, the neglect of the Irish language; he set an English standard before the country; he helped to turn the Irish into imitators of another country, ashamed of their own traditions and ideals."

His *Lalla Rookh* (1817) and *Loves of the Angels* (1823), in the vein of Byronic Orientalism then so much in vogue, furnished Byron himself with some warrant for the epithet which he applied to his friend, when he called him "the melodious apostle of lust." His total unfitness to write the *History of Ireland* (between 1839 and 1846) is revealed in the fact that he had no suspicion of it until the memorable day when the sight of O'Curry at work on the ancient MSS in the Royal Irish Academy startled him into the abashed admission to Petrie: "I had no right to have undertaken the *History of Ireland*."

Moore has been charged with altering some of the traditional airs in order to fit them to his English words, but he has also been credited with catching in his poetry something of the Gaelic rhythms. In this case, as Mr. Strong points out, it was the air that taught him all he knew.

After their first collaboration a quarrel had broken out between Moore and Bunting, since Moore and his other collaborator, Sir

John Stevenson, had freely borrowed from Bunting's later collection, a procedure which Bunting resented, while Moore dismissed as "a mere mess of trash" anything that he did not use.[1]

The title page of the 1809 edition of Bunting's work, which is the only one of his publications I have been able to examine, runs as follows: *A General Collection of the Ancient Music of Ireland arranged for the Piano Forte, some of the most admired melodies are adapted for the voice, to Poetry chiefly translated from the Original Irish Songs by Thomas Campbell Esq. and other eminent poets: To which is prefixed Historical and Critical Dissertations on the Egyptian, British and Irish Harp,* by Edward Bunting. The most important of Campbell's contributions to this volume is the famous *There came to the beach,* commonly known as *The Exile of Erin,* set to the music of *Blaith na sead* (*Thou Blooming Treasure*). In addition, the volume contains several of Carolan's fine airs, such as *Bumper Squire Jones, Bridget Cruise, Mild Mable Kelly* and *I'll follow you over the mountain,* but as for the verse, the only thing less Irish than Campbell's is that of Miss Balfour, who, to the grand tune of *Cailin beg cruitin na mbo* (*The pretty girl milking her cow*) supplies a poem of which the first stanza is typical:

> The moon calmly sleeps o'er the ocean
> And tinges each white bosom'd sail,
> The barque, scarcely conscious of motion,
> Glides slowly before the soft gale.

Moore may not have been able to rise to the level of the music which inspired much of his verse, but assuredly the verse itself stood on sturdier poetic feet than did Miss Balfour's. Commenting on the relative merits of the work of Walker and Bunting, O'Curry says that Walker was assisted in his conclusions chiefly by his imagination, whereas Bunting relied on induction assisted by a high musical education.

Their work in this field was supplemented by the publication in 1831 of James Hardiman's *Irish Minstrelsy, or the Bardic*

---

[1] Graves, *Irish Literary and Musical Studies.*

Remains of Ireland with English Poetical Translations. The sources of Hardiman's selections are never clearly indicated, but they are thought to have been taken down from MSS that were in current use until the extinction of the harpers. Hardiman was born in Connaught about 1790 and died in 1855 in Galway, where he was librarian of Queen's College. Although not a profound scholar, he made an important contribution to the effort to preserve ancient Irish music. He was likewise the author of a *History of Galway* (1820), and for the Irish Archeological Society he edited O'Flaherty's *Iar Connaught* (1846).

Another interesting figure of this period is Hercules Ellis, who engaged in a correspondence with Campbell on the subject of his authorship of the *Exile of Erin.* Ellis, who was born about 1808 in Dublin, where he died in 1879, was educated at TCD, was admitted to the bar and published the following works: *Songs of Ireland* (1849), of which he was the editor, *Romances and Ballads* (1850), and *The Rhyme Book* (1851).

It was perfectly natural, though the reason may not at first be apparent, that the effort to preserve Irish music should have been allied with the movement to promote the study of the Irish language, a movement which at first amounted to little more than an attempt to halt its utter dissolution and decay. To this end a number of societies were organized of which one of the earliest was the Gaelic Society (1806), in the organization of which Joseph Cooper Walker was instrumental. Its secretary, Theophilus O'Flanagan, had edited a volume which contained the tales of the *Children of Lir* and the *Sons of Usnach,* thereby providing Moore with the subjects for *Silent, O Moyle,* and *Avenging and Bright.*

The Society had a distinguished membership, most of whom contributed something towards the preservation, if not the complete restoration, of Irish. Among them was William Halliday (b. 1788), who learned Gaelic and, under the pseudonym of O'Hara, published an Irish grammar (1808). He also published a translation of the first volume of Keating's *History* and at the time of his death (1812) was engaged on a dictionary of Irish.

He was a brother of Charles Halliday (1789-1866), who, despite antiquarian studies which resulted in the publication of a *History of the Scandinavian Kingdom of Dublin,* made a large fortune in business.

Still another member of the Gaelic Society was Sylvester O'Halloran, already mentioned as the author of a *History of Ireland* that nearly a hundred years later was to exert an influence out of all proportion to its intrinsic value. It was published in London and, as the author explains in his Foreword, it was necessary to print the Irish quotations in English characters, since there was in London no font of Irish type. The book is addressed with possibly unconscious irony to "the mere English" reader with the assurance that, "However ambitious I have been to rescue my native history from the hands of ignorance, and to draw it forth from that oblivion to which it has been so long and so shamefully consigned, yet I am not conscious in any single instance of aiming to do it at the expense of truth."

O'Halloran was mainly intent upon the task of salvaging as was also his friend, Rev. John Lanigan (1758-1828), who in 1794 returned to Ireland penniless after completing a brilliant course of ecclesiastical studies in Rome. After thirty years labour his *Ecclesiastical History of Ireland* appeared in 1822, by which time he had begun to exhibit symptoms of the insanity which eventually led to his being placed under restraint.

Even at that early date, however, there were far-sighted and intrepid souls who thought in terms not merely of survival but of revival. One of these was William Farmer, who came to Dublin in 1810 and with Edward O'Reilly opened a school for the teaching of Irish. With an ingenuity not unworthy of comparison with Champollion's in deciphering the Rosetta Stone, O'Reilly had prepared himself for this task by purchasing some MSS from which he taught himself Irish. But since the task of teaching others was rendered formidable, not to say impossible, by a total lack of books, in order to remedy that condition at least in part, O'Reilly compiled an Irish-English Dictionary, the Supplement to which was afterwards made by John O'Donovan. O'Reilly was likewise the author of a *Catalogue of Irish Writers, The Brehon Laws* and the *Poems of Ossian.*

Philip Barron, as Desmond Ryan well shows[2] in pages that deserve to be read to their last syllable, was no mere salvager, but a man of vision and dauntless if impractical courage. Born in Waterford in 1797 of a family of Geraldine stock, he dreamed of such a bourgeoning of Irish culture that in the endeavour to promote it he went bankrupt and had to withdraw to France, where he is said to have died.

His projects included a press for the printing of Irish books, among its products being O'Reilly's *Dictionary*; the purchase of a newspaper; the foundation of a periodical (*The Annual Register*), and the establishment of an Irish college. Not only that, but he urged (Mr. Ryan says "demanded") the teaching of Irish in all the schools and colleges of Ireland and the teaching of the literary classics through the medium of Irish. So certain was he of the success of his ventures that he had the courage to assert that from the year 1835 "we shall have to date the revival of learning in Ireland." When it is recalled how utterly those ventures failed, so that of his college there remained in 1913 "only a thin fringe of broken wall," the chapter which Mr. Desmond devotes to Barron is only too appropriately entitled *Sixty Years Too Soon*. And yet Arthur Griffith called him "the first Gaelic Leaguer."

Although Gaelic had long since ceased to be the literary language of Ireland, the medium used by scholars, historians, poets, and *shanachies*, it continued to be spoken, mostly by the peasantry, who, on the witness of Canon Ulick Bourke (*The Aryan Origin of the Gaelic Race and Language*), during the first quarter of the nineteenth century, "spoke their native tongue with the same sweetness and grammatical exactness with which it was spoken in 1631 when the Four Masters penned the Annals of Ireland." Another witness to this fact is John Banim, who in *Crohoore of the Bill-Hook*, after reporting Terence Delaney's

[2] *The Sword of Light. From the Four Masters to Douglas Hyde.* 1636-1938 (1939).

dying words, remarks that if the language appeared too refined
for one of his station in life, it had been literally translated from
the Irish, in which "there is nothing of what is known by the
name of vulgarism; its construction even in the mouths of the
peasantry, who to this day use it, has been and can be but little
corrupted; nor could the familiar colloquy of the meanest among
them be rendered, in English, into commonplace or slang." This
fact is further emphasized by Mr. Robin Flower, who was wont
to pursue his own Gaelic studies among the peasants of the Great
Blasket and who pays tribute to one of the women as "one of the
finest speakers in the island; she has so clean and finished a style
of speech that you can follow all the nicest articulations of the
language on her lips without any effort; she is a natural orator,
with so keen a sense of the turn of phrase and the lifting rhythm
appropriate to the Irish that her words could be written down
as they leave her lips and they would have the effect of literature,
with no savour of the artificiality of composition."[3]

But in the early nineteenth century even among the peasantry
its use was waning, partly because the Irish themselves had come
at last to regard it as a mark of cultural backwardness. The very
schoolmasters whose love for the Gaelic had helped to keep alive
this organ of their native culture now strove to discourage its
use, maintaining to this end a system of penalties incurred by
students whose parents reported an infringement even at home
of the master's ban upon Irish.

At this point it becomes imperative to introduce the name of
Daniel O'Connell, since he is held to have been largely responsible for so drastic a change in the Irish attitude towards the
ancestral language. Daniel O'Connell was unquestionably the
greatest of Irish orators, if he was not indeed one of the greatest
orators of all time, not of course in the sense in which Burke
and Grattan or even Curran were orators, although he had some
of the qualities of all three. Like them he was trained to the bar
and to parliamentary procedure and address, but skilled though
he was in the art of pleading, his greatest triumph was the fruit

[3] *The Western Island, or the Great Blasket* (1945).

of native genius rather than training, and his true sphere was neither the court room nor the halls of Parliament, but the hustings or the public hall or even an open field, into which could be gathered the vast throngs that came to stand under the "impetuous hailstorm" of his words.

O'Connell was, of course, essentially an agitator (that is what he called himself), and the purpose of his agitation was first of all Catholic Emancipation, and with that achieved, as it was in 1829, the Repeal of the Union. Born in Co. Kerry in 1775, he was educated at first abroad, and then, as a consequence of the relaxation of the penal laws, which permitted Catholics to enter the professions, he undertook the study of law and was admitted to the bar in 1798. A life of unprecedented success and glory, culminating in the enactment of Catholic Emancipation, as a result of which he was hailed as the uncrowned king of Ireland, was saddened towards the end, which came in 1847. He died at Genoa while on a pilgrimage to Rome, where his heart is buried. His body rests in Ireland.

O'Connell himself knew Irish, but it was English that he chose to make the medium of his eloquence, English that he established in a position of pre-eminence by emphasizing the fact that all prospects of worldly advancement and success, to which the way had been opened by Emancipation, lay with the English speech, so that the time came when even Catholic Emancipation was deplored by Irish nationalists insofar as it had helped to further this idea. As a matter of fact, even the Catholic clergy to a certain extent supported this point of view, because of their fear of Irish as an instrument of proselytism, a use to which it had actually and repeatedly been put. On the witness of Dr. Douglas Hyde and others, some of the bishops even went so far as to drive teachers of Irish out of their dioceses, a fact which enabled Dr. Hyde, in reviewing the movement for the preservation of the Irish language (*Beside the Fire*), to remark on the irony of the situation which had developed when a knowledge of his ancestral tongue exposed a man to the danger of being suspected as an "enemy."

This was the situation that obtained at the period referred to, when as a consequence of the Act of Union, the country had been reduced to the condition of a British colony, an English-speaking colony, administered by English laws, with social institutions and manners modelled upon the English pattern and a copious literature recognized as constituting a part of the literature of England. The religion of the majority of the population was no longer (after 1829) penalized. They were no longer debarred from education, no longer excluded from the professions, nor denied the cultivation of the liberal arts, but they were still for the most part paying the price of dire poverty for their stability in the faith; they were still reduced by barbarous land laws to a state of extreme economic distress, which rendered their eligi- bility for education of little practical use, while to such as suc- ceeded in becoming educated every inducement was offered that it should be along English lines and through the medium of English speech.

One of the immediate consequences of Catholic Emancipation, therefore, was an inclination to forget the past, to regard the Irish nationalistic spirit as hopelessly idealistic and foolishly impractical; it was a tendency to look forward to a prosperous future along Anglo-Saxon lines, which, though still subject to certain limitations, the Irish were at last in a position to share with the Anglo-Saxons.

And yet in the Ireland of that very time there was developing a tendency to look backward, an inclination to delve into the Irish past, to scrutinize the very countenance of the country itself and to question the countless ancient monuments which lay scattered about it in ruinous mystery. An important centre of such inquiry was the Dublin household of the distinguished Dr. William Stokes (1804-1878). Recognized as one of the great- est physicians of his day in Europe, he was also a scholar and a friend of scholars. His daughter, Margaret (1832-1900), was an artist who shared her father's antiquarian interests and herself won distinction in this field (see below), while his son, Whitley (1830-1909), became one of the most brilliant philological scholars of his generation.

To the Stokes home as to a centre of intellectual activity came all the leading Irish scholars of the day, and suddenly Dublin seemed to be full of them. Among them were Todd, Ferguson, Reeves, Lord Dunraven, but most important of all, George Petrie, one of the giants of the movement that was now rapidly getting under way. Born in Dublin in 1789, Petrie was a man of exceptional ability and forceful personality. The son of a portrait painter, his early education was received at Samuel White's school in Dublin. Then he too began the study of art, for which purpose he attended the Art School of the Dublin Society. He became proficient and successful as a landscape artist, participating in several exhibitions and selling numerous pictures. At an early age, as a result of his travels in search of picturesque scenery, he began to be interested in Irish antiquities, of which he beheld on every hand so many interesting specimens.

At the second exhibition of the Royal Hibernian Academy in 1827 he was represented by a picture of the *Round Tower of Kilbannon,* which, apart from its artistic merits, derives interest from the fact that a few years later Petrie published an important essay on the Irish Round Towers. In 1830 he became librarian at the Hibernian Academy, in 1832 joined Caesar Otway[4] in the editorship of the *Dublin Penny Journal,* and in 1842 became sole editor of the *Irish Penny Journal,* one of the most important contributors to which was John O'Donovan.

In 1828 Petrie had become a member of the Royal Irish Academy, founded in Dublin in 1786 for the purpose of promoting the study of Irish literature, antiquities and science. In 1831, in an effort to improve its library and museum, Petrie successfully engineered its acquisition of the MS of the *Four Masters* and the great Cross of Cong. From 1832 to 1848 he was attached to

---

[4] Caesar Otway, born in Tipperary in 1780, received his B. A. degree at TCD in 1801, became a popular preacher and engaged in several journalistic enterprises in Dublin, having been one of the founders of the *Christian Examiner,* to which Carleton became a contributor, besides being associated with Petrie in the *Dublin Penny Journal.* He was the author of *Sketches in Ireland; In Ennis and Tyrawley;* and *A Tour in Connaught.* He died in 1842. He was, it has been noted (p. 114), instrumental in promoting Carleton's apostasy from the Catholic Church.

the Ordnance Survey, which gave him both the incentive and the opportunity to carry on intensive studies of subjects such as Tara, on which he published in 1837 an essay in which he took issue with Sir William Betham, who, lacking Petrie's scholarly magnanimity, was seriously affronted.

Petrie's essay on the Round Towers, eventually published in 1845 under the title, *The Ecclesiastical Architecture of Ireland,* stirred up a heated controversy because it was awarded a medal for which a rival competitor had been Henry O'Brien (1808-1835), a Trinity man whose dissertation on the Round Towers had been enlarged to prove that they were Buddhistic remains, a claim that relegates him to the fantastic company of General Vallancey and justifies Thomas Davis's reference to "poor Henry O'Brien's enthusiastic ignorance." Vallancey was a French Protestant engineer engaged in a military survey of Ireland, who became interested in the country's language and history and in 1772 published an essay and grammar, in the course of which he asserted the resemblance of Irish to Punic, Kalmuck and Algonquin. Not only that, but he afterwards published a six-volume work in which he proved the facts of Irish history from Sanskrit literature and traced a likeness between Irish and Egyptian, Persian and Hindustani. After this, Petrie's claim that the Round Towers were once Christian ecclesiastical buildings must have resembled an anticlimax, but the solidity of the scholarship which substantiated that claim was generally recognized by all who were competent to appraise it.

He had already (in 1816) published an *Essay on Music,* and in 1855 issued his invaluable study of *The Ancient Music of Ireland.* But in the long list of Petrie's achievements perhaps nothing is more important nor of more enduring significance than his association with Eugene O'Curry and John O'Donovan, "my warmest and most attached friends," for by that association, by his large-minded recognition of their gifts and his unflagging friendship, he shared in a major contribution to Irish learning.

Eoghan (Anglicized Eugene) O'Curry was born (1796) in Co. Clare, "the last county in Ireland that was governed by Brehon laws administered by native judges." Not only was it a Gaelic-speaking section, but O'Curry's peasant father, like many of his neighbours, possessed a fine collection of ancient MSS, which, for lack of school masters, the young men of the district used to study in one another's houses in the winter evenings. It was only in mature years that O'Curry came to appreciate his father's knowledge and the value of his collection, and this appreciation was largely due to the inspiration of Petrie, with whom he became associated in the Ordnance Survey. When this work was suspended in 1837, O'Curry's learning was next employed, again through the offices of Petrie, on MSS at the Royal Irish Academy and in the library of Trinity College. He edited and translated several texts published by the Celtic Society (see below) and wrote a MS Catalogue of the Irish MSS in the British Museum, where he spent the years 1849-1855.

When the Catholic University of Ireland was founded, its rector, the great Newman, gave additional proof of his greatness by appointing O'Curry to the chair of history, despite his lack of formal academic training. In this capacity O'Curry delivered the series of lectures, every one of which Newman attended, which were afterwards published in the volumes on which the Irish scholar's fame chiefly rests. That on the *Manuscript Materials of Ancient Irish History* was published in 1860 at the expense of the university. The master died in 1862 after his last lecture, which was on the subject of Irish Music and Dancing. In 1873 his lectures on the *Manners and Customs of the Ancient Irish* were published under the editorship of W. K. Sullivan, whose Introduction constitutes an entire volume.

John O'Donovan, whom Mr. Desmond Ryan (*The Sword of Light*) calls "the fifth master," was born in Co. Kilkenny in 1809 of ancient Irish lineage, of which, in characteristic fashion, his father reminded him from his death-bed, since such descent was regarded as a heritage to be cherished. He was educated in Dublin at the expense of his brother, Michael, but acquired his love of his country's antiquities from an uncle. In 1826 he entered the employ of the Irish Record Office, from which in 1829 he went to the Irish Ordnance Survey, then under the direction of Petrie, who was quick to recognize his genius.

Here also he came into contact with O'Curry, whose sister he married.

His work, which required him to examine MSS in order to decide topographical nomenclature, took him on numerous journeys throughout Ireland. His greatest work, a truly monumental performance, is his translation of the Four Masters, on which he was engaged from 1848 to 1851, and for whose seven quarto volumes Petrie designed the type. Among the other works which he translated and edited were *The Circuit of Ireland by Muircheartach Mac Neill*, a poem written in 942; *The Tribes and Customs of Hy Many*, commonly called O'Kelly's country, taken from the Book of Lecan (1418), and published in 1843; *The Genealogies, Tribes and Customs of Hy Fiachrach*, commonly called O'Dowda's country, printed from a MS of Duald Mac Firbis (published 1844). He edited various works which were published under the auspices of the Irish Archaeological Society (founded 1840) and the Celtic Society, and in 1845 published an Irish grammar for the use of the Senior classes at St. Columba's College, a work which included what has been called "the most interesting treatise on modern and medieval Irish as a spoken tongue." He worked extensively on the ancient Irish laws, of which he made transcripts which fill 2491 pages, but he died in 1861, without having edited any part of this work.

The scholarly achievements of O'Curry and O'Donovan help to throw into strong relief the high-minded liberality of Petrie and one to whom O'Curry referred in one of his lectures when he said, "You have an example of a Protestant gentleman, a clergyman of the Protestant Church, a Fellow of the Protestant University of Dublin, casting away from him all unworthy prejudices of creed, caste, and position . . . like a true scholar and a man of large mind and understanding, endeavouring to recover for his native country as much of her long-lost and widely dispersed literary remains as he can."[5]

This was James Henthorn Todd, born in Dublin in 1805, and active in every scholarly enterprise of the time, not only a

[5] *MSS Materials*, p. 174.

scholar in his own right, but expending time and fortune in the promotion of the scholarly labours of others, oblivious of credit to himself. He participated in the Protestant controversy concerning education and helped to found St. Columba's College (1843), where provision was made for the teaching of Irish. As librarian at Trinity, he not only performed invaluable services for the library, but took advantage of his office to befriend James Clarence Mangan (see below). Dr. Todd edited *The War of the Gaedhil with the Gaill, or the Invasions of Ireland by the Danes and Other Normans.* The volume, which was published in London in 1867 under the direction of the Master of the Rolls, contains the original Irish text as well as Dr. Todd's translation and Introduction. He was likewise the author of a *Life of St. Patrick.*

Speaking in the capacity of professor of Irish History and Archaeology, O'Curry pointed out that while he had no difficulty in procuring material on the ancient Irish period, he was embarrassed when it came to the Christian ages, and begged that something might be done to procure for Ireland at least true copies of the numerous Christian MSS scattered through the libraries and museums of the Continent. In attempting to give some idea of the situation by which Irish students were confronted, he described how in 1842 a scholar had found at St. Isidore's alone twenty volumes of Irish MSS, and, acting in collaboration with O'Curry, had taken steps to purchase them, but various factors, including the death of the scholar and the famine, had brought the venture to nothing.

Meanwhile, upon the rumour of other finds at Louvain, Dr. Todd at once set out for Brussels, and in 1849 succeeded in procuring from the Belgian government the loan of documents, some of them incontestably the work of Michael O'Clery, which O'Donovan forthwith proceeded to edit and translate.

The story of the recovery of the MS which enabled him to perform his greatest feat, the translation of the *Annals of the Four Masters*, introduces two other names into the record. The first is that of Charles O'Conor of Belanagare, a Catholic gentleman who traced his descent to a brother of Roderick O'Conor, last king of Ireland. Charles was born in 1710, and was taught to read and write Latin and Irish by a Franciscan friar who knew no English. Barred from the professional success which his talents warranted, Mr. O'Conor nevertheless engaged in scholarly pursuits, especially the collecting of Irish MSS, and acquired a reputation as an antiquary. He died in 1791, his MSS and his antiquarian tastes descending to his grandson, also Charles O'Conor (1764-1828).

As a preliminary to becoming a priest this gentleman studied in Italy, and for some years after his return acted as chaplain to the Marchioness of Buckingham, to whose husband, the Marquis, his grandfather had sold the MS of the *Four Masters*. At her death he remained at Stowe as librarian. According to the elder O'Conor's account, on which Petrie casts doubt, the document had been taken to Spain by a member of the O'Gara family and there given to a kinsman of the O'Conors, who presented it to the elder Charles.

What Petrie questioned was the manner of its acquisition, which he had reason to believe was by purchase at a sale in Ireland itself; that it was the authentic work of O'Clery was never in a moment's doubt. Rev. Charles O'Conor included a translation of it in his *Rerum Hibernicarum Scriptores* (1814-1826), a translation which O'Donovan criticized with extreme severity. This was the MS which Petrie purchased (1831) out of his own pocket, for presentation to the library of the Royal Irish Academy and it thus became the basis of O'Donovan's masterly edition.

Some years later Rev. Dr. O'Conor was suspended by his bishop for unsound views, possibly explained by the fact that he eventually had to be placed under restraint, owing to mental infirmity. He died, however, at his brother's seat at Belanagare, having had the melancholy pleasure in his confinement of the company of his old schoolfellow, Father Lanigan.[6]

[6] Of O'Conor's contribution Dr. Kenney has this to say: "O'Conor's knowledge of the Irish language and of Irish history was inadequate, and both his texts and his translations are filled with errors, but he made available to the public in some form a most important body of historical sources, and in the case of the Annals of Boyle and of Innisfallen his text remains the only one in print. He also began the vindication of

This chapter could not be more appropriately concluded than by the addition of some details concerning the work of Margaret Stokes, another of Petrie's friends, since her work serves to illustrate further the extent to which his genius consisted in the ability to inspire the genius of others. At first her services to Irish culture took the form chiefly of embellishing the books of other writers, as instanced by the illustrations and illuminations which she supplied for Ferguson's poem, *The Cromlech of Howth*. She edited Lord Dunraven's *Notes on Irish Architecture* and performed the same service for *Christian Inscriptions in the Irish Language*, chiefly collected and drawn by Petrie, *Early Christian Architecture in Ireland* (1878) and *Early Christian Art in Ireland*. She spent six months in the Apennines engaged in what she called a *Pilgrimage in Search of Vestiges of the Irish Saints in Italy*, and in 1895 devoted three months to a similar quest in the forests of France. In that same year she published *Notes on the Cross of Cong* and at the time of her death was engaged on a series of illustrations for a book on the High Crosses of Ireland.

This was the situation, paradoxical and inexplicable, in the early years of the nineteenth century. Everything had been done to destroy Irish as a living tongue, but despite all this and the penalties to which it was still subject, it continued to subsist. Everything had been done, and with unqualified success, to make English the language of Ireland; yet in the very hour in which things seemed most propitious for English culture, the old language, with the ancient cultural tradition of which it was the symbol, seemed to speak from the tomb, as the dead tongue of Fergus spoke to restore the lost *Tain* to the bards. Not the least curious feature of this phenomenon lay in the fact that while it was the Gaels, the O'Currys and O'Donovans, who unlocked the treasure, the initiative in the matter was taken by non-Gaels, by Petrie and Todd and Stokes, figures out of the Ascendant House itself.

But indeed it was not only from the tomb that the Gaelic was

Ireland's title to those many and important early Irish manuscripts in European libraries which Continental scholars in the days of Irish national eclipse had been classifying as Anglo-Saxon" (op. cit., p. 62).

heard, for while all these matters were in process of development, a blind man tapping the roads of Connacht was singing Irish songs of his own composition, pausing at fairs and "patterns" to assemble an audience with the music of his violin, now denouncing tithes, now paying poetic tribute to O'Connell. He was Anthony Raftery, whom De Blacam calls "the greatest of the popular poets of the West." Born at Kiltimagh in 1784, he lost his sight in the same manner as O'Carolan, through an attack of smallpox. There, however, the resemblance to O'Carolan ends, for he became a folk poet, to whom it never occurred to demand recognition as a member of a privileged class. He died in 1834, leaving his poetry to be discovered and collected by Douglas Hyde[7] and his grave to be honoured with a tombstone by Lady Gregory.

[7] *Songs Ascribed to Raftery*. Being the fifth chapter of Songs of Connaught, now for the first time collected and translated by Douglas Hyde. 1903.

Chapter X. THE CALL OF THE EAGLE

> *I stood on Derrybawn in the Autumn,*
> *And I heard the eagle call,*
> *With a clangorous cry of wrath and lamentation*
> *That filled the wide mountain hall.*
>
> > *Ferguson,* Lament for Thomas Davis

THERE IS HOWEVER something rather paradoxical in the fact that in the midst of all the delving into Irish antiquities, the concern with an apparently dead and buried past, a movement was begun under the leadership of men with whom, it was said, "a new soul came into Ireland." This was the movement that came to be known as Young Ireland, a title bestowed upon it in jest by English journalists, but eagerly adopted by the band of enthusiasts whose one ambition was to restore their country's youthful vigour and glory.

Young Ireland was intrinsically a political and nationalistic movement, but much historical water had flowed under Irish bridges in the half century previous to its rise. The abortive rebellions of 1798 and 1803[1] had been followed by the agitation for the repeal of the penal laws, culminating in Catholic Emanci-

---

[1] The story of the manner in which Robert Emmet's rebellion was manipulated from behind the scenes has recently been narrated in a volume which is a marvel of painstaking research, *The Pursuit of Robert Emmet*, by Helen Landreth (1948). It is a terrible and almost incredible story, even to those who were already prepared for the facts. Not the least of its merits attaches to the author's quest for those facts and the excitement which she contrives to share with the reader in describing their tracking down. A chapter which throws light on many a dark corner of the human heart as well as of Irish history is entitled, "Informers and How They are Made."

pation, the immediate consequence of which was the movement
for the repeal of the Union. Young Ireland, as a matter of fact,
grew directly out of a certain disappointment with O'Connell's
handling of Repeal, but its pertinence to the subject of this book
lies not so much in its political character (it was directly responsible for the insurrection of 1848), as with its cultural influence, for in order to spread and promote its ideas, the group
established the famous periodical called *The Nation*, at first under
the editorship of Charles Gavan Duffy and later under that of
the truly great Thomas Davis.

The purpose of the *Nation*, which was only one of numerous
periodicals established in Dublin during the first half of the
nineteenth century, was to make Ireland a nation again, to fuse
all the diverse factions into a united people. In the words of
T. W. Rolleston, in part quoting Duffy, "It told the people of an
Ireland they had never heard of before; not the Ireland of
burlesque or bigoted misrepresentation inhabited by Handy
Andies and Scullabogue murderers, but an old historic island,
the mother of soldiers and scholars whose name was heard in the
roar of onset on a thousand battlefields, for whose dear sake
the poor homeless exile in the garret or cloister of some foreign
city toiled or plotted . . . the one mother country which a man
loves as he loves the mother who held him to her breast."

The means by which the editors of the *Nation* sought to effect
this end was the publication of prose and poetry,—vigorous
prose articles on every phase of the national question, and poetry
that was not so much patriotic as national in spirit, recalling, it
is true, the country's ancient political greatness, her bitter wrongs
and grievances, but above all carrying the insistent reminder of
a great literary and cultural past. The *Nation* prose was on the
whole better than its poetry, which was not always of the highest
literary quality. But it was no part of the editors' purpose or intention that it should be, since they were addressing themselves
chiefly to a public that had been rendered incapable of savoring
literary excellence, at least in the English language, and who, if
they could read at all, could read no other. Many of the poets

themselves were of the deprived class, Charles Duffy (*Young Ireland*), recalling, for instance, that "John Keegan's fine peasant verses came to us in a hand on which the scythe and spade had left their broad mark." The *Nation* poetry had about it nothing of the Gaelic character, except an occasional phrase. How should it have been otherwise when to the men who wrote it the Irish was no longer a living speech, and to the generation for which they wrote the literature of which Irish was once the medium was unknown?

Charles Gavan Duffy, founder of the Young Ireland party, of which the *Nation* became the mouthpiece, was born in Monaghan in 1816, and during his long life (he died at Nice in 1903) he had a most active and variegated career. Arrested for participation in the disturbances of 1848, he was tried five times, and although no conviction was ever obtained, the *Nation* was suppressed. In 1855 Duffy emigrated to Victoria, Australia, where he rose to be prime minister, and having been knighted in 1873, returned a few years later to London, where he became president of the Irish Literary Society, out of which developed the Gaelic League and in great part the Irish Literary Revival.

During the *Nation* period Duffy was a frequent contributor of poetry, usually on some stirring aspect of Ireland's history, which it was the object of the periodical to keep before the Irish mind, since, as Davis complained, the Irish schoolboy was taught "not one word of the ancient fame, the literature, the chivalry and history that have at last obtained an audience in the country of their growth."[2] For this reason such fiery verses as Duffy's *Muster of the North* and his *Irish Rapparees* served a purpose, even a cultural purpose, that would scarcely have been served by verse of higher literary merit. If Duffy did not act on Davis's suggestion that he write a ballad history of Ireland, he did publish (1843) a collection of Irish ballad poetry.

In addition to his contributions to the *Nation* Duffy wrote several prose works which give a first-hand account of the move-

[2] Arthur Griffith, ed., *Thomas Davis, the Thinker and Teacher* (1916), p. 43.

ment which he founded and with which he was so intimately associated. These are *Young Ireland* (1880), *Four Years of Irish History* (1883), *Life of Thomas Davis* (1890), and *My Life* (1898). For an age which was somewhat given to prolixity, his was an exceptionally forthright style, characterized by aphoristic sayings, such as, "If treason is to prosper it must not be uttered a day before it is acted"; and "The imagination of a Celtic race is an appetite almost as imperious as hunger." It was a style apt for summarizing a situation or analyzing a character, as is especially well exemplified in his appraisal of O'Connell, which should be read alongside Mitchel's: "He was gifted with a noble daring, when daring was rare and precious among a people still struggling for the fundamental rights of civilised men, and a stability of purpose not commonly allied with a mobile sensibility and vehement passions. He was laborious and patient, energetic and full of resources; and his life was a model of persistent industry. If he had set his nation an example of sober truth in word and action—an example so needful among a people escaping from the degrading shifts and subterfuges of long dependence—and an example of unselfishness like that by which George Washington has exalted and ennobled a national contest, he would have died as he had lived—the undisputed leader of his race; and his memory would have been an inspiration to every succeeding generation.

"His distrust was easily awakened and this was a deficiency which left evil results. He rarely fostered independent thought, and his death bequeathed a great memory to his country, but not a great party."[3]

Since the insurrection of '48 was in great measure precipitated by the desperation born of the Famine, of which Duffy was an eyewitness, some of his comments on it, as well as a reference to the emigrations which followed it, may serve to further illustrate his style:

"The people saw the harvest they had reaped carried away to another country without an effort, for the most part, to retain

[3] *Four Years of Irish History*, pp. 398-399.

it. The sole food of the distressed class was Indian meal, which had paid freight and storage in England, and had been obtained in exchange for English manufactures. Under a recent law, a peasant who accepted relief forfeited his holding, and thousands were ejected under this cruel provision. But landlords were not content with one process alone; they closed on the people with ejectments, turned them on the roads, and plucked down their roof-trees. . . . In more than one county rents falling due in November for land, which no longer yielded food to the cultivator, were enforced in January. In the South-West the peasantry had made some frantic efforts to clutch their harvest and to retaliate for their sufferings in blind vengeance but the law carried a sharp sword.

"The people fled before the famine to England, America, and the British colonies. They carried with them the seed of disease and death. In England a bishop and more than twenty priests died of typhus, caught in attendance on the sick and dying. The English people clamoured against such an infliction, which it cannot be denied would be altogether intolerable if these fugitives were not made exiles and paupers by English law. They were ordered home again, that they might be supported on the resources of their own country; for though we had no country for the purposes of self-government and self-protection, we were acknowledged to have a country when the necessity of bearing burdens arose. . . ."

The founder of the *Nation* was Duffy, but its heart and soul was Davis. Born in Mallow, Co. Cork, in 1814, he was educated at Trinity College, Dublin, where he became a lover of literature, to follow which as a profession he abandoned the law. When he died of scarlet fever in 1845 there was universal lamentation among the people whose heads and hearts he had already lifted up.

He himself wrote a great deal in both prose and verse and lost no opportunity to address public gatherings on the principles of Young Ireland and the *Nation*. "Educate that you may be free," was his constantly reiterated maxim, and in the realization of the stupendousness of the educational task which confronted him he did not make the mistake of writing above the heads of his public. His poetry, which always follows the conventional English form, is obviously intended for popular consumption, but even so it is often suffused with a sincerity that is in itself a kind of inspiration, often marked by a distinction that lifts it out of the commonplace. All of it reflects his peculiar power of stirring the soul, as do certain stanzas of his *Lament for Owen Roe O'Neill*:

> Wail him through the island! Weep, weep for our pride!
> Would that on the battlefield our gallant chief had died!
> Weep the victor of Beinn Burb—weep him, young men and old!
> Weep for him, ye women,—your beautiful lies cold.

Of this poem it is not precisely accurate to say that its rhythms are purely English, for they falter somewhat as with the sobbing of the Irish keen.

Davis's prose was forceful and eloquent, but restrained, for all its latent fire, and he wrote on every phase of the subject that he held dear, the rebuilding of a native Irish culture. "There is," he said, "an absenteeism of the Irish mind, a draining away of the ingenuity and learning—an emigration of the wit, wisdom and power of our land constantly going on." Among the projects suggested by him as means of halting this terrible waste were a ballad history of Ireland, the encouragement of a national art, in which he went so far as to compile a list of subjects suitable for historical pictures, and the writing of appropriate verses for the surviving Irish tunes. Knowing no Gaelic, he nevertheless envisioned a return of the language as essential to the realization of Ireland's nationhood, and to this end joined with Hudson in the foundation of the Celtic Society (1845). Nor was that all, for he wrote vehemently in behalf of Irish as "our national language." "Is it befitting," he asked, "for the fiery, delicate-organed Celt to abandon his beautiful tongue, docile and spirited as an Arab, 'sweet as music, strong as the wave,' is it befitting in him to abandon this wild liquid speech for the mongrel of a hundred breeds called English, which, powerful though it be, creaks and bangs about the Celt who tries to use it?"

Surely there was a subtle irony in the situation which enabled the mongrel tongue to be used so effectively in behalf of the outlaw language.

This single passage might serve to illustrate the nervous strength of Davis's style, but it would be easy to cite a hundred others, as these from his article on *The State of the Peasantry*: "In a climate soft as a mother's smile, on a soil fruitful as God's love, the Irish peasant mourns. . . . His consolations are those of the spirit—his misery includes all physical sufferings, and many that strike the soul, not the senses." This essay is brought to a dramatic conclusion in a passage in which he implores the aristocracy of Ireland to remember the Irish poor.

His critical power is shown in his description of Ferguson's *Wicklow War Song* as "condensed, epigrammatic and crashing," and in his plea for a recognition of the superiority of Irish popular ballads to what he calls "the faded finery of the West End, the foul parodies of St. Giles's, the drunken rigamarole of the Black Helots—or, as they are touchingly called in the streets, 'sentimental, comic, and nigger songs.'"

He concludes this essay (On *The Library of Ireland*) with an impassioned defence of Ireland as a source of culture: "This country of ours is no sand bank, thrown up by some recent caprice of earth. It is an ancient land, honoured in the archives of civilisation, traceable into antiquity by its piety, its valour, and its sufferings. Every great European race has sent its stream to the river of the Irish mind. Long wars, vast organizations, subtle codes, beacon crimes, leading virtues, and self-mighty men were here. If we live influenced by wind and sun and tree, and not by the passions and deeds of the past, we are a thriftless and a hopeless People."

When it is recalled that from a cultural standpoint Davis himself was so thoroughly Anglicized that he had no real conception of it, his death, before he had come to such realization, in the light of which he would assuredly have laboured to a fuller purpose, is exceptionally regrettable. It would be difficult to overestimate Davis. His intellectual power is manifest in his forceful, clear thinking, his grasp of issues, his simultaneous perception of a goal and the means adequate to its attainment. His literary power is shown not only in both his prose writings and his speeches, in which nothing is introduced merely for rhetorical effect, but also in his verse, which if it is not great, not only is never trivial or banal, but has positive qualities of distinction and charm. But his real greatness consisted in an elevation of character that is impressed upon everything that he wrote and said and did, to such a degree that in the hero-worshipping Irish it inspired a passionate love and loyalty which his death turned into an impassioned grief.

As editor of the *Nation* Davis was succeeded by John Mitchel, a man whose meeting with Davis in 1842 "first filled his soul with the passion of a great ambition and a lofty purpose," and who relinquished his profession as a solicitor in order to devote himself to the cause of Young Ireland. Born in Derry in 1815, he was educated at TCD, and after having served for a time as Davis's successor as editor of the *Nation,* quarrelled with the other members of the group and severed his connection with the *Nation* in order to found another periodical, *The United Irishman.*

It was his contributions to this publication that led to his arrest in 1848 on a charge, new to the statutes, of "treason-felony." He was tried by a frankly packed jury, sentenced to twenty years' transportation and within an hour was on his way to the convict depot at Spike Island, the scene of his memorable interview with Edward Walsh, and thence to his ultimate destination, Van Diemen's Land, by way of Bermuda and Cape Town. However, he escaped to the United States, where he founded several newspapers, through which he engaged in numerous heated controversies. In 1872 he returned to Ireland, where he was elected M.P. for Tipperary, dying that same year at Newry. In literature he is represented by his famous *Jail Journal* and his continuation of the Abbé MacGeoghan's *History,* "From the Treaty of Limerick to the Present Time." He gave as his reason for undertaking this work, which was published in New York (1868), his conviction that the Abbé "would desire the dark record of English atrocity which he left unfinished to be duly brought down through all its subsequent scenes of horror and slaughter, which have been still more horrible after his day than they were before."

In view of the circumstances under which it was written, for the most part under restraint, either aboard the convict ship or as a ticket-of-leave man, the *Jail Journal* is an amazing performance. The book abounds in such allusions as come spontaneously to the literary mind, certifying in Mitchel's case to his broad education and prodigious memory. Throughout his experiences, even in the midst of hardship and physical agony (he was a martyr to asthma), he makes the sensitive man's quick response to natural beauty. Thus he writes under date of April 6, 1850: "The mountainous southern coast of Van Diemen's Land! It is a soft blue day; soft airs, laden with all the fragrances of these antarctic woods, weave an atmosphere of ambrosia around me. As we coast along over the placid waters, passing promontory after promontory, wooded to the water's edge, and 'glassing their ancient glories in the flood,' both sea and land seem to bask and rejoice in the sunshine. Old Ocean smiles—that multitudinous rippling laugh seen in vision by the chained Prometheus. Even my own sick and weary soul (so kind and bounteous is our Mother Earth) feels lightened, refreshed, uplifted. Yet there, to port, loom the mountains whereunto I am to be chained for years with a vulture gnawing my heart. Here is the very place, the Kaf, or Caucasus, where I must die a daily death and make a nightly descent into hell."

The work bristles with Mitchel's political opinions and convictions, particularly his hatred of England. In comparing him with Davis, Duffy said, "Davis loved Ireland; Mitchel hated England." Assuredly he hated England, whose queen is always in his pages the Famine Queen or Nicé, queen of Carthage, but that he also loved Ireland is testified over and over again, notably in the words with which on the first day of his exile he records by way of culmination of the losses that his banishment will entail: "And may never, never—never more, O Ireland!—my mother and queen!—see vale or hill or murmuring stream of thine!"

Perhaps not even Davis expressed deeper love for his countrymen than glows in the following passage: "There are nearly two hundred Irish amongst these prisoners—the famine-struck Irish of the Special Commission; many who have not a word of English, and most of them so shattered in constitution by mere hunger and hardship, that all the deaths among the prisoners, ever since we embarked, have been Irish. . . . What a fate, what a dreary doom has been spun and woven for you, my countrymen. They were born these men, to a heritage of unquenched hunger, amongst the teeming plenty of their motherland—hunted like noxious beasts from all shelter on her hospitable bosom—driven to stay their gnawing enemy with what respectable fed men call their 'property.' . . . Many of them, I believe, being without families, are glad of this escape, as they might be glad of any escape from the circle of hunters that chased them at home. But then there are many others (boys from twelve to seventeen years of age, and some of them very handsome boys, with fine open countenances, and a laugh so clear and ringing) whom it is a real pain to look upon. . . . But in poor frail huts, on many an Irish hill-side, their fathers and mothers dwell with poverty and labour, and sorrow, and mourn for their lost children, with a mourning that will know no comfort till they are gathered to their people in the chapel-yard."

Mitchel's style is not always so emotional. For the most part it is appropriate to his comments and observations on political economy and international politics, which are sagaciously sound. His references to his political associates are far from generous, but the lengthy recital is exceptionally interesting, and for sheer excitement and suspense it would be difficult to surpass his account of his escape from Van Diemen's Land. The following is his famous analysis of O'Connell: "Poor old Dan!—wonderful, mighty, jovial, and mean old man! with silver tongue and smile of witchery and heart of melting ruth!—lying tongue! smile of treachery! heart of unfathomable fraud! What a royal yet vulgar soul! with the keen eye and potent swoop of a generous eagle of Cairn Tual—with the base servility of a hound, and the cold cruelty of a spider! Think of his speech for John Magee! the

most powerful forensic achievement since before Demosthenes
—and then think of the 'gorgeous and gossamer' theory of moral
and peaceful agitation, the most astounding *organon* of public
swindling since first man bethought him of obtaining money
under false pretences. And after one has thought of all this and
more, what then can a man *say*? what but pray that Irish earth
may lie light on O'Connell's breast—and that the good God who
knew how to create so wondrous a creature may have mercy upon
his soul."

Duffy has drawn an engaging picture of the *Nation's* editorial
room, "lighted up with the enthusiasm of youth devoted to a
generous cause, with the gaiety of hearts at ease with themselves
and with the world." To it flocked the men and women who were
prominent in the intellectual life of Dublin, bred for the most
part in the English tradition, but fired with an eagerness for an
Irish cultural resurgence, of whose form they had as yet no very
definite idea. Many schemes were hatched there that had only
cultural ends in view: the inauguration of the Library of Ireland,
for instance, the reissue of certain Irish books, the bringing back
for Irish burial of Ireland's "illustrious dead," Grattan from
England, Duns Scotus from Cologne, O'Neill from Rome,
O'Donnell from Spain, Sarsfield from Belgium; and the publication of an Irish historical series and a series of Irish biographies.
One writer projected a book on the peasant population; a cor-
respondent called attention to the dramatic *Lamentation for the
Death of Christ* held annually in Holy Week in the Glens of
Antrim; Mangan came with practical suggestions and excruciating
puns. One of their projects was the publication (1843) of a
volume entitled *The Spirit of the Nation*, in which was collected
the work of its most representative poets. Read thus collectively,
the literary level attained is seen to be remarkably high. Certainly they never fall into mere doggerel or cant, but on the
other hand, although they are so numerous, they speak with a
unanimity that might have become monotonous, except that
what they so invariably utter is the spirit of rebellion and defi-
ance. It is so stirring that one wonders that it should have taken

so long to provoke a rising, but that the utterance did not fall on deaf ears is attested by the fact that the volume went into upwards of sixty editions.

But the *Nation* itself was the object of their chief care, and in that connection a most important occasion of solicitude was the poetry which embodied its spirit, so that the Poets of the *Nation* came to constitute a significant literary group, a group which of course included Duffy and Davis, as well as others whom they persuaded to write or otherwise encouraged.

Prominent not only among the *Nation* writers, but in the political disturbances of the time was Thomas D'Arcy McGee, who, born at Carlingford in 1825, went to America in 1842, where for a time he edited the Boston *Pilot*. On his return to Ireland he joined the movement headed by Duffy and Davis and in 1848 fled the country with a price on his head. He went to Canada, where he rose to an official position under the Crown. He later underwent such a complete change of political convictions that, having returned to Ireland at the time of the Fenian movement, he denounced it so vehemently that he came to be regarded as a traitor, the lamentable result of which was his assassination at Ottawa in 1868. Such poetry as his *To Duffy in Prison*, in which he complains of "the land that will not rise," leaves no doubt of his ardent nationalism, although by the time he wrote on *The Dead Antiquary O'Donovan* his sentiments had become less militant. He was the author of several historical works and some *Memoirs* of Duffy, but he is of literary interest chiefly as a poet of the *Nation*.

John Keegan was typical of much that the *Nation* was striving to accomplish. He was a peasant, born in Queen's Co. about 1809 and educated at a hedge school. His poetry is characterized by pathos and simplicity, but it occasionally blazes up into such lines as these:

> There's nothing but rags and green rushes for me.
> O mild Virgin Mary!
> O sweet Virgin Mary!
> Who keeps my rough hand from red murder but thee?

Two women poets, known respectively as "Mary" and "Eva" of the *Nation*, won considerable renown for their contributions to its pages. "Mary" was in private life Ellen Mary Patrick Downing, daughter of a physician in Cork, where she was born in 1828. Her imagination stirred by the life and writings of Davis, she tried her own hand at writing poetry, which was declared to be "like the carol of a lark." She wanted desperately to write in the Irish vein, but this she could not achieve.

"Eva" (Mary Kelly) was born in Co. Galway in 1825 and was a supporter of Young Ireland principles, to the extent of urging her lover, Kevin Izod O'Doherty, on trial for implication in the Rising of '48, not to accept the freedom that he was offered as the price of pleading guilty. He was consequently transported to Van Diemen's Land in 1849, where he was later joined by Mitchel (he is the "St. Kevin" of the *Jail Journal*), was released two years later, and returned to Ireland, his marriage to "Eva" of the *Nation* taking place in two days' time. He was afterwards not only a successful medical man in Australia, whither his wife, of course, accompanied him, but a member of the Australian Parliament. "Eva" is known especially for the poem beginning *Were you ever in sweet Tipperary?*

Among the women who submitted verse was one who signed the pseudonym *Speranza*, and who turned out to be Jane Francesca Elgee, daughter of an Anglican archdeacon. She was a girl whom the spectacle of Davis's funeral with its accompaniment of universal grief had awakened to a realization of the nationalist ideal, of which she had hitherto known nothing, and turned her into a "volcano of sedition." She married the later famous eye surgeon and antiquary, Sir William Wilde, Oscar Fingal O'Flaherty having been born of the union. *Speranza* was the author of the article in the *Nation* for which Gavan Duffy was prosecuted.

These names do not exhaust the list of the *Nation* poets, but they are representative of the most important features of the *Nation* poetry. Obviously it was not great poetry. It was too partisan for that. Obviously, also, except for its themes, it was not Irish. It was second-rate English verse, written by men and women whose flaming sincerity had to stand them in the stead of the divine afflatus. There was a constant iteration of the unhappy facts of Irish history, all too many of which, far from being far-off, were vividly present and contemporary. In the *Nation's* pages there was no retelling of any of the bardic tales, no attempt to put to poetic use any of the vast store of material, so recently recovered by O'Curry and O'Donovan.

There were of course during this period poets other than those who contributed to the *Nation*. Some of them, like Lover with his *Widow Machree* and *Rory O'More* and Lever with the *Widow Malone*, wrote in the same vein of burlesque that characterizes their novels. Although John Banim did not contribute to the *Nation* his poetry resembled that of the *Nation* poets, as exemplified in *Soggarth Aroon* and the fierce attack on the same Duke of Wellington to whom the O'Hara Tales were dedicated.

> He said that he was not our brother—
> The mongrel! he said what we knew.

He attempted, rather feebly, for his poetic power was slight, to tap Gaelic literary sources in a poem called *The Celt's Paradise*, which is a version of the dispute between St. Patrick and Oisin, emphasizing Oisin's sojourn in Tir-nan-oge. It is practically the same as Comyn's *Lay of Oisin*, except for being cast in dialogue form.

In *Deirdre* (1877) Robert Dwyer Joyce handled the great Sorrowful Tale in such commonplace English metres that the strangeness and splendour of the epic could scarcely be suspected. It was not that he lacked the Gaelic, because we know from his brother, Patrick Weston Joyce, of their early familiarity with the language, but that he lacked the poetic fire. However, his *Ballads of Irish Chivalry*, the subjects of which are taken either from Irish history or Irish fairy-lore, give off occasional sparks.

Joyce was born in Co. Limerick in 1830. He began to write poetry while he was a medical student, and continued when, after emigrating to the United States, he was engaged in a large medical practice in Boston. His health failing, he returned to Ireland, where he died in 1883. Besides the works mentioned, he is the author of *Legends of the Wars of Ireland; Irish Fireside Tales;* and *Blanid.*

Gerald Griffin wrote decidedly graceful and affecting lyric verse, such as *A Place in Thy Memory, Dearest,* which became widely popular when set to music. He occasionally wrote words for Irish airs, such as *Shule Aroon* and *Eileen Aroon,* the latter a version of O'Daly's famous song.

Certain poets at this time were contributing to periodicals other than the *Nation* specimens of what eventually developed into a large body of verse, written to extol the natural beauties of Ireland or in commemoration of local scenes. It is mostly sentimental, as such verse naturally tends to be, and again, in most cases, except for the subject, is not particularly Irish. Perhaps the most famous example of this type of verse is *The Bells of Shandon,* by "Father Prout," as Francis Sylvester O'Mahoney chose to be known. Born in Cork in 1804, he became a priest, but neglected, if he did not wholly abandon, the ecclesiastical state for the literary career for which he was better fitted, at least by his tastes. His collected poems, published in 1876, are sufficient evidence that he was not a poet.

The amount of poetry that has thus far been considered is rather extensive. Since none of it added anything to the glory of either English or Irish letters, the literary outlook in Ireland about the middle of the nineteenth century would seem to have been depressingly dark. Yet even then there were gleams of light. There was, for instance, Jeremiah Joseph Callanan (born in Cork in 1795), another spoiled priest in the sense of his having left Maynooth before ordination, but whose literary gifts were far in excess of his achievement. He never became a wastrel of anything but himself, but he had certain talents which might have been used to advance the Revival by at least a generation. In the first place he knew Irish, and so he was the first to draw directly from Irish sources in such translations as *The Dirge of O'Sullivan*

Beare and *The Outlaw of Loch Lene*. The Gaelic accent is unmistakable in the second of these, especially in the lines which
express the outlaw's mindfulness of the love from whom he is
separated:

> 'Tis down by the lake where the wild tree fringes its sides
> The maid of my heart, the fair one of heaven, resides;
> I think as at eve she wanders its mazes along
> The birds go to sleep by the sweet wild twist of her song.

The Gaelic gives colour and fire not only to such translations,
but to his own *Gougane Barra*, all of them set to measures that
fall strangely on an ear accustomed to English rhythms. He
died in Lisbon, whose climate he had sought for reasons of health,
in 1829.

George Fox, about whom practically nothing is known, deserves mention for his *County of Mayo*, of which the original
Irish published by Hardiman, and somewhat contemptuously dismissed by MacDonagh, is one of those heartbroken songs of exile
of which Ireland has produced so many. This is the first stanza
of Fox's English rendering as preserved by Ferguson, which
contrives in some mysterious way to be an Irish keen:

> 'Tis my grief that Patrick Loughlin is not Earl in Irrul still,
> And that Brian Duff no longer rules as Lord upon the hill,
> And that Colonel Hugh MacGrady should be lying dead and low,
> And I sailing, sailing swiftly from the County of Mayo.

And then there was Mangan, who although he did some of his
best work for the *Nation*, was not in the strict sense of the word
a *Nation* poet. That he was a tragic figure no one knew better
than he; in fact it is to be feared that he rather dramatized
that realization, not only in his dress, which played up every
aspect of his emaciated frame and haunted countenance,

> that sunken charnel cheek
> And spectral eye
> And drooping horizontal head,

but in his poetry as well. He wrote of himself as destined for
"the gulf and grave of Maginn and Burns," but he was rather in

the direct line of Donnchadh Ruadh and Carleton, geniuses driven in upon themselves by poverty and the desperation born of a constant diet of one's own heart.[4] His eccentricity of appearance and behaviour and his well-known faculty for dressing up the truth, or rather his inability to distinguish between the truth and the phantoms of his drug-befogged imagination, make it difficult to get at all the facts of his life. However, it is generally agreed that he was born in Dublin in 1803, the son of "a man of some education and refinement," who seems to have been unequal to the successful conduct of the grocery business which he acquired by marriage, and in which he consequently failed.

His family was thus reduced to poverty and his son, Clarence, afterwards complained of his neglect and even brutality, but this indictment he revised to the extent of reducing his father's crimes to a single head—improvidence. The boy got some education at various Dublin schools, for a time under the direct tutelage of a learned priest, but although several people, including himself, had inklings of his genius, when the time came for him, at fifteen, to stand between his family and starvation, the best post that could be secured for him was an apprenticeship to a scrivener. In this establishment he was wretchedly unhappy, as he was also in the office of the attorneys by whom he was later employed. When he became a copyist for the Ordnance Survey in 1838 he began that process of steady drinking which not only hastened his death but cast an even darker shadow upon his spirit. As a matter of fact, he was always unhappy, although that seems too mild a term to apply to his capacity for a black dejection, which only he could attempt to describe, and to which even he does not pretend to do justice, in either prose or verse. There were, of course, reasons for this unhappiness, among them wretched physical health, insufficient food, and the terrible "remedy," opium, whose black ensign overshadows so much of his work.

He began quite early to write verse, contributing to the various periodicals in which Dublin abounded in the 'thirties, and eventu-

[4] D. J. O'Donoghue, *Life and Writings of James Clarence Mangan* (1897).

ally he was one of the *Nation* poets, incomparably the greatest.
He knew German, from which he made some verse translations,
and his love of mystification led him to pretend the authorship
of some translations from Oriental languages, of which he knew
nothing, but through the medium of German he had apparently
become sufficiently acquainted with Eastern poetry to make a
number of satisfactory paraphrases. What is most important is
that he knew no Gaelic, and yet he made English renderings of
certain Irish poems that have been described as miraculous. The
way of it was that O'Curry made literal translations from the
Gaelic originals and the Gael in Mangan's blood did the rest.
Not that he attempted to reproduce in English, as Sigerson and
Hyde afterwards did, the Irish metrical forms. Indeed, although
O'Curry vouched for Mangan's fidelity to his translations,
O'Donovan contended that of those translations Mangan's
verses were not "the shadow of a shade," in this intending
to give Mangan all possible credit for what amounted to a new
creation. However that may be, it is undeniable that the rhythms
of his early paraphrases, *Woman of Three Cows, O'Hussey's Ode
for the Maguire* and *O Woman of the Piercing Wail*, contributed
to the *Irish Penny Journal*, fell upon the ear with a strange, enchanting sound, signalizing a new era in Irish poetry. Nowhere,
despite the use of the standard Saxon tongue, is the radical difference between Celt and Saxon more clearly demonstrated than
in these stanzas from *Dark Rosaleen:*

> Oh! my dark Rosaleen,
>   Do not sigh, do not weep!
> The priests are on the ocean green,
>   They march along the deep.
> There's wine from the royal Pope
>   Upon the ocean green,
> And Spanish ale shall give you hope,
>   My dark Rosaleen!
>   My own Rosaleen!
> Shall glad your heart, shall give you hope,
> Shall give you health, and help, and hope,
>   My dark Rosaleen!

Woe and pain, pain and woe,
  Are my lot, night and noon,
To see your bright face clouded so,
  Like to the mournful moon.
But yet will I rear your throne
  Again in golden sheen;
'Tis you shall reign, shall reign alone,
  My dark Rosaleen!
  My own Rosaleen!
'Tis you shall have the golden throne,
'Tis you shall reign, and reign alone,
  My dark Rosaleen!

. . . .

Oh! the Erne shall run red
  With redundance of blood,
The earth shall rock beneath our tread,
  And flames wrap hill and wood,
And gun-peal and slogan-cry
  Wake many a hill serene,
Ere you shall fade, ere you shall die,
  My dark Rosaleen!
  My own Rosaleen!
The Judgment Hour must first be nigh,
Ere you can fade, ere you can die,
  My dark Rosaleen!

After the termination of the Ordnance Survey, Mangan had to seek for other employment, which he found, temporarily at least, in Trinity College Library through the good offices of James Henthorn Todd. With the founding of the *Nation* in 1842 Mangan became a contributor to that journal, although his work did not appear there frequently until 1846, in which year he is represented by *Dark Rosaleen, Shane Buie* and *A Vision of Connaught in the Thirteenth Century*, as well as by a number of non-Irish poems. Outstanding among his "translations" are his rendering of Donnchadh Ruadh Mac Conmara's *The Fair Hills of Eire* (quoted above), and the traditional Aisling poem, *Kathaleen ny Houlahan*, which were done for John O'Daly's *Poets and Poetry of Munster*.

The Jacobite dream is eloquently expressed in *Kathaleen*:

Long they pine in weary woe—the nobles of our land
Long they wander to and fro, proscribed, alas and banned;
Feastless, houseless, altarless, they bear the exile's brand,
    But their hope is in the coming-to of Kathaleen Ny-Houlahan.

       . . . .

Sore disgrace it is to see the Arbitress of thrones
Vassal to a Saxoneen of cold and sapless bones!
Bitter anguish wrings our souls—with heavy sighs and groans
    We wait the Young Deliverer of Kathaleen Ny-Houlahan.

       . . . .

He who over sands and waves led Israel along—
He who fed, with heavenly bread, that chosen tribe and throng,
He who stood by Moses when his foes were fierce and strong,
    May He show forth His might in saving Kathaleen Ny-Houlahan!

Mangan was reduced to private if not public beggary by final lack of employment, as well as by the habits which prevented his keeping employment. He was therefore already homeless when in 1849 he fell a victim to the cholera then prevalent in Dublin. He was first taken to the sheds, whence he was discharged as cured, only to be found a few days later dying in a cellar. He was then removed to a hospital, where the great Dr. Stokes, who had vainly tried to befriend him, watched beside him, "lovingly," says his daughter, for three days until he died, fortified by the last sacraments and murmuring "O Mary, Queen of Mercy!"

Conspicuous among the picturesque figures in what must have been an exceptionally picturesque era in Dublin's history was John O'Daly, important for his unselfish devotion to the language movement, in the course of which he was of inestimable assistance to Mangan, by providing him with many of the translations on which he based his Irish poems and by publishing his work. Born in Co. Waterford in 1800 and educated at a hedge school, he was a native speaker who worked for a time at a Wesleyan school in Kilkenny, and spent the rest of his life trying to live down the reproach attached to that employment. He finally left it to go to Dublin, where he set up a publishing and book-selling business in Anglesea St., the shop becoming a centre for Irish scholars and the press turning out such important works as *Poets and Poetry of Munster,* which included some of Mangan's "translations," and Walsh's *Reliques of Irish Jacobite Poetry* (1844). O'Daly, who was also active in various learned societies (see below), died in Dublin in 1878.

Edward Walsh, compiler of the above-mentioned *Reliques,* was a singularly unfortunate though admirable character. He was born in Derry in 1805, married happily, but was most unhappy in his work, which was that of a teacher, at one time in the convict depot on Spike Island. When Mitchel was brought thither on his way to the convict ship, Walsh approached him to shake his hand and to assure him that he, Mitchel, was the happiest man in Ireland. In consequence of this act he was dismissed from Spike Island, but secured another teaching post, this time in a workhouse, an environment that must have been most distasteful to a man of his temperament and tastes, but in which he remained until his death in 1850. Many of the Jacobite poems which he collected and translated are by the Munster poets represented in O'Daly's volume, which is much more comprehensive in scope. One of the anonymous and untranslated songs contained in Walsh's collection is addressed to Prince Charles Edward under the title of *An Chraobhin Aoibhin,* the gentle young branch, which it is scarcely necessary to identify as the pseudonym later adopted by Dr. Douglas Hyde.

Among the Dublin men of letters who had befriended Mangan was Samuel Ferguson, whose own poetic work now demands attention. While his poetry no longer arouses the almost ecstatic praise with which it was first received, it undoubtedly warrants the claim made by Alfred Percival Graves that Ferguson was "the Irish poet of his time who most powerfully influenced the literary history of his country." Of Scottish ancestry, he was born in Belfast in 1810 and educated at TCD. He was called to the Irish bar, but his health breaking under the arduous practice of his profession, he spent the year 1845-46 on the Continent, where he followed the traces of early Irish missionaries and scholars, making voluminous notes of his findings. In 1848 he married, settled in Dublin and founded the Protestant Repeal Association, but later abandoned all political activity. In 1867 he relinquished his legal practice in order to become Keeper of Irish Historical Records, a post which gave him fuller opportunity to engage in the studies and literary activities to which he was already devoted.

Ferguson was intensely interested in everything Irish, and throughout his life contributed articles to various periodicals on such subjects as Irish music, Irish art and certain phases of Irish antiquities. His early verse is commonplace enough and he never became a great poet, but what distinguishes his work as a whole is the fact that he knew Irish, and therefore much of it is translated from the Irish, drawn from Irish sources or in some way affected by his familiarity with Irish speech, so that there was warrant for the claim that in it "was decisively begun the great work of restoring to Ireland the spiritual treasure it had sacrificed in losing the Gaelic tongue." He was already known as the author of much miscellaneous prose and verse when, in 1864, he published *Lays of the Western Gael,* a series of poems on ancient Irish subjects cast into the English ballad form, a form which was, of course, unknown to the ancient Irish poets. *Congal,* which appeared in 1872, is an epic tale in which the poet writes with considerable power on an old Irish heroic theme, its source being the *Tale of Cath Muighre Rath* or the Battle of Moyra, in which pagan heroism makes its last stand against Christian chivalry. It was a superb subject, to which Ferguson's powers did not quite rise, but the poem marked an advance of the Gaelic movement by its tapping of those great stores of bardic inspiration, and it is interesting besides for the use which Ferguson makes of a number of typically Celtic preternatural elements such as the Washer at the Ford.

Typical of both his lyric form and his relation to the Gaelic Revival is his *Lament for Thomas Davis,* the best stanzas of which are the following:

I walked through Balinderry in the spring-time,
  When the bud was on the tree;
And I said, in every fresh-ploughed field beholding
  The sowers striding free,
Scattering broadcast forth the corn in golden plenty
  On the quick seed-clasping soil,
"Even such, this day, among the fresh-stirred hearts of Erin,
  Thomas Davis, is thy toil."

I sat by Ballyshannon in the Summer,
  And saw the salmon leap;
And I said, as I beheld the gallant creatures
  Spring glittering from the deep,
Through the spray and through the prone heaps
      striving onward
  To the calm clear streams above,
"So seekest thou thy native founts of freedom, Thomas Davis,
  In the brightness of strength and love."

I stood on Derrybawn in the autumn,
  And I heard the eagle call,
With a clangorous cry of wrath and lamentation
  That filled the wide mountain hall,
O'er the bare deserted place of his plundered eyrie;
  And I said, as he screamed and soared,
"So callest thou, thou wrathful-soaring Thomas Davis,
  For a nation's rights restored!"

                  . . . .

Oh, brave young men, my love, my pride, my promise,
  'Tis on you my hopes are set,
In manliness, in kindliness, in justice,
  To make Erin a nation yet;
Self-respecting, self-relying, self-advancing,
  In union or in severance, free and strong—
And if God grant this, then, under God, to Thomas Davis,
  Let the greater praise belong.

In these lines Ferguson catches something of Davis's high and
indomitable courage. The stanzas which are not quoted are not
nearly so good as poetry, perhaps because they reflect more of
Ferguson's own characteristic spirit, which, when all is said and
despite his genuine sympathy with the nationalist cause, inclined

to a compromise that would have been inconceivable to Davis.

The Revival was well under way by the time Ferguson published his *Poems* (1880), in which he draws upon an even more remote source than that which gave him the story of *Congal*, for in this volume, together with such verses as *The Morning's Hinges* and *The Widow's Cloak* (the "widow" being Queen Victoria), the volume contains poems on various phases of the great Ulster cycle, such as *Mesgedra, Fergus Wry-mouth, The Naming of Cuchullin, Conary* and *Deirdre*. These, with certain others from the same source, such as *The Healing of Conall Cearnach, Deirdre's Farewell to Alba, Deirdre's Lament for the Sons of Usnach*, were included in the posthumously published *Lays of the Red Branch*. It is interesting to compare Ferguson's version of *The Fair Hills of Ireland* with Mangan's, since Ferguson's close adherence to the Irish shows with what "careless rapture" Mangan wrote. Besides the works already mentioned he was the author of the three-volume *Hibernian Nights Entertainment*. He was knighted in 1878 and died in 1886.

Another poet of this period who made use of the ancient bardic material was Aubrey De Vere, the third son of Sir Aubrey De Vere, born in 1814 at Curragh Chase, where he died in 1902, having witnessed in his lifetime a tremendous literary revolution. To a certain extent he could boast that he was a part of all that he had seen, for although he was thoroughly steeped in the English literary tradition, having enjoyed the friendship of Wordsworth and Tennyson, a fact which is perceptible in his work, he was intensely interested in everything Irish. This was especially noticeable after his conversion to the Catholic Church in 1851, which not only ranged him with the still aggrieved majority of his countrymen, but provided him with more essentially Irish themes and a more sympathetic point of view, as instanced in *The Little Black Rose*, whose Celtic quality is recognized even by the exacting MacDonagh, and *The Year of Sorrow: Ireland, 1849*.

Especially impressive are the *Spring* stanzas of the second poem, commemorating the dreadful year of the Famine. The following lines succeed a series of lovely verses which enumerate the recurrent glories of the season, the cuckoo's call, the anemones, "trembling like a bridal veil," the released waters.

> From ruined huts and holes come forth
>   Old men, and look upon the sky.
> The Power Divine is on the earth:
>   Give thanks to God before ye die!
>
> And ye, O children, worn and weak,
>   Who care no more with flowers to play,
> Lean on the grass your cold thin cheek,
>   And those slight hands, and whispering say:
> 'Stern mother of a race unblest,
>   In promise kindly, cold in deed,
> Take back, O Earth, into thy breast,
>   The children whom thou wilt not feed.'

There is something almost overwhelming about the slow, deliberate measures in which the poet records the disasters of that year, something that recalls the implacability of time and the calloused human heart.

But De Vere's most ambitious work was done in such compositions as *The Foray of Queen Meave*, which is appropriately inscribed to the memory of Eugene O'Curry. Despite the fact that in every sense of the word it is English verse, written by a man who knew no Gaelic, it is not unworthy of association with O'Curry's distinguished name, for it is one of the first fruits of his lectures, and there must have been many to whom it brought a first acquaintance with these noble stories, many whom it stirred to a closer and more extensive knowledge of a culture with which they felt not only the kinship of the mind, which all men feel with that of Greece, but a kinship of the blood and of the heart of which the Gael had been for too long deprived. To this writer, at least, Aubrey De Vere's *Combat at the Ford* still marks so signally the dawn of a literary *vita nuova* as to make it impossible to dwell coldly upon his shortcomings as a poet.

Of Joseph Sheridan Le Fanu, born in Dublin in 1837, author of numerous tales of horror and mystery (*Uncle Silas; Green Tea*) and eminently successful as a journalist, it was said that although he belonged to the Ascendancy by birth and education, he became a rebel when he wrote poetry, a claim which seems to be further substantiated by the novel, *Shemus O'Brien,* a tale of the rebellion of '98.

William Allingham is generally ranked as an Irish poet on the strength of his famous poem *The Fairies,* beginning:

> Up the airy mountain
> Down the rushy glen,
> We daren't go a-hunting
> For fear of little men.

Needless to say, despite the fact that they "stole little Bridget," these "little men" bear not the slightest resemblance to the Irish *sidhe.* Happily Allingham's fame rests on more solid foundations, though they are never intrinsically Gaelic. He was born in Bally-shannon, Co. Donegal, a place which he loved and celebrated in his verse, of which he published many volumes. His earliest employment was that of a clerk in the bank of which his father was manager, after which he was for some years a customs official, most of his life after 1847 having been spent in England. There Dante Gabriel Rossetti was one of his closest friends, and Allingham's verse could not but bear some mark of that association. Nevertheless, he never considered himself anything but Irish, and in *The Winding Banks of Erne* and *The Banshee* he writes effectively on Irish themes.

His most memorable Irish poem, however, is *Lawrence Bloomfield in Ireland* (1864), in which, as he says himself, he ventures to handle "the Landlord and Tenant question in decasyllabics." He declared his intention of making this work "Irish in phraseology, character and local colour, with as little as might be of a corrupt dialect, and with no deference at all to the stage traditions of Paddyism," an intention which he succeeded, despite minor defects, to a remarkable degree in carrying out. It is a narrative poem in which Allingham describes the efforts of an Irish landlord, a member of the Ascendancy, to be a good landlord. The subject was one which not only involved some portrayal of native character, of both landlord and peasant class, but a considerable study of local conditions, social, economic and religious. All of which required of the author a knowledge and understanding of one of the major problems of Irish life, the land question, whose complexities had in great part developed out of the Famine. Both the land problem and the Famine were merely aspects of the single situation, unjust and intolerable.

In all of this Allingham strives to be strictly impartial, and while his Father John Adair is anything but an ingratiating personality, the poet has nothing but praise for the priesthood in general, and especially for the Church, if only on the score of its hold on the popular imagination:

> Imagination to the Church must cling.

Unquestionably he understood many of the finer qualities of the Irish character, especially the native love for learning, as is shown in his description of the eagerness with which the long defrauded people hastened to avail themselves of educational opportunities.

> Learning she loves as long ago she loved.
> The peasant, sighing at his own defect
> Would snatch his children from the same neglect;
> From house and hut, from hill and plain, they pour
> In tens of thousands to the teacher's door.

Neither is there the slightest doubt of his love for the land itself, a love which he shared with the most harassed of his countrymen.

> O Ireland! home of hardship! why do yet
> Thy children cling to thee? thin cheeks are wet,
> Hearts long oppressed with care feel poignant woe
> As hence from gloom to brighter climes they go.

Thomas Davis had been nearly twenty years in his grave when *Lawrence Bloomfield* was published, but surely even in its staid decasyllabics it is possible to detect an echo of that eagle's cry. Whether or not Allingham succeeded in handling the vexed question of landlord and tenant, he did succeed in making the poem Irish in a sense of which most writers of his class had had no inkling until Davis began to infuse the Spirit of the Nation into Irishmen of every class.

Chapter XI. THE GAELIC TONGUE

Erin will be joyful and her strongholds will be merry,
And the learned will cultivate Gaelic in their schools.

From the Irish of Egan O'Rahilly

If anyone wants to know on which side I shall be, I'll be on the side of Owen Roe.

Douglas Hyde

ALTHOUGH THOMAS DAVIS resented the fact that the Irish people of his day, three quarters of them of Celtic blood, were compelled to speak "a medley of Teutonic dialects," he conceived of the restoration of Irish as "a dream of what may happen a hundred years hence," and so he set about utilizing that Teutonic medley as the weapon of his crusade, while often expressing the hope that the time would be shortened: "The bulk of our history and poetry are written in Irish, and shall we, who learn Italian, and Latin, and Greek, to read Dante, Livy and Homer in the original—shall we be content with ignorance or a translation of Irish?"

The work of such men as O'Curry and O'Donovan did not at first sight seem calculated to hasten the realization of his dream, for they were to a certain extent merely survivors or even throwbacks. Their work, brilliantly learned though it was, was largely the result of the fact that they were Gaelic-speaking, born of families in which the ancient tradition lived on, but in which it was with difficulty kept alive. They and several of their associates were, as it were, engaged in the task of burrowing amid the ruins of the past in the hope of salvaging such remnants as could be saved.

As O'Curry himself says in his Preface to the *Lectures on the*

Ancient MSS, deprecating his fitness for the office in virtue of which he had delivered those lectures: "My studies had always been of a silent kind: I was engaged, if I may so speak, in underground work, and the labours in which I had spent my life were such that their results were never intended to be brought separately before the public in my own individual responsibility. No person knows my bitterly felt deficiencies better than myself. Having been self-taught in all the little I know of general letters, and reared to mature years among an uneducated people (though a people both intelligent and fond of learning when opportunity permits them to apply themselves to it), I always felt the want of early mental training and of early admission to those fountains of knowledge which can be approached only through the medium of languages which, though once generally cultivated in my native province, had, under sinister influences, ceased to exist in the remote part of the country from which I come, not very long before I was born."

This is not the tone of one who felt that he was promoting a resurrection of such training or who regarded such a resurrection as at all likely, and yet even then various efforts towards that end were being energetically carried on. One of the most noteworthy of these was the foundation of societies for the study of Gaelic and the translation of works written in that language, although the direct purpose of such groups was certainly not the restoration of Irish as a spoken tongue.

The earliest of these was the Archaeological Society, founded in 1840 by Dr. Todd, chiefly for the purpose of publishing documents illustrative of Irish history on which scholars had long been at work and which might, if such publication were delayed, become unavailable to students. In the early years of its existence, the Society published twenty-one such volumes, among them O'Donovan's translation of Cormacan Eigeas's *Circuit of Ireland*, the *Battle of Magh Rath*, and the *Accounts of Hy Many* and *Hy Fiachrach*; Hardiman's *Statute of Kilkenny*, and his edition of O'Flaherty's *Description of Iar Connaught*. The Miscellany of the Society, published in 1846, is of exceptional interest, as including MSS edited by O'Donovan, Hardiman and Dr. Todd, while the year 1851 was signalized by the publication of Archbishop Colton's *Visitation of the Diocese of Derry in 1397.*

The editor of this important work was Dr. William Reeves, born in Charleville in 1815 and educated at TCD for the Anglican ministry, to which he was ordained in 1838. The generosity which was his life-long characteristic was manifested in his division among his brothers and sisters of the landed estate which he inherited from his father. A man of scholarly tastes, he was the author of an *Ecclesiastical History of Down and Connor and Dromore,* which was immediately accepted as the authoritative work for that diocese, as the above-mentioned acts of Bishop Colton became for Derry.

While Dr. Reeves was not acquainted with Gaelic, later developments would seem to indicate that his failure to secure the post of professor of history and later that of librarian at Trinity is traceable not to this lack, but to his zeal in the cause of Irish studies. He was appointed by Dr. Todd to a perpetual curacy, in which he acted at the same time as librarian of Armagh, until his appointment in 1886 as Bishop of Down and Connor. With the generosity already referred to, he purchased the *Book of Armagh,* which he presented to Trinity College. In 1891 he was elected president of the Royal Irish Academy, his death occurring in Dublin in 1892.

Next in order was the Celtic Society, founded in 1845 by John O'Daly, with the active assistance of Thomas Davis and William Elliott Hudson. Hudson was born in 1796 at his father's country residence at Rathfarnham, across the road from the home of John Philpot Curran. Educated at TCD, he was admitted to the bar, where he followed in the footsteps of a distinguished father. In addition to his profession, he had interests which impelled him to draw upon his ample fortune to assist every movement for the preservation and promotion of Irish culture. Thus, it was he who paid the editors of the Celtic Society, as he had discharged a debt contracted by the Archaeological Society, he who paid for the publications of the Ossianic Society as he had already defrayed the cost of printing *The Spirit of the Nation.*

Like the Archaeological Society, the Celtic Society had as its purpose the publication of ancient MSS, the documents issued prior to 1853, when both were merged into the Ossianic Society, consisting chiefly of works edited by O'Donovan, including *The Book of Rights,* and O'Curry, Dr. Todd's edition of the *Liber Hymnorum,* of inestimable importance for the early Christian period, since it contains St. Sechnall's *Hymn* in praise of St. Patrick and the *Alphabetical Hymn* in praise of St. Brigid; Dr. Reeves's edition of Adamnan's *Life of St. Columba,* and Dr. Todd's *War of the Gaedhail and the Gaill.*

The declared purpose of the Ossianic Society was "the publication of Irish MSS relating to the Fenian period of our history, and other historical documents, with literal translations and notes." The seventh annual report (17 March, 1860), sets forth the reasons why the Society's publications were calculated to become popular: "Less dry than strictly historical books, they throw open the Portals of the Past to the reader, and bring him among the majestic forests of ancient Erinn—there to behold the enchantment of Fairy-power, to accompany Finn and the Fianna in the chase and the battle-raid, to admire the chivalry of Oscar, the 'gold-deeded,' the *beau-ideal* of magnanimity, and list to the melodious harps and sweet lays of the later bards." The "other historical documents" included tales from the earlier cycle, that of the Red Branch, and some from history.

The tone of the Transactions of the Society clearly indicates that the documents issued, important though they were, were generally unfamiliar, not to say completely unknown. Thus the *Pursuit of Diarmuid* is described as "a curious specimen of ancient Irish romance," while the *Tain* was so far lost to Irish memory that a reference to it in Professor Connellan's edition of the *Tract on the Bardic Institution* had to be identified in a footnote, which describes it as "a composition of a very ancient period, regarded by some of our Archaeologists as the detail of a cattle raid, and by others as a purely mythical relation, a contest between two opposing sects of ancient pagans."

Foremost among the early members of the Society, and for a

time its president, was Standish Hayes O'Grady, to whom was entrusted the publication of the most important of the Fenian documents, *An Account of the Pursuit of Diarmuid.* The son of Admiral O'Grady and a kinsman of that Standish O'Grady who had prosecuted Robert Emmet, Standish Hayes O'Grady was born in 1832, and spent his boyhood among Irish speakers, so that by the time he went to Rugby he was deeply versed in Gaelic. He attended TCD, but left without a degree. He was closely associated with the ventures of John O'Daly, but his literary career was apparently broken off when, in 1857, upon completing the engineering studies he had undertaken after leaving college, he went to the United States, where he became interested, first in gold mining and then in running a coastal schooner. He was recalled by his father about 1862 and spent most of the remainder of his long life in England, always, however, retaining his keen interest in Gaelic studies, on which he became a recognized authority. Invited to continue the work of O'Curry and O'Donovan on the Brehon Laws, he declined, but his application for the chair of Celtic studies at Edinburgh University was denied.

Under the name of S. Hayes, O'Grady published (1853) *The Adventures of a Luckless Fellow,* by Donnchadh Ruadh Mac Conmara, but O'Grady's most monumental work, planned as early as 1886, consists in his great *Catalogue of Irish MSS in the British Museum,* most of which was printed between 1889 and 1892. Forced to desist by ill health, he completed only the first volume, the second being the work of Mr. Robin Flower (1926). Even greater than the *Catalogue* is O'Grady's *Silva Gadelica* (1892), based on MSS in the British Museum, in which he shows himself not only a great master of Irish epigraphy, but a genial personality whose humour saves his extremely learned work from pedantry and makes these compilations attractive to the general reader, while at the same time they are invaluable to the scholar. Thus he describes the poems listed in the *Catalogue* as "poems of a kind that in former ages high training produced for the delectation of minds by culture and practice fitted to appreciate them." He died in 1915.

To his edition of *The Pursuit of Diarmuid* is appended a series of poems entitled *The Lamentation of Oisin after the Fenians,* including the old pagan's dispute with St. Patrick, of which O'Grady's rendering is delightfully spirited, and to which he adds the information that the poem is based on his own collection of Fenian poetry "written by Martin Griffin of Kilrush in the year 1845," and on a MS made by Thomas Geoghan of Limerick in 1820.

Like all translators from the Irish, O'Grady is under the necessity of explaining the practical impossibility of success, his being one of the earliest protestations of the inadequacy of the result, of which there have been so many throughout the course of the Gaelic Revival. "The Irish," he says, "is exceedingly copious and expressive in all directions in which it has been cultivated; and powerful and rich as the English language is, it cannot describe with the same copiousness, variety, and nicety the gradations of the passions and feelings, all the face of nature, battles, and other things which engaged the attention of the Irish when their language flourished. Let any one, who is in any degree acquainted with the tongue, reckon how many words there are in it to express various degrees of love, of joy, of sorrow, of hatred; how many names for a hill, how many words to denote generosity or penury, bravery or cowardice, beauty or ugliness, then try to match each with an English equivalent, and the truth of what has been said must appear."

Some of the most important enterprises of the Ossianic Society were confided to Owen Connellan, professor of Irish at Queen's College, Cork (1846-1869). He was born in Sligo in 1800, the son of a farmer who claimed descent from King Laeghaire Mac-Neill. Connellan early acquired a reputation for his ability as a transcriber of Irish MSS and as a translator, in which capacities he was employed by the Royal Irish Academy. In 1822 he was appointed Irish Historiographer Royal because of his translation into Irish of King George IV's *Letter to the Irish People*. Shortly before O'Donovan issued his Irish grammar Connellan published one, as in 1846 he published a translation of the *Four Masters,* the first in English, two years before the publication of O'Donovan's work, which, however, was immeasurably superior to Connellan's, whose inferiority O'Donovan was the first to point out.

For the Ossianic Society Connellan edited the Tract on the *Proceedings of the Great Bardic Institution*, published in 1860, the volume including an essay on MacPherson's *Ossian*, and several specimens of bardic verse translated by Connellan. Some of these were so ancient that he could not read the language in which they were written and had to base his translation on the medieval glosses of the original text. In the case of Ward's *Lament for O'Donnell* he wisely utilized Mangan's superb version, *O Woman of the Piercing Wail*.

Still another name on the illustrious roster of the Ossianic Society is that of W. K. Sullivan (1820-1890), professor of chemistry at the Catholic University and editor of O'Curry's great series of lectures, to which he contributed the Introduction to the *Manners and Customs* which fills the entire first volume. At the time of his death he was president of Queen's College, Cork.

In all such movements there seems to be at least one figure who serves to link his generation with both the past and the future. In the Ossianic Society this was John O'Mahoney, an Irish scholar and a political agitator. He was born in Co. Cork in 1816, of a family with revolutionary traditions, his father and uncle having been "out" in '98. The son attended Trinity, but did not receive a degree.

After leaving college he devoted himself to the study of Hebrew and Sanskrit, but above all, of Gaelic, in which his scholarship won recognition. In that capacity he translated (1857) Keating's *History*, which, despite its merits, gives evidence of having been hastily done.

Early in life O'Mahoney became interested in the Repeal movement, joined the Young Irelanders and was with Smith O'Brien in the uprising of 1848. He escaped to France, but later joined Mitchel in New York, where he became the founder of the Fenian organization (Irish Revolutionary Brotherhood), resigning his colonelcy in the famous 69th New York regiment in order to work for the cause. He took no active part in any phase of the insurrection, after the suppression of which he devoted himself to literary pursuits. He had been reduced to extreme poverty when he died in New York in 1877, his proud spirit refusing to accept any proffer of help. His body was returned to Ireland and he was buried in Glasnevin cemetery with a public funeral.

Since Standish O'Grady owed his first introduction to Celtic studies, as distinguished from his knowledge of spoken Irish, to the German scholar Windisch, it would seem imperative to attempt at this point some slight description of the impetus which the cultivation of Gaelic received from Continental scholars. One of the consequences of the science of anthropology, which originated with the discovery of Sanskrit and was definitely formulated by the publication in 1833 of Franz Bopp's *Comparative Grammar of the Sanskrit, Zend, Armenian, Greek, Celtic and Slavonic Languages,* was the development of that branch of learning known as Comparative Philology. This subject proved especially attractive to German savants, many of whom concentrated their attention on the Celtic tongues and their allied cultures.

Foremost among such scholars was Johann Caspar Zeuss, known as the founder of Celtic philology. Born in 1806, in Upper Franconia, he was educated for the priesthood, but preferring the field of secular study, especially philology, in which he had early displayed exceptional aptitude, he became a professor at Munich. His labour on his gigantic *Grammatica Celtica* was interrupted by serious illness, and he withdrew to Bamberg, where he completed the work which lifted the study of Irish out of the realm of political controversy into that of high and disinterested scholarship.

Zeuss was followed by a long line of German, French and Irish scholars, under whose auspices Irish learning began to be restored to the place it had once held in Ireland. Of signal distinction among the Germans was Ernst Windisch, born in Dresden in 1844 and at various periods professor of Sanskrit and Celtic philology at the Universities of Leipzig, Heidelberg and Strassburg. He was an honorary member of the Royal Irish Academy, and was instrumental in directing the choice of a career not only for Standish O'Grady, but for Whitley Stokes (1830-1909), son of that Dr. Stokes who has already been described as the friend of Petrie and the benefactor of Mangan. Whitley Stokes was educated at TCD and admitted to the bar, but devoted his life to the study of comparative philology, especially as far as it concerned Gaelic. His philological writings are too numerous to list. Running to nearly two hundred items in the *Bibliography of Irish Philology and Literature*, published in 1913, they include editions of *Cuchulain's Death*, abridged from the *Book of Leinster* and reprinted in Miss Hull's *Cuchullin Saga* (1890); *The Destruction of Da Derga's Hostel* (1902), from the *Yellow Book of Lecan*; *The Colloquy of the Two Sages* (1905), from the *Book of Leinster*; *The Training of Cuchulainn* (1908). His most important single work was the *Irische Texte* (1884-1909), done in collaboration with Windisch.

Heinrich Zimmer, born at Castellaun in 1851, became professor of Celtic philology at the University of Berlin and wrote numerous articles on the early Irish Church, some of which have been translated into English, e.g., *The Celtic Church in Britain and Ireland* and *The Irish Element in Medieval Culture*.

Of the German scholars the most voluminous writer was Kuno Meyer (1858-1919), who became director of the School of Irish Learning in Dublin, Todd Professor of Celtic Languages at the Royal Irish Academy and McCollum Lecturer in Celtic at the University of Glasgow. While his philological theories and literary ascriptions have not gone entirely unchallenged, his works, which include such interesting books as *The Triads of Ireland, A Primer of Irish Metrics* and *Ancient Irish Poetry, The Voyage of Bran, The Battle of Ventry, The Vision of MacConglinne* and the *Law of Adamnan*, bring us into the full tide of the literary revival which he did so much to promote.

While the Germans were the principal Continental authorities on philological and allied subjects, they did not by any means have the field entirely to themselves. Thus the French anthropologist, Henri d'Arbois de Jubainville, was the author of revolutionary studies in Celtic mythology, in which he identifies the figures of the Irish pantheon with their counterparts in classic and other mythologies. Born at Nancy in 1827, he studied history and philology at the Collège Royal de Nancy and the University of Königsberg, and law at Paris (1850), where he became archivist for the department of l'Aube (1850-1880). In 1882 he became professor of Celtic languages and literature at the Collège de France. Of his numerous works the most important is his *Le Cycle Mythologique Irlandais et la Mythologie,* translated into English by Richard Irvine Best and published in 1903. The translator described it as the best and fullest treatment of the subject, and it is unquestionably essential to any serious study of the religion of pagan Ireland, although Professor O'Rahilly has thrown discredit on certain of de Jubainville's theories.

That the language movement in Ireland itself was not entirely dependent upon the exertions of foreign scholars is evident from the foundation in 1876 of the Society for the Preservation of the Irish Language under the patronage of the great John McHale, archbishop of Tuam, whom O'Connell called "the lion of St. Jarlath's," from which Society the Gaelic League directly stemmed. John McHale was a native speaker of Irish, born in Co. Mayo in 1791, and during his long and active life a fearless agitator for the restoration of Irish as a living speech. It was an address he delivered at Maynooth that stirred up one of its students, Eugene O'Growney, to such interest in the subject that he afterwards became professor of Irish in that institution, the author of Gaelic text-books and an active member of the Gaelic League. Failing health obliged him to seek the warmer climate of California, where he died in 1899.

Archbishop McHale meanwhile was pursuing his own labours in Irish, into which he translated the *Pentateuch, Moore's Melodies* and the *Iliad.* His cousin, Canon Ulick Bourke, was another Catholic priest who did everything in his power to promote Irish scholarship. He had studied the language under Hardiman, compiled a grammar while still a student at Maynooth and as president of St. Jarlath's College, an office which he filled from 1865 to 1877, saw to it that the students were taught Irish. His most important book, *The Aryan Origins of the Irish Race,* is clearly abreast of the current philological research, although some of his theories are now antiquated. His work was influential in popularizing the findings of the Continental scholars.

As already indicated in the chapter on the early Irish novel the term was a misnomer, chiefly because the so-called Irish novel was actually a branch of the English novel. At the time when the novel as a literary form was reaching its fullest development, the Irish were in no position to show what it might have become in their hands, since under constant threat of the penal code they were furtively dragging out behind the hedge such cultural life as they retained. That, given the opportunity, they might have made something memorable of the form is evident from the fact that from time immemorial the function of the *shanachie* or story-teller was traditional among them. So that if they did not produce novels it was not because they could not tell a story or enjoy listening to one. "One thing the Irish *seanchaidhe* or *file* could do supremely well," says Professor MacSweeney,[1] "and that was tell a story. From childhood he was accustomed to hear them; not a winter's evening passed over without some new effort of the *seanchaidhe's* art being revealed to him; and when he came of age to adopt the profession himself, he was already well on the road to perfection."

It was therefore perhaps only natural that one of the earliest results of the interest in Gaelic as a spoken tongue should be the publication of collections of folk tales, a subject which had become one of the major interests of the science of anthropology. It may be difficult for those whose childish imaginations were fed upon the fairy tales of the brothers Grimm to realize that the collecting of these tales was the result of serious scholarly research, and not of mere playful fancy. In this connection it is of interest to note that in 1856 the Ossianic Society records with satisfaction the admission of its vice-president, John O'Donovan, as a member of the Royal Academy of Berlin on the motion of

[1] Introduction to his edition of *The Martial Career of Conghal Clairingh-neach,* Irish Texts Society, V, xxix.

Jacob Grimm, "the greatest of living philologists, and the man best capable of appreciating the importance of a knowledge of the Celtic language and literature to the philologist and the ethnologist" (Third Annual Report).

As a matter of fact, even before the development of anthropology as a science, the field of Irish folk-lore had proved itself exceptionally rich and rewarding. While still a boy, Crofton Croker (b. Cork, 1798), had collected material which he sent to Tom Moore, and his first compilation, *Fairy Legends,* was published anonymously in 1825. It was followed by *Legends of the Lakes* (1829) and *Killarney Legends* (1831).

In 1832 and 1834 Samuel Lover published his *Legends and Stories of Ireland,* to which is added *National Proverbs* and *Irish Sketches.* Of this, as of similar books, Dr. Hyde complained, when eventually he asserted his mastery over the whole field of folk-lore, that they were not sufficiently authoritative. Among the collections cited by Dr. Hyde as unsatisfactory are those of Croker, who was, he says, too often his own original; Carleton and Lover, whose work is called incidental and largely manipulated; Patrick Kennedy's *Legendary Fictions of the Irish Celts* (1866) and *Fireside Stories of Ireland* (1870), for which no sources are given; Lady Wilde's *Ancient Legends of Ireland* (1888), to which is assigned neither authority nor locale.

In Jeremiah Curtin's *Myths and Folk Lore of Ireland* (1890), Dr. Hyde deplores the lack of information concerning sources, especially since Curtin had "approached the fountain head more nearly than any other." Curtin was American-born, a Harvard graduate, and an exceptionally proficient ethnologist who is known particularly for his translations from the Russian and Polish, notably the novels of Sienkiewicz, as well as for his studies among the American Indians.

Of the above-mentioned folk-lorists Croker was born in Cork in 1798 and died in London in 1854, having in the interval established a considerable reputation as an antiquary. He helped to found the Camden Society, the Percy Society and the British Archaeological Association. "I give them as I found them," he says of the stories in the *Fairy Legends,* but no reader will have difficulty in accepting Dr. Hyde's charge that they were manipulated for the English market, not only in form but in subject. Besides the works already mentioned he also assembled a collection of *The Popular Songs of Ireland* (1839) in which, according to his statement in the Preface, he sought to steer a middle course between the vulgar ballad and "the exquisite compositions of Moore and Lover." In the course of this same Preface, however, he cites some scathing words of criticism against Moore's "audacity" in prefixing the word *Irish* to his *Melodies.* The airs are admitted to be Irish enough, "but as for his songs, they in general have as much to do with Ireland as with Nova Scotia." Croker groups the items in his collection of Songs under headings such as *St. Patrick, The Shamrock, The Potato, Whiskey, The Irish Oak* and *Local Songs,* among which he includes *Gougane Barra, the Groves of Blarney* and *Garryowen.*

Patrick Kennedy, who wrote under the pseudonym of "Harry Whitney," was born in Wexford in 1801 and died in 1873. Like O'Daly, he kept a bookshop in Anglesea St. and wrote with great fidelity on aspects of rural life with which he was familiar, but Dr. Hyde maintains that his tales have been impaired and stunted by being "filtered through an English idiom."

Lady Wilde, who in the later days of the *Nation* had written poetry under the pen-name of "Speranza," was born in Wexford in 1826 and died in London in 1896.

To this list may be added Joseph Jacobs' *Celtic Fairy Tales,* published in 1891, and afterwards enlarged and improved until it could be pronounced "the most representative and attractive collection of Celtic Fairy Tales ever published."[2] As also the work of William Larminie (born in Co. Mayo in 1849; died in Bray, 1900), whose *West Irish Folk Tales and Romances* (1898) had been taken down word for word in the Irish of the peasants of Galway, Mayo and Donegal. But by that time the illustrious example of Hyde had put the whole subject on a new footing.

The advent of Dr. Hyde was foreshadowed by the publication

[2] Brown, *Ireland in Fiction.*

in 1888 of a volume entitled *Fairy and Folk Tales of the Irish Peasantry,* edited by W. B. Yeats, whose only previous publication had been his *Mosada.* The prose volume was a compilation drawn from various sources, such as the collections of Crofton Croker, Lover, Patrick Kennedy, Carleton and Lady Wilde, with the stories grouped under such headings as *Trooping Fairies, Solitary Fairies, Ghosts, Witches,* etc. An item of special interest is the tale entitled *The Countess Kathleen O'Shea,* first because it seems to be Yeats's only contribution, which he describes as "quoted from a London newspaper," and second, because it is the germ of *The Countess Cathleen,* which was not only Yeats's first play, but the first play produced under the auspices of what developed into the Abbey Theatre.

Of even greater significance, however, is the fact that the volume, which incidentally is dedicated to "my mystical friend, G. R.," contained three tales directly translated from the Irish by Mr. Douglas Hyde, accompanied by the statement that they had not been published before but would appear in his forthcoming book, *Leabhar Sgeuluigheachta,* the publication of which was an event of major importance in the Irish Literary Revival.

In fact, the appearance of Douglas Hyde upon the Irish literary scene altered not only the appearance of the scene itself, but, despite Dr. Hyde's aloofness from politics, the subsequent course of Irish history. He gathered up the strands of numerous earlier efforts, of divers purposes and cross-purposes, and wove them into a unified and durable fabric in which all the ancient symbols and sacred colours are blended with the later sadder hues into a pattern in which even the beggar's nondescript fluttering rags are an essential element.

Douglas Hyde was born at Castle Hyde, French Park, Co. Roscommon, in 1860, of Norman or possibly pre-Norman stock, the family belonging, of course, to the Anglo-Irish ascendancy.[3] His father, a clergyman of the Established Church, was practically his sole teacher, to whom he owed his love of reading and especially his proficiency in the Classics. Most of his boyhood was

[3] Diarmuid Coffey, *Douglas Hyde, President of Ireland.*

spent in the company of the peasantry of the district, by whom he was received on terms of friendship and from whom he acquired not only the Irish language but a knowledge of all that the language stood for, which was a world from which most of the members of his class were excluded.

The Trinity to which the Gaelic-loving Hyde was admitted for his higher studies was violently antagonistic to that language and that world, a circumstance which seemed only to increase the fervour of the young student's devotion, so that he lost no opportunity to assert his position, even boasting that he dreamed in Irish.

It was intended at first that, like his father, he should enter the ministry, but although his studies in that field were successful, he soon turned to the humanities and to law, in which he earned a doctorate, although he had no intention of practising that profession. After graduation he spent some months in Canada, teaching English literature at the University of New Brunswick. But more and more his interests were being concentrated on the study of Irish, and in 1878 he joined the Society for the Preservation of the Irish Language, leaving it in the same year in order to help in the formation of the Gaelic Union, whose members devoted themselves to the study of Modern Irish.

The task upon which these enthusiasts were engaged, in whose behalf they published a monthly called the *Gaelic Journal,* seemed almost hopeless, but since like their predecessors they had the wisdom to realize that they must encourage not merely the revival of the language but every form of Irish culture, for which reason music and dancing were among the interests which they promoted, the enthusiasm so aroused was extended to the language itself.

Consequently all previous efforts to preserve and sustain the Irish tongue came to fruition in 1892 when at a meeting of the National Literary Society of Dublin, of which he was president, Douglas Hyde organized the Gaelic League.

The chief difference between the League and all the earlier bodies devoted to the study of Irish is that its activities were not confined to Dublin, but were intended to be nationwide. Neither was its purpose the same as that of the earlier societies, the rescue and publication by scholars of ancient documents, although such a purpose would necessarily be served by the restoration of Irish among the people. Hence, as president of the League, an office which he held until 1915, when he resigned because of his fear that the organization was becoming involved in the political agitations of that time, Dr. Hyde not only travelled through Ireland organizing branches of the League, but toured the United States, delivering lectures for the purpose of making it known and raising funds for its support.

From the outset he made it quite clear that its chief object was the de-Anglicizing of Ireland, the necessity for which he emphasized in an address delivered in 1894 before the Irish Literary Society of London, in which he bore witness to the persistence of Irish speech and the survival of the native literary tradition, affirming that he himself had heard persons reciting Irish poems by a poet who died sixty years before Chaucer was born, and claiming that throughout the penal times every one of fair education had training in this art. The Irish language, he insisted, was worth knowing, or why would the greatest philologists of Germany, France and Italy be so emulously studying it?

While blaming O'Connell and Maynooth for the decline in the use of the native tongue, Dr. Hyde took occasion to refer proudly to "my friend, Father O'Growney," then engaged in teaching Irish at Maynooth. Despite his life-long determination to remain aloof from politics, he made it clear on this occasion that he did not consider it in any sense a political matter to help the Irish race to become "what it was of yore, one of the most original, literary and charming peoples of Europe."

The place of Irish in the national curriculum was an occasion of academic controversy, conducted for the most part with unacademic heat. Thus in 1900 Dr. Mahaffy, president of Trinity, and several of his colleagues, opposed the inclusion of Irish in secondary education, their opposition being expressed in the most puerile terms and manifesting an ignorance that would have disqualified them as scholars had they been discussing any subject but Irish. Dr. Hyde's speech before the Educational Commission disposed of the matter so effectively that Irish thenceforth became a part of secondary education. The establishment of the National University in 1908, in compliance with the demands of Catholics for an educational institution other than Trinity, implied, as far as most Catholics were concerned, the inclusion of Irish in the curriculum, but to this there was violent opposition, emanating sometimes from the most amazing quarters.

Dr. Hyde, who foresaw more trouble ahead, this time concerning the compulsory teaching of Irish and with the issues largely political, prophesied that there would be a fight as there had been in the seventeenth century between the new Irish and the old Irish, between Ormonde and Owen Roe O'Neill, and he added, "If anyone wants to know on which side I shall be, I'll be on the side of Owen Roe."[4]

Next to Hyde and Eoin MacNeill, then vice-president of the Gaelic League, the most indomitable figure on the side of Owen Roe was Rev. Michael P. O'Hickey, professor of Irish at Maynooth, whose vigorous advocacy of the cause, or rather his ill-advised reference to those of his ecclesiastical superiors who were against it, resulted in his removal from the chair at Maynooth in which he had succeeded Father O'Growney.

The League was well organized and spread steadily if not rapidly. The local branches conducted classes in which the language was studied, and the League as a body sponsored, but did not control, "Summer colleges," situated in remote districts and closely resembling an Irish university of the early Middle Ages. An important feature of the movement was the *Oireachtas*, an annual festival lasting for several days during which competitions and games were held.

An immediate consequence of the League's successful fight for the compulsory teaching of Irish was Hyde's appointment as professor of Modern Irish in University College, Dublin, where Eoin MacNeill, vice-president of the League and a close friend

[4] Coffey, op. cit., p. 95.

of Hyde's, was assigned to the Chair of Early Irish History, a post formerly held by O'Curry.

Douglas Hyde was already known as a writer, and it is characteristic of him that he should have made his entrance into the literary world through the subject of folk-lore. His first published work was the Gaelic *Leabhar Sgeuluigheachta,* a collection of stories collected by himself from the lips of the peasant narrators. This was followed in 1890 by *Beside the Fire,* which the distinguished bibliographer, Rev. Stephen Brown, S. J., describes as "the first really scientific treatment of Irish folk-lore." It consists of about half the stories contained in the earlier and wholly Gaelic volume, with others, English versions of all being supplied.

A poet in his own right, Hyde chose to restrict his poetic gifts to the English rendering of the important collections of songs which he had gathered from among the peasantry of Connaught. These are *The Love Songs of Connaught* (1893), *The Religious Songs of Connaught* (1906), and the *Half-Rann.*

In 1895 his *Story of Early Gaelic Literature* was included in the New Irish Library, and in 1899 appeared his *Literary History of Ireland,* which is really a history of Gaelic Literature in Ireland down to the eighteenth century. *Legends of Saints and Sinners,* consisting chiefly of stories of early Irish saints, appeared in 1915.

His best work is to be found in the *Songs of Connaught,* all of which are printed in the same manner, with the Irish text, consisting in part of the recovered poems, in part of Hyde's commentary, on the left-hand page, and the translation of both on the right. The poems themselves had been cherished in the memory of the peasantry, but their authors were men cultured in the use of language and familiar with the traditional poetic forms.

These poems, as well as his literary histories and his edition of the *Three Sorrows of Story-telling,* had an incalculable effect in arousing both Irish and non-Irish readers to a realization of the Irish literary heritage. His dramatic work will be treated below in the chapter dealing with the theatre. In all that he did, and it is impossible to do more than touch on his multiple activities, he had only one real object, and that was to assist in the restoration of Irish as a spoken tongue and a literary medium. The extent to which he identified himself with the ancient native tradition is evident from the dedication of *Beside the Fire*, which is inscribed: "To the memory of those truly cultured and unselfish men, the poet scribes and hedge schoolmasters of the last century—men who may well be called the last of the Milesians— I dedicate this effort to preserve even a scrap of that native lore which in their day they loved so passionately and for the preservation of which they worked so nobly but in vain."

The completeness with which Hyde himself has been included among the "Milesians" was foreshadowed in his youth by their whole-hearted acceptance of him when he ranged the Irish hills or sat beside Irish firesides, not as a Stranger, but as "one of ourselves." Their recognition of his quality is expressed in the widespread use of his literary name, not only by the learned and the literary, but by the people, the same people who devised such terms as the Blackbird and *An Craobhin Aobhin* to describe the object of their fealty and devotion, sentiments which were given their fullest possible expression when on May 6, 1938, Douglas Hyde was elected first President of Ireland. He died on July 12, 1949.

Chapter XII. *THE RETURN OF THE HEROES*

> *The dead under the grasses*
> *Ask "Is it time?" and she answers "Yes."*
> > Katharine Tynan

IN THE POEM on Spring from which the above lines are quoted, Katharine Tynan makes use of an old legend which describes Finn and his warriors as drowsing in an ancient cave in Donegal, clad in full armour, with horses panoplied and weapons at hand, awaiting the summons to arise and join the great Earls and the other heroic Irish dead in striking the blow that will restore forever Ireland's lost freedom. The literary development which this book has undertaken to chronicle, at last and with apparent abruptness reached a point where the ancient heroes seemed to reply to some such summons by making a sudden return to literature.

The signal which aroused the heroes may have been first sounded by the scholarly labours already described, particularly those undertaken by the Ossianic Society. It is, however, rather generally agreed that the final awakening, not only of the heroes themselves, but of the generation of writers who welcomed them back, was due chiefly to the work of one person, Standish James O'Grady, kinsman of the author of *Silva Gadelica*. Born in 1846 at Berehaven, and educated at TCD, where he was graduated in 1868 after a distinguished scholastic career, he was called to the bar in 1872, but, feeling an attraction to letters, became under a pseudonym a contributor to the *Gentleman's Magazine*.

So completely was he of his class that later he was able to say that throughout his life he had never read one word about

189

Irish history and legend, nor heard a syllable on such subjects from either his pastors or his masters, so that at the age of twenty-three he would have accepted Brian Boru as a mythical character. And then, in the course of an inclement week-end at a country house he read O'Halloran's *History of Ireland* (Cf. supra p. 132), in which he made the discovery, to quote Mr. Ernest Boyd, "that Ireland had a great past."[1] To a man with his imaginative gifts this discovery was in the nature of a revelation, which completely changed the direction of his intellectual life. The concrete result was a long and active literary career, in which O'Grady attempted to bring to life something of that forgotten past, that lost greatness. Consequently, the publication in 1878 of his *Bardic History of Ireland*, the first of several treatments of Ireland's legendary and historical past, was an event of such importance that it is generally regarded as the corner-stone of the so-called Gaelic Renaissance.

In his own way, and although he was so dissimilar in background and spirit, he was not unlike those old annalists who worked against time and chaos in order to record the history of their country. Of course, O'Grady's was not scientific history any more than theirs was; it was much more than that: the re-creation of the figures of that lost heroic age, by a man who was in Yeats's phrase "at once all passion and all judgement," whose function it was not to write history but to make literature. If he never completely fulfilled this function, because he lacked the courage to pursue his own method, fearing the adverse criticism of the pedants, he nevertheless performed an inestimable service by revealing "the fire and beauty of the bardic imagination" to a waiting generation of writers, including Katharine Tynan, Eleanor Hull, T. W. Rolleston and W. B. Yeats, to mention only those who specifically acknowledged their indebtedness to him. This was because, again despite great differences, he himself possessed not a little of that bardic imagination.

Besides the *Bardic History* he is the author of *Early Bardic Literature* (1879); *History of Ireland: Cuculain and His Con-*

[1] *Ireland's Literary Renaissance* (1922), p. 27.

temporaries (1880); *History of Ireland: Critical and Philosophical*, Vol. I (1882). He later re-cast the *Bardic History* into a three-volume version of the Cuchulain cycle, entitled respectively *The Coming of Cuculain*, *The Triumph of Cuculain*, and *The Passing of Cuculain*.

Some idea of his way of handling his material may be derived from the following passage: "Now this was the manner of Lavarcam. When upon her shining feet she had bound the white sandals which were a gift from her foster-father, Mananan Mac Lir, she was the swiftest thing in the whole world; the winged lightning not swifter. Her footprints as she sped did not mark the still surface of the sea or burst a bubble of its rolling waves; neither did the bearded barley bend beneath her flying feet. She was young and lovely to look upon, and the wisest knew not the place and time of her birth. Her by his spells of power and druidic art did Concobar bend to his ministry and service and in all things she obeyed him" (*The Passing of Cuculain*).

There are many noteworthy passages throughout the narrative, notably those which describe Fergus identifying for Meave the great champions of the Red Branch as the host approaches; Lugh offering to Cuchulain his choice of long and happy life, or "this day victory and a great deliverance for thy people and afterwards an early, a violent and a solitary death"; above all, Cuchulain making ready for the death of which he has already received the wound, by binding himself to the pillar stone in an upright position so that even in death he might seem to the enemy to be still alive.

Under the titles of *Finn and His Companions* (1892) and *The Departure of Dermot* (1917), O'Grady submitted the Fenian cycle to similar treatment, while various phases of actual rather than legendary history are the subject of *Red Hugh's Captivity* (1889); *The Chain of Gold* (1895); *In the Wake of King James* (1896); *Ulrick the Ready* (1896); *The Flight of the Eagle* (1897); *In the Gates of the North* (1901). Of *The Bog of Stars* (1893), he himself said that the tales it contains are "not so much founded on fact as in fact true." His object in assembling them, he stated, was to bring modern Irish readers into closer and more sympathetic relation to the Elizabethan age, because it was one which more than any other seemed to have determined the destiny of Ireland. This is the age which is passed under review in his edition of the *Pacata Hibernia*[2] in the introduction to which he reveals himself as on the side of the "pacificators," in whose behalf he was endeavouring to arouse sympathy.

The *Pacata Hibernia*, whose original sub-title was *Ireland Appeased and Reduced,* is an account of the reduction of Munster by Sir George Carew, whom Elizabeth had appointed president of Munster in 1599. Editing it involved the discussion of some nice textual problems, especially that involving authorship. The narrative was written by one who was obviously an eyewitness of the events which he records. O'Grady believes that Lieutenant Thomas Stafford who served under Carew is "almost certainly" the author, whom he identifies with the professed editor of the MS, which was found among Carew's papers.

The work itself, despite its wholly English and Protestant outlook, is interesting, but O'Grady's Introduction is peculiarly so, for the light it sheds on his attitude towards the nationalist issue. Although he points out that when the Tudor dynasty came to the English throne, "the kings of England, though titular lords of Ireland, were only so in name," he clearly believed that the conquest had been completed by the Tudors, much as he despised the methods by which it was accomplished, for example the assassination by poison of Hugh Roe O'Donnell. He likewise despises many of the Irish leaders, and indicates, although not with such purpose in mind, that the conquest was facilitated by their quarrels among themselves, thus bearing out Dr. MacNeill's charge that the Irish were destroyed by their own pride.

For the priests, especially the Jesuits, he has nothing but words of praise, rejoicing that Ireland which had produced

[2] *Pacata Hibernia*, or A History of the Wars in Ireland during the reign of Queen Elizabeth, especially within the province of Munster under the government of Sir George Carew. Edited with an Introduction and Notes by Standish O'Grady. 1896.

so many "noble-ignoble" men, could produce "men capable
of devoting themselves body and soul to the cause which seemed
to them to be the highest" (lxii). Indeed it is not only here, but
everywhere throughout his work, that O'Grady gives evidence
of the division in his allegiance, of the fact that with his mind
he accepted the conquest and the Union, while his imagination
was drawn to the Brightness of Brightness as powerfully as was
the heart of any hedge-poet or wandering bard. This, at any
rate, is the vein in which he writes of Ireland: "Beginnings, ever
still beginnings, noble actions without end that shine and vanish,
characters as great as any but resultless, movements full of hope
leading no-whither, flashing glories ever dimmed and blasted,
travail and labour unceasing, expectation and resolution ever
baffled; through all the centuries Ireland labouring to bring
forth the Irish Nation, and that nation yet unborn. . . . When
Ireland at last emerges, standing out clear on the world's horizon,
her conscience will be clear indeed—that will never fail—but
it will also be the conscience of the Earth. None can hate her,
none ever will or can. Because of her own millennium-enduring
tragedy she will love this suffering world, and because of her
sufferings, her patience, her faith, her hope, and her heroic and
unconquerable resolve, the world will love her."[3]

That O'Grady was not completely successful even in his handling of the pagan elements in Irish literature is indicated by
Thomas MacDonagh, who, while according full recognition to his
initiative and his literary gifts, takes exception to his accuracy:
"For the poets of the Irish Mode," writes MacDonagh, "it was he
who found the dún in which the wild riders of ancient Irish
hero-lore were confined. It was he that let them forth, them or
phantasies of them. . . . Others have gone into the dún and have
found no such mystery—they have been mistranslated. Not for
the first time has the world owed a beautiful thing to a mis-
translation of genius." Considering O'Grady's work as a whole
it is not surprising that Yeats, looking back upon those aspects
of the movement for whose organization he was responsible,

[3] Quoted in Introduction to *In the Gates of the North.*

could say, although twenty years O'Grady's junior, "I wanted him among my writers."

The group to which Yeats thus so possessively referred constituted the nucleus of what presently came to be known as the Gaelic Renaissance, a movement of which it is customary to call O'Grady the father. Certainly it was directly due to his influence that it acquired the predominantly pagan character which marked its earlier stages, since with his Ascendancy background and outlook it was natural that he should have overlooked the Christian, that is the Catholic, cultural heritage to which Ireland owed the preservation of even the pagan elements of her great past. As a matter of fact, as these pages have shown, that past was not at all the profound and unsuspected secret that O'Grady supposed it to be, since for generations men of learning had been working steadily and quietly, though not in complete obscurity, to rescue and preserve its monuments, and some of the greatest of such scholars, Protestants like Petrie, Todd, Reeves, and O'Grady's own kinsman, had been quick to recognize and pay tribute to the Catholic origin of such monuments.

The tolerance which is characteristic of all true scholarship is exemplified in the work of the Catholic, Patrick Weston Joyce, whose *Old Celtic Romances* was published a year after O'Grady's *Bardic History*. In spite of its dissimilarity, this book, which sought to do chiefly for the Fianna what O'Grady had done for the Red Branch, was bound to have a somewhat similar influence on literature, since Joyce too re-tells the Three Sorrowful Tales, as O'Grady had dealt with the Fenian story. Despite its lack of the "fire and beauty" that are so indisputably the marks of O'Grady's style that they were largely responsible for his powerful appeal to the poetic imagination of his generation, the very simplicity and lack of adornment of Joyce's helped to bring the old epics within the ken of those who could not read them in the original, thus providing the creative among them with abundant matter upon which to work.

Joyce, a brother of Robert Dwyer Joyce, was born at Ballyorgan, Limerick, in 1827, and for many years served as a teacher in the national schools. He had already (in 1863) published a book on school management, and in 1869 came three extremely interesting volumes on *The Origin and History of Irish Names of Places*, in which a wealth of local lore and legend is identified and explained. Indeed, this volume, too, had no small share in facilitating the return of the heroes, by pointing out that they had never really gone away, never at least left Ireland, since their names and their memory were stamped upon so many features of the Irish scene, on hill and wood and river, on cromlech and dun. Without intending to do so, this book makes it clear that from Irish place-names alone it would be possible to reconstruct a whole world of legend and heroic story, the whole of Irish myth and history that are rooted in the "dark backward and abysm of time."

There is no hint of enchantment in Joyce's presentation of his data, which he has assembled industriously, basing his findings mostly on the documents published by the Celtic and Ossianic Societies, and classified clearly, but there is enchantment not only in the beauty of such a name as *Assaroe*, but in the fact that the name itself enshrines the memory of a legendary Irish king who was drowned in the cataract three hundred years before Christ; as there is in names which carry reminders of the race which withdrew to the *sidhes* or hills, or of the fairy music that has been heard in the vicinity of such hills, or the dread nearness of such beings as Cliodhna, queen of the fairies of South Munster, or Aebhinn, regnant over those in the North of that province. Nevertheless, under the impact of Joyce's facts, even as elucidated by philology, enchantment entered, or rather a spell seemed to be broken, the hills and raths and brughs were thrown open and the fairy race emerged, the heroes shook off their enchanted slumber and stood forth in the light of day, Cuchulain from Loop Head (Cuchulain's Leap), Conchobar from Arduchar (the Ford of the Cast), while Finn moved from cromlech to cromlech in pursuit of the lovers whose resting places the stones were set to mark.

When Joyce retired from teaching in 1893 it was to devote the remainder of his life to Irish studies, to which department of learning he made a number of distinguished contributions. He is the author of several historical works, the most important being his *Social History of Ancient Ireland* (1903).

In all these works he had the advantage of knowing Irish and therefore of having access to important original sources. He had a further advantage in the place of his birth, which, as he later recalled, was situated in a part of Limerick in which music, singing and dancing were favourite amusements. Music and song were part of the atmosphere of his home at Glenosheen; they were in the very air of the Valley. Consequently he was, so he declared, the sole legatee of a long accumulating treasure of melody, of which he became aware when he discovered how many of his tunes were unknown to Petrie. He not only wrote down all that he carried in his own memory, but went among the people collecting others and in 1872 published the results in his important work on Irish Music.

In a number of respects, therefore, Joyce supplements the work not only of Petrie, in the field of both music and antiquities, but of the folk-lorists and anthropologists, although strictly speaking neither his work nor O'Grady's belongs to the realm of folk-lore. O'Grady re-told, and glorified in so doing, the old sagas, while Joyce translated a group of them into rather colourless prose which makes no attempt to reproduce any aspect of their original beauty. It is none the less true that by his other works, particularly his *Place Names* and his *Social History*, he built up a background against which the heroic sagas might thenceforth be seen in better perspective.

It is also true that although originally the epic tales were anything but folk-lore, they had come in the course of time to partake of its character. Thus, in the Introduction to his first collection of *Celtic Fairy Tales* (1891), after noting that there was nowhere so large a body of oral tradition about national and mythical heroes as among the Gaels, Mr. Joseph Jacobs declares that the stories of Finn alone, *as told by the Irish peasantry*, that is, of course, as distinguished from the bardic versions preserved in MSS, deserved an entire volume, while those concerning

Cuchulain would easily fill another. As a matter of fact, Finn had always been a popular hero, while the champion of Ulster had remained a literary figure, but since by the time of which Mr. Jacobs writes both of them had become part of the oral tradition of the people, they had to that extent at least become incorporated in the common stock of folk-tales.

The following circumstances will convey some notion of the process by which the material which had thus found a place among the folk acquired a literary status. Almost simultaneously with the publication of O'Grady's *Bardic Literature* and Joyce's *Old Celtic Romances*, an unimportant book was printed in New York City by an obscure publisher, Mr. A. J. McGee. The volume, which was called *The Zozimus Papers*, consisted of a series of comic and sentimental stories and legends "the edited, unedited and pilfered works" of Michael Moran, the Blind Story-Teller of Dublin. The pilfering, it will be understood, was done by Moran, who, born in Faddle Alley, Dublin, in 1794, and blind from infancy, had made his living by telling stories, most of them tall and in the hedge-school style, or improvising verses and songs, many of which the publisher declared he had heard sung "within the classic walls of old Trinity or at the fancy dress balls of the Rotundo." The most famous of his tales, and that whence he derived his pseudonym, was the story of the penitent, St. Mary of Egypt, who had been attended on her deathbed by Bishop Zozimus, but most of the tales were vulgar enough, many of them quite ribald.

Moran's songs belong to the class known as ballads or "Come-all-ye's," most of which are of anonymous authorship and include such famous examples as *Willy Reilly, Johnny, I hardly knew ye,* and *The Night before Larry was Stretched*. The fact of the matter is that for all his poverty and ignorance, Moran had unquestionable gifts, which he sold for profit in the streets instead of employing them for the entertainment of the neighbours beside the fire. It is not too much to claim that he was in the direct line of the *shanachie* and the *file*, but his compositions belong to the realm of folk-lore rather than to literature.

Into that realm, however, he was presently exalted, by the publication in 1894 of a small volume entitled *The Celtic Twilight, Men and Women, Dhouls and Fairies*, by W. B. Yeats. The frontispiece consists of a Pre-Raphaelite drawing by J. B. Yeats entitled *The Last Gleeman*. The caption is explained by the fact that this is the title of one of the chapters of the book, the subject of which is no other than Michael Moran, otherwise known as Zozimus. Despite the fact that he is depicted in all his native vulgarity by the author (who does not, however, minimize his gifts), and that Yeats's account of him is more factually correct than Mr. McGee's, Zozimus has nevertheless undergone a sea-change, for not only has the Dublin singer been idealized beyond recognition in a frontispiece which shows him seated on a flowery bank with two cherub's heads appearing over his left shoulder and a couple of haloed, lily-bearing figures of indeterminate sex emerging out of the mist at the right, but the author could wind up his account of Zozimus in all seriousness with the words, "Perhaps he may have found and gathered, ragamuffin though he be, the Lily of High Truth, the Rose of Far-Sight Beauty."

In other words, the alchemic symbol, the language of a pseudo-mysticism, had entered Irish literature, and that by way of folk-lore, but in such a way that an atmosphere of misty twilight, of esoteric philosophy, has ever since been identified with things Celtic, and has all too frequently been regarded as inseparable from the Irish Revival. The extent to which such assumptions are warrantable will be discussed in a later chapter.

At this point the development of Irish literature, especially as far as the Gaelic Revival is concerned, was complicated by the merging of various streams, both the purely scholarly and the imaginative treatment of the bardic material and the presentation of the same subjects from the standpoint of folk-lore.

A link between the earlier movement, as represented by the Ossianic Society, and the artistic phase of the Revival is found in George Sigerson, who while still a medical student undertook, under the pseudonym of Eironnach, M.D., the translations for a second series of O'Daly's *Poets and Poetry of Munster* (1860).

Of ancient Norse descent, and therefore a Gall (speaking on the same platform with him in 1894, Charles Gavan Duffy called him "the last Dane. . . . an unmitigated Dane"), he was born in Strabane in 1838, followed a course of brilliant medical studies in Dublin and Paris, and by his biological researches attracted the favourable attention of Darwin and Tyndall. But he was primarily interested in Ireland, especially Irish culture, and despite his busy professional life was active in the Literary Revival. His major contribution to this came in 1897 with his anthology, *Bards of the Gael and the Gall*, which Dr. Hyde described as an extension into the past of his *Poets and Poetry of Munster*, showing what a continuous process the Revival was. The noteworthy feature of these translations is that they are "done into English after the modes and metres of the Gael," an achievement which helped to drive home a realization of the inadequacy of English metres for the rendering of Irish verse. The book has additional importance, inasmuch as it covers a wide range of Irish poetry down through the Fenian, the Christian and the penal ages, its value being greatly enhanced by the scholarly discussion of the whole subject wihich constitutes the Introduction. In 1913 he published *The Saga of King Lir*, a poem in blank verse.

Dr. Sigerson also attracted attention by his treatise on the *Carmen Paschale* of Sedulius, an author whom he identifies with the fifth-century Irish scholar. *The Last Independent Parliament of Ireland*, published in 1918, is dedicated to his daughter, Dora Sigerson Shorter (see Chapter XIII). Dr. Sigerson died in 1925.

Likewise representative of what may be called the "direct" stage of the movement, that is the unelaborated rendering of an Irish text, is Kuno Meyer's translation of *The Voyage of Bran, the Son of Febal*, to which is appended Alfred Nutt's *Essay on the Happy Otherworld and the Celtic Doctrine of Rebirth* (1895). One of the earliest writers to follow in O'Grady's footsteps by dealing creatively with the bardic tales was "Ethna Carbery" (in private life Anna Johnson, the first wife of Seumas Mac-Manus), who died "in her high, bright noontide" in 1902. Her *In the Celtic Past* is a collection of tales including *The Pursuit of*

Diarmuid and Grainne, The Death of Diarmuid O'Dubhine, How Oisin convinced Patrick the Cleric, and *The Red Whistler.* They are not translations, but original versions of episodes in the old sagas, several of which have the quality of folk-lore, as have all the stories in her other prose work, *The Passionate Hearts.*

This, as a matter of fact, is the quality which pervades Lady Gregory's versions of the bardic tales. Isabella Augusta Persse was born in 1852 at Roxborough, Galway, the daughter of a wealthy landowner. In 1881 she married Sir William Gregory of Coole, like herself a strong nationalist. Lady Gregory was a woman of brilliant intellectual parts, of vigorous character and liberal principles, whose home at Coole became the hospitable centre for most of the figures of the new movement which she did so much to promote. Her meeting with Yeats in 1898 was a momentous occasion for both of them, since it led directly to the venture which developed into the Abbey Theatre and inaugurated a friendship and association that was only broken by her death in 1932.

By re-telling the bardic tales in a dialect which she called Kiltartan, and as she said herself, "in the same way as my old nurse used to be telling stories long ago," she brought them within the boundaries of folk-lore. This, of course, did them no harm, except perhaps to convey the impression that they had never had any other status, whereas originally they had conformed to literary standards of a difficult and exacting kind. Lady Gregory's most important books of this type are *Cuchulain of Muirthemne* (1902), which weaves together into a fascinating narrative not only the principal Red Branch Tales, but most of the subsidiary stories; and *Gods and Fighting Men* (1904), in which she performs the same service for the Fenian cycle.

Yeats declared her *Cuchulain* the best book that had come out of Ireland in his time, and while Yeats's judgment of any performance of Lady Gregory's was not likely to be impartial, there can be no hesitation in recognizing the importance of her work as a whole, and especially as it is exemplified in these two books, which have a value not only in themselves, but also to the extent that they directed attention to a strangely enchanting body of literature, which for all its apparent newness was not of yesterday. Apart from Lady Gregory's plays, which will be dealt with below, her works include *Poets and Dreamers* (1903), *A Book of Saints and Wonders* (1906), *The Kiltartan History Book* (1909), *The Kiltartan Wonder Book* (1910), *Visions and Beliefs in the West of Ireland*, and *Our Irish Theatre*.

That Irish scholars had no intention of permitting the great epics to survive merely as folk-lore is certified by A. H. Leahy's *Heroic Romances of Ireland* (1905-06), which he describes as "an attempt to give to English readers some of the oldest romances in English literary forms that seem to correspond to the literary forms that were used in Irish." Disavowing any intention of dressing up the old tales, each of which, he contends, was able to speak for itself as it had originally done, Mr. Leahy nevertheless contrives to present a nearly literal translation which is at the same time colourful. An interesting feature is the Introduction in verse, in which, despite his Cambridge fellowship, he manifests the soundness of his Irish learning by protesting against the tendency of some exponents of the Revival to find in the old romances

> mystic gleams
> And traces of the "moody Celt."

Foremost among those who were concerned for the preservation and elucidation of the ancient texts was Eleanor Hull, daughter of Professor Edward Hull, long director of the Geological Survey of Ireland. Although the thoroughness of her scholarship has sometimes been impugned, she nevertheless became the founder of the Irish Texts Society (1899), of which she was for years the honorary secretary, and which numbered among its members some of the most distinguished Gaelic scholars who have ever lived. Miss Hull was also president of the Irish Literary Society of London. She compiled the *Cuchullin Saga* in English, a collection of fourteen stories by various authors, for which Miss Hull supplied the Introduction. This is an essay which should be read by every serious student of this subject, since it provides so much valuable information concerning the historical and mythological aspects of the saga.

Besides writing *Cuchulain, the Hound of Ulster*, an arrangement of the story for younger readers, and a *Text Book of Irish (Gaelic) Literature* in two parts (1906, 1908), the first part dealing with the Red Branch and the second with the Ossianic and Jacobite period, Miss Hull is the author of *Pagan Ireland* (1908), and *Early Christian Ireland*, and compiler of an anthology entitled *The Poem Book of the Gael* (1912).

Among the most important publications of the Irish Texts Society are: *The Feast of Bricriu; The Poems of Egan O'Rahilly;* Keating's *History*, ed. David Comyn; *The Martial Career of Conghal Clairingneach; Duanaire Finn* (Ossianic Poems), ed. Eoin MacNeill; *The Poems of David O'Bruaidair*, ed. MacErlean; *The Poems of Turlough O'Carolan; The Contention of the Bards*, ed. L. McKenna.

In his Preface to *The High Deeds of Finn* (1910), T. W. Rolleston explained that since Miss Hull had devotel a volume to Cuchulain as one of the two most conspicuous figures of ancient Irish legend, he felt that his should bear the name of Fionn, the second of those figures. He has nevertheless included considerable earlier material and he has omitted the most important single Fenian tale, the *Pursuit of Diarmuid and Grainne*, partly because his volume is intended for younger readers. It is, however, far from being a juvenile and can certainly not be overlooked in any study of the bardic literature in English.

Thomas William Rolleston was born at Shinrone in 1857 and after completing his courses at Trinity spent some time studying in Germany, on whose literature he became an authority. On his return to Ireland he founded the *Dublin University Review*, and, despite an active and semi-official career in Ireland, wrote voluminously on German and Gaelic literary subjects, being the author of a volume of poems entitled *Sea Spray* (1909) and *Myths and Legends of the Celtic Race* (1911). The best-known of his poems is the beautiful translation entitled *The Dead at*

Clonmacnois, in which the magic of names once more evokes the sense of racial continuity. In 1908 he took up his residence in London and died at Hampstead in 1920.

Ella Young's *Celtic Wonder Tales*, for which the original decorations were made by Maud Gonne, are not so much translations as "re-tellings" of the old stories, or at least parts of them, somewhat after the manner of O'Grady. They are charged with great beauty, a beauty that derives in part from the tales themselves, but in part also from the teller's sense of that beauty, from her awareness of kinship with its first fashioners.

The Irish movement had by now acquired two aspects, one of which predominated over the other. Unquestionably the heroes had returned. The old gods had come back in such numbers and with such magic powers as almost, it seemed, to have recovered the dominion which had been wrested from them by the Christian saints. They were reasserting their ancient wizardry, this time through literature, especially the ranns of the poets. Oisin, it seemed, was in the way of worsting St. Patrick, so that there was danger of overlooking the fact that the pagan was only one aspect of Irish culture, that the golden age of Irish letters was in reality the height of the Christian era, since it had been Christian scribes, probably labourers in monastic scriptoria, who first recorded the pagan epics, the ancient bardic songs, and thus preserved them from passing into oblivion. So great indeed had been the Christian service to Irish pagan culture that there is even warrant for the legend which credited the great Columba with the recovery of the *Tain* when it had passed from the memory of the bards. This is made abundantly clear, not only by such a work as Dr. Kenney's *Sources for the Early History of Ireland*, but by Dr. Flower's *The Irish Tradition*, especially in the delightful chapters entitled "Exiles and Hermits" and "Ireland and Medieval Europe." See also Helen Waddell's *The Wandering Scholars* (1927), in which she says, with the understanding that preserves her great learning from any shadow of pedantry: "That fierce and restless quality which had made the pagan Irish the terror of Western Europe, seems to have emptied itself into the love of learning and the love of God; and it is the peculiar distinction of Irish medieval scholarship and the salvation of literature in Europe that the one in no way conflicted with the other."[4]

That this aspect of the matter might not be lost sight of, a great Catholic scholar like Archbishop Healy paid tribute to his predecessors in the Irish Church, not only by his masterly account of the monastic schools entitled *Insula Sanctorum* (1890), but by numerous other writings, notably his *Life of St. Patrick* (1905) and *Irish Essays* (1908). John Healy was born in Ballinafad, Sligo, in 1841, and was educated at Maynooth, where after his ordination he became professor of the Classics. Made Archbishop of Tuam in 1903, he died there in 1918.

Another worker in the field of Catholic scholarship was that Canon John O'Hanlon who, under the pseudonym of *Lageniensis*, had published *Irish Local Legends* (1896). Born at Stradbally in 1821, he was educated at Carlow, but ordained in the United States in 1847. As parish priest of Irishtown, he devoted many years of his life to his monumental *Lives of the Irish Saints*, a work of enormous erudition. Of a projected twelve volumes, nine were completed at the time of his death in 1905.

The works of these two men are permanently important, but it would be absurd to maintain that they had any immediate effect on the literary movement. Indeed, it would be safe to say that their direct literary influence was almost negligible, and that when in the later stages of the movement Christian themes became the inspiration of creative writers, the inspiration derived rather from life itself, from the enduring Christian sense of the Irish race, which never stood in need of revival, than from any literary source.

Nevertheless works of pure scholarship continued to be produced and to help forward the intellectual life of Ireland. Indeed, far as this was from his intention, Lecky's *History of Ireland in the Eighteenth Century*, which is said to have made a nationalist of everyone who read it except its author, helped to emphasize the Irish character of the new literary developments. William Edward

[4] Op. cit., p. 28.

Hartpole Lecky was born at Newtown Park near Dublin in 1838. After his graduation from TCD he became interested in theological studies, which became the basis of such works as his *History of Rationalism* (1865) and *History of Christian Morals* (1869). His marriage in 1871 led to his taking up his residence in England, where he devoted many years to his *History of England*, five of its volumes constituting the Irish portion of the work, *The History of Ireland in The Eighteenth Century*, a thoroughly uncompromising presentation of the facts of that terrible era, remarkable for its accuracy and impartiality. In 1895 he was elected M. P. for Dublin, and it is characteristic of him that although he advocated reforms in Ireland and especially freedom of education for Catholics, he was opposed to Home Rule.

Meanwhile what Arthur Griffith called "an Ireland the demigods of the hour despised," was being served by such men as William Rooney, who died in 1901 at the age of twenty-four in consequence of his tireless though unobtrusive labours in behalf of the Gaelic League. Born in Dublin, he became an enthusiast for the cause in boyhood, and despite the fact of constant employment in a solicitor's office, traveled throughout Ireland in its behalf. Under the pseudonym of *Fear na Muinntire* he wrote a good deal of unpretentious verse (*Poems and Ballads*, edited by Arthur Griffith, 1901), invariably on Irish themes. His forthright prose, which represents the lectures and addresses he delivered under the auspices of the Gaelic League, contains excellent criticisms of the literary movement then well under way. As a Gaelic scholar he was eminently qualified to speak on such subjects as *Gaelicism in Practice* (1901), and it was natural and reasonable that he should stress the element of Gaelicism in the literary movement, as he does in *A Recent Irish Literature* (1899). It was also natural that he should take exception to certain fantastic manifestations that were being accepted as typically Irish, as he does when he declares that "No mystification, no introspective or metaphysical ramblings can pass current for Celtic style or spirit."

It seems appropriate at this point to introduce the name of

the distinguished scholar, Robin Flower (1881-1946), already
mentioned as the continuator of Standish O'Grady's *Catalogue
of Irish MSS* in the British Museum (1928). He was of English
birth and of mixed Irish and English blood, born at Meanwood,
Leeds, Yorkshire, and educated at Leeds Grammar School and
Oxford University. He became one of the best palaeographers of
his time, being generally recognized as an authority not only on
Gaelic but also on Anglo-Saxon and Middle English. Although he
devoted his life to intensive study and filled it with numerous
scholarly activities, there is no hint of pedantry about his writings, which not only manifest his learning, but reveal his possession of poetic gifts and the charm of his personality.

In the pursuit of his Gaelic studies he was accustomed to
sojourn among the Blasket islands, an experience which had
among its fortunate results the publication of his delightful *The
Western Island* (1945), and his translation (1934) of *The
Islandman*, the autobiography of Tomas O'Crohan. His works also
include *The Exeter Book of Old English Poetry*, with R. W.
Chambers and Max Foerster (1933), *Eire* (1910), *Love's-Bitter-
Sweet*, poems and translations (1931), and *The Irish Tradition*,
posthumously published in 1947. To those who knew his work
his death was the occasion of the keenest regret that he should
thus have been prevented from writing the work on the history
of Irish literature which he had long planned.

Chapter XIII. *THE HAZELS OF POETRY*

> *In the same hour their fruit, and their blossom and their foliage break forth, and then fall upon the well in the same shower, which raises upon the water a royal surge of purple.*
>
> The Voyage of Bran, *ed. Meyer and MacNutt*

THE IRISH RENAISSANCE broke upon the world in the 1890's with an effect of suddenness that must have stirred many an observer of its phenomena to something of a wild surmise, but that the movement was far from being a sudden outburst it has been in part the object of this book to show. On the contrary, it had been a long, slow, gradual process, so that the manifestations which first challenged attention of the reading world, especially outside of Ireland, were not necessarily its most authentic expression. The Irish Literary Revival was the result of many factors,—the long Irish memory, for one, the strengthening of national consciousness, the rediscovery of Ireland's cultural past, especially the realization of her achievement in the field of letters, art and music, the recovery of her vast store of imaginative lore, both written and oral, the diffusion of the language movement.

Taken all together, it was a heady brew, which found its earliest expression in poetry, so that what first attracted attention was the purple surge upon the well of inspiration, a circumstance which probably delayed participation in its deeper waters on the part of both poets and readers.

Looking back over Irish poetic accomplishment in English as summarized in his *Treasury of Irish Poetry* (1900), Stopford Brooke pointed out what seemed to him its salient characteristics:

its nationalism, its religious tone, its spirit of rebellion. At that time the Revival was still young, and many of its now unmistakable traits were as yet in process of development, so that it was too early for the recognition of those marks which enabled Thomas MacDonagh, writing in 1915, to describe what he calls Anglo-Irish literature, whose poetry is written in the Irish mode.

Such a literature, he maintains, could only have come into existence in Ireland when English had become the language of the Irish people, mainly of Gaelic stock, and it would necessarily demonstrate the radical difference between Irish and English ways of life and thought, while its form, particularly its poetic form, would necessarily reflect the character of the Irish language, particularly its rhythm. Even the earliest poetry of the Revival substantiates Mr. MacDonagh's claims, although not to the same extent as its most recent productions, while much of the more recent poetry likewise answers to Mr. Brooke's description.

To those who first became aware of the Irish Literary Revival it meant the poetry and personality of William Butler Yeats. Both are factors which have continued to dominate the movement to the point of being at least to a certain extent responsible for the impression of a purple surge, as they have also been responsible for most of the misconceptions concerning the movement as a whole.

Born in Sligo in 1865 of Cromwellian Protestant stock, the son of the Pre-Raphaelite artist, John Yeats, the future poet grew up in a household which knew nothing of the work that was being done in the field of Irish scholarship by such men as Petrie, O'Curry and O'Donovan, but as a young man in Dublin he made the acquaintance of Douglas Hyde, Stephen Gwynn, Stockley, and George Russell, whom he met at art school. Since already at eighteen he had declared his inclination to believe in all that had ever been believed, there was nothing strange about his becoming active in the Theosophic Movement, which, as far as its Dublin aspect was concerned, had originated in a visit of Annie Besant and in a discussion at Professor Dowden's home of A. P. Sinnett's work on *Esoteric Buddhism*.

This was the beginning of an interest which dominated Yeats's whole life, and which his official biographer, Joseph Hone, attributes to an innate love of secrecy and mystification, possibly inherited from his Masonic maternal relatives. However that may be, the outcome was the organization of a society for the promotion of Oriental religions and Theosophy, of which the Dublin lodge was established in 1886 after an interview with Madame Blavatsky. Later, in association with other Theosophists, he was a member of a group of "Christian" Cabbalists known as the Society of the Golden Dawn, but in his earlier Dublin days, he and a number of other young men, calling themselves the Hermetic Society, of whom George Russell was one, engaged a room "near the roof in York Street," in which they read papers to one another on Oriental and other aspects of what they called "mysticism." Yeats and Russell wrote poetry in this vein, so that they came to be known as "the Dublin mystics," their "mysticism" being regarded, by themselves and others, as having literary as well as religious significance.

Another member of the group who accepted its doctrines, was imbued with its spirit and made numerous contributions, notably *Celtic Wonder Tales* (1910), to its literary output was Ella Young. She devotes the early chapters of her autobiography, *Flowering Dusk* (1949), to an account of the activities of the Hermetic Society and their earnest endeavours to revive the pagan beliefs and way of life, which had been overthrown by St. Patrick in the fifth century. The book as a whole presents a highly readable first-hand account of the chief literary and political figures and events of her time, as well as of the Revival, of which she writes exultantly, "The National Spirit has more than stirred, it has lifted its voice and   shouted." The book is pervaded by her implicit belief in the reality of the old gods and the fairies, whose visible manifestation was for her and the other members of the Hermetic Society not only part and parcel of the Irish Revival but an article of abiding religious faith to which Miss Young adhered even after coming to America in

1925, where she became associated with the Theosophists of Point Loma, California, under the direction of Mrs. Tingley.

This was the type of "mysticism" which Yeats at last carried to a degree where he believed himself to be in more or less constant communication with disembodied elementals. He also believed in and practised spiritualism to a point where he succeeded on more than one occasion in obtaining public verbal communications, though for the most part his friends took his word for his "supernatural" experiences. His final experiments in this field are the subject of the treatise entitled *A Vision*, of which more will be said later.

During the years when he was becoming an adept in these matters he made the acquaintance of the old Fenian, John O'Leary, then president of the Young Ireland Society, who had been made a patriot by the poems of Thomas Davis, despite his realization that their literary quality was not of the highest order. Through O'Leary and those he met at his home, especially O'Leary's intrepid sister, Ellen, Yeats became aware of nationalist issues, especially as they had influenced literature, so that later he was able to give O'Leary credit for all that he himself had attempted in that field. Not that Yeats ever to his last day became a nationalist in the fullest sense of the word, but he did come to have a certain degree of imaginative sympathy for the Gaels as a race, especially certain picturesque aspects of the race, above all its legendry and superstition, which he too often mistook for religious conviction, something of which he seems to have had not the slightest perception.

Yeats was active in the foundation in 1892 of the National Literary Society of Dublin, of which Dr. Hyde was first president, and before which at the end of the first year Hyde delivered his address on the de-Anglicization of Ireland, which resulted in the organization of the Gaelic League. Obliged by family circumstances to spend part of each year in London, Yeats determined, in what he liked to think was a moment of supernatural insight, to attempt a similar organization of the numerous Irish authors and journalists then residing in the British capital. Out of a meeting which he called for the purpose at his father's house grew the Irish Literary Society of London, which was the factor chiefly instrumental in calling attention to the new Irish movement.

John O'Leary was the Society's first president, its membership presenting an interesting cross-section of Irish racial descent, background, achievement and opinion, from Standish O'Grady, whom Yeats wanted among "his" writers, Charles Gavan Duffy, a returned Odysseus, Dr. Hyde, already known as *An Craobhin*, to Lionel Johnson, the English Catholic poet and critic, with his strange gift for being articulately Irish on the strength of a drop of Irish blood. Or was it on the strength of the religious faith which he shared with the majority of the Irish?

As early as 1886 Yeats had published a volume of poems entitled *Mosada*, but it was not until 1889 with the publication of *The Wanderings of Oisin* that readers generally became aware not only of a new poetic talent, but of a new source of poetic inspiration, fascinating by its very strangeness and rendered more fascinating by the spell-like cadences fashioned for its utterance.

The subject of *Oisin* was not new to Irish writers; neither did it belong among Ireland's earliest poetic sources, since the work upon which Yeats based his verses was apparently the eighteenth-century *Lay of Oisin*, translated somewhat later by Thomas Flannery. But to the English reader to whom Yeats chiefly addressed himself it was, despite Macpherson's attempt to turn the Irish poet into a Scotsman, both startlingly new and mysteriously ancient.

Before *Oisin* (at first spelled *Usheen* by Yeats), he had written ballads and lyrics, some of which were strange and mysterious too, but in a most un-Celtic way, since they were expressions of Hindu, that is, Theosophical, pantheism, than which nothing could be farther removed from the concreteness of Celtic thought, even pagan Celtic thought. It would seem to be impossible to exclude this quality of concreteness from a work dealing with such an individualist as Oisin, but the poem is nevertheless pervaded by the trance-like quality, the almost mesmeric rhythms, of Yeats's earlier verses on Hindu themes. As a matter of fact this poem sounds the first notes in a prolonged incantation, even though such treatment necessarily does violence to the dynamic Fianna, not to mention the Danann Aengus, who is described as being perpetually sunk in a Druidic dream.

Yeats himself felt that in his earlier ballads he was not at his best, but the publication in 1897 of *The Secret Rose* showed an increase in the characteristics that made for the strangeness and myteriousness in *Oisin*. The volume contained many verses whose meaning seemed clear and even obvious, but as a whole it conveyed the unavoidable impression that for all the poet's desire to be accounted one with Davis and Mangan and Ferguson, his rhymes told more than their rhyming of a most un-Irish philosophy, which would have been strange and even repugnant to the elder poets.

This impression was confirmed by such succeeding volumes as *The Wind among the Reeds* (1889), *In the Seven Woods* (1904), *The Shadowy Waters* (1906), all of which are under the enchantment of the Rose, the esoteric symbolic rose, whether the subject be the rose itself, or the *Fiddler of Dooney*, or, as in the poems of a somewhat later date, *Baile and Ailinn* or *The Old Age of Queen Meave.*

Since the above summarizes the characteristics of most of Yeats's earlier and much of his later verse, it will do no harm at this point to consider those traits in some detail, if only for the sake of examining the extent to which they include those marks listed by Stopford Brooke and Thomas MacDonagh as characteristic of Irish poetry.

Yeats himself declared that the one way in which he was different from his generation was that he was very religious, and in writing of the group of young Irish writers as represented by himself and Lionel Johnson he maintained that what distinguished them was the spirituality of their outlook, which would certainly seem to be in agreement with Stopford Brooke's description of Irish poetry as religious. But in Yeats's case such spirituality was completely divorced from dogmatic religion. Inasmuch as true mysticism is by its very nature inseparable from belief in a Supreme Being, and, in its historical aspect, inseparable from the pursuit of moral perfection, such as characterizes the lives not only of the great Christian saints but even of many of the Hindu religious leaders, Yeats's pantheistic hedonism can scarcely be said to have had any religious significance whatever, although he persisted in his cultivation of Cabbalism to a point where he enraged Edward Martyn by his incantations at Tulira Castle and stirred even the patient Russell to violent dissent by his invention of a "system" based on the Great Year of the Ancients, in which the cycle of Anima Mundi is shown to be the equivalent of 26,000 years of our time, a theory which Russell found difficult to relate to life.

Developing when it did and in the environment into which he was brought by his father, Yeats's talent, however, was subjected to several influences that had nothing to do with Cabbalism or druid dreams. One of these was his admiration for William Morris, which coloured not only his poetry but especially his prose; another was the French Parnassian movement, whose distinctive mark was indefiniteness and whose use of symbols, so brilliantly studied by Mr. Edmund Wilson in *Axel's Castle* (1931), made poetry "so much a private concern of the poet's that it turned out to be incommunicable to the reader."

In the chapter which he devotes to Yeats Mr. Wilson recognized the extent to which this type of symbolism accounts for the strangeness of Yeats's early verse, as well as the extent to which maturing experience helped him to discard it. Mr. Wilson also devotes some pages to the completely ineluctable type of symbolism which the poet developed late in life and which he sets forth in *A Vision* (1924), the work in which he recounts with almost scientific precision the story of his intercourse with the "communicators" and the system of philosophy which he developed out of their "revelations." The story has been told so often that it is almost superfluous to repeat it here, but this attempt to account for the various elements in the poet's work would be incomplete without at least a brief summary of a matter by which he set such store, especially as the declared purpose of the "communicators" was to provide him with poetic assistance.

In the Introduction entitled *A Packet for Ezra Pound,* and dated March and October, 1928, he relates how four days after his marriage his wife surprised him by attempting automatic writing, with such results that he persuaded her to devote an hour or two a day to taking down what came from the invisible speaker, this, according to Yeats, being generally exciting and sometimes "so profound." When he offered to devote the rest of his life to piecing together the piecemeal fragments, the offer was declined by the spirits with the assurance that their purpose was to supply him with metaphors for poetry.

In the course of time a system of symbolism strange to both Yeats and his wife developed, and when he inquired how long it would take to complete it he was told it would take years. At last Mrs. Yeats became wearied and bored, and the method of communication changed from the written to the spoken word, for suddenly during a lecture tour in the United States Yeats heard his wife begin to talk in her sleep, not in her own person but as the mouthpiece of the communicators. There were other manifestations, frequent audible and visible phenomena, such as loud whistling, chairs and tables being violently struck and a succession of sweet odours, such as violets and incense.

The communications in sleep came to an end in 1920 and Yeats thereupon began the task of mastering the contents of fifty copy-books of script. In order to give what he considered a plausible setting to the fantastic experiences, he invented the implausible story of an Arabian traveller (*Michael Robartes and His Friends*), part of the myth being the supposed discovery of an ancient book, *Speculum Angelorum ad Hominem,* written by a certain Giraldus and printed at Cracow in 1594. This was the source out of which he developed his philosophy of the Great Wheel, a Cabbalistic system of cones based on mathematics and astronomy, in which every date was foretold by his instructors.

It is noteworthy that most of the events recorded were of literary or artistic importance, the kind of thing, that is, in which

Yeats would be most interested. Also noteworthy is the statement made by his "instructors" early in their intercourse: "Remember we will deceive you if we can." At this point the benighted Irish peasant, filled with a wholesome dread of the Father of Lies, would probably have reached for the holy water, but it never seems to have occurred to Yeats that they might have succeeded in their design.

This, then, was the book concerning which Yeats assured Pound that when it was finished it would reveal a new divinity, but the one fact it does reveal is the author's complete ignorance of philosophy. Happily, it is not necessary to master its perns and gyres in order to realize the extent to which the ideas it contains colour the poetry written subsequent to his marriage.

There was still another factor which helped to enrich and colour Yeats's poetry, if it did not actually assist in moulding and maturing his poetic gift, and this was no symbol from the world of dream, no phantom out of a region of mist, but a concrete fact of human experience: his love for Maud Gonne. It was his strange fate to love a woman who did not love him, at least not well enough to marry him, although she did not dislike him enough to dismiss him with any degree of finality, and it was part of that fate that he who loathed politics and all forms of agitation and who never became a complete nationalist, should have become enamoured of one of the fieriest of Irish rebels, a woman whose beauty, money, talent and time were expended in behalf of insurrection for the cause of Irish freedom. She is the subject of most of his love poetry, which on the whole is the least metaphysical of his verse. She is unequivocally the subject of his best lyric, *The Rose of the World*, which contains his two most felicitous lines:

> Troy passed away in one high funeral gleam,
> And Usna's children died.

As for the element of nationality, so stressed by Stopford Brooke, although Yeats wrote and talked a good deal about Ireland and Irishry, he was no Celt, and despite his friendship for

O'Leary, he never whole-heartedly shared O'Leary's convictions, while on more than one occasion he outraged those of Maud Gonne, notably in his poem on the Easter Rebellion of 1916, which he called a casual comedy.

Nevertheless, after the establishment of the Free State, he was elected to the Irish Senate on the strength of his having once been a member of the Irish Revolutionary Brotherhood. As a senator he allied himself strongly on the side of "Protestant rights," especially on the question of divorce, although hitherto his Protestantism had consisted chiefly in the fact that he was a member of no other denomination. He was, however, Protestant enough to maintain that Irish civilization had been retarded by Catholic women, who, he declared, had repeatedly checked the development of any refinement in Catholic households. He maintained that a continuity such as that which distinguished Coole (Lady Gregory's residence) had in consequence been impossible in any Catholic family since the Middle Ages. No one, it would seem, with either a knowledge of history or a sense of humour would have made a claim which makes the continuity of Coole stand out in glaring and discreditable contrast to the circumstances under which Catholic households maintained their precarious existence.

In 1917 Yeats married Georgie Hyde Lees, an Englishwoman whose mediumistic powers led to the writing of *A Vision*. Towards the end of his life his interest in the occult not only became intensified, but was merged in his interest in sex. As a matter of fact, his mystical theories were by this time almost wholly reduced to terms of sex, so that his biographer can say that eventually he came to see the mystical as the sexual life. To judge from his later poems, it would be more accurate to say that he regarded sex as the sole mystical experience. Certainly his *Last Poems* (1940) are the songs of a lecherous senility. What has he, he asks, save lust and rage to spur him into song? *The Herne's Egg*, a play written two years before he died, was considered too ribald to be produced.

In 1924 he was awarded the Nobel Prize for Poetry, and in 1932 was active in the organization of the Irish Academy of

Letters, the invitations to prospective members having been
signed by him and George Bernard Shaw. He died on January 28,
1939, at Roquebrune, France, where he was buried, the outbreak
of the second World War having prevented burial in Ireland. In
1948 the poet's body was brought back to Ireland, where he was
given a public funeral and buried with many honours.

There remains to be considered the matter of Yeats's poetic
form, as the basis of his claim to be regarded as a representative
Irish poet. Unquestionably that form is part and parcel of his
"Celticism." But is it any more authentic than his mysticism? He
does not, of course, qualify under the first of MacDonagh's requirements, since he was not of Gaelic stock, and knew no Gaelic,
except for an occasional phrase which he could scarcely have
avoided. His early poems, however (as MacDonagh himself con-
cedes, although he charges him with lacking a musical ear), have
certain melodious qualities that seem attributable to Irish speech,
"wavering rhythms" that belong to the very essence of Irish verse,
and which both speech and poetry owe to the racial character of
Irish music. Knowing no Gaelic, he could not have been directly
influenced by Irish versification, although in the course of time
a knowledge of its intricacies was pretty widely diffused by Hyde
and others, who strove to reproduce them in English.

The form of Yeats's verse in what may be called his middle
period was simplified out of all resemblance to his earlier style.
Even his mystical poems have a certain lucidity, while those that
are not cryptic have the clarity of good prose or of Pope's couplets, without the wit which made their clarity to shine. Instances
in kind are *His Phoenix* and *In Memory of Alfred Pollexfen*. From
this time to the end of his life, however, his verses take on a new
kind of obscurity, which is the result of the fact that so many of
them are private, being concerned with subjects of interest
chiefly to himself and his friends. The list of his later works
follows: *The Green Helmet* (1910); *Responsibilities* (1914);
The Wild Swans at Coole (1919); *Michael Robartes and the
Dancer* (1921); *The Tower* (1928); *The Winding Stair and
Other Poems* (1933); *Words for Music, Perhaps*.

That Yeats's fame and prestige continue to grow is evidenced by the increasing amount of critical writing of which his work is the subject. An impressive collection of this has been published in a volume entitled *The Permanence of Yeats* (1950), to which twenty-five distinguished contemporary critics have contributed. Their appraisals constitute a paean of praise in which there is not a dissenting note, unless something of misgiving is to be detected in the essays of J. Middleton Murry and T. S. Eliot. The pages from Mr. Edmund Wilson's *Axel's Castle* included here still seem to me to be the best treatment of Yeats's symbolism. Under the title of *The Golden Nightingale* (1949), Professor Donald Stauffer of Princeton has made a brilliant study of Yeats's poetic principles. *W. B. Yeats, Man and Poet,* by A. Norman Jeffares (1949) is not only a full-length biography which utilizes considerable new material, but a detailed critical study.

In my opinion the best of these works is *The Lonely Tower. Studies in the Poetry of W. B. Yeats,* by T. R. Henn, Fellow and Tutor at St. Catherine's College, Cambridge, where he is University lecturer in English. Among the qualifications which Professor Henn has brought to his exhaustive scrutiny of Yeats and his work are certain similarities of background, among them Irish birth, the social and political outlook of the Ascendancy and the profession of the Protestant religion. Under some circumstances these apparent advantages prove to be disadvantages, as they sometimes were for Yeats, but on the whole Professor Henn's book is an indispensable guide for readers of Yeats to whom his system of symbolism constitutes an obstacle to his meaning. Especially valuable in this respect are the chapters entitled *Myth and Magic, The Phases of the Moon,* and above all *The Vision,* in which he interprets Yeats's interpretation of history.

Detraction is the term (surely a strange one for a critic), which Professor Henn uses to describe opinions unfavourable to Yeats. Some of the opinions he lists are personal, such as insincerity, with which is linked the snobbery which Yeats himself made no attempt to conceal; some literary, such as the charge of obscurity, which surely implies no moral obliquity. The question of whether Yeats's poetry is out of touch with the world about him is a point on which it would seem to be possible to form an objective opinion without falling into the sin of detraction.

George Russell (universally known as AE because these were the only two letters of the Greek name, Æon, which he first chose as his pseudonym, that the printer could decipher), was a close associate of Yeats from their early Hermetic days. Like him he was a professed "mystic" in the Oriental sense of the word, although there was always a considerable difference in their outlook and methods. Born at Lurgan, Co. Armagh, of Protestant parents, at ten he went with his family to live in Dublin, which was thenceforward his home. He attended the Rathmines School, and later, at intervals, the Dublin school of art, where he met Yeats. At seventeen he became a clerk in a Dublin office, and for years earned a modest living as a cashier in a bank.

Unquestionably this obscurity of life was in great part due to Russell's so-called mystical ideas, which inspired him to a holy indifference to both fame and fortune.[1] He eventually became not only famous, but the best-loved literary personality in Ireland. As a matter of fact, although he was most active in the field of literature, it did not absorb his interest to the exclusion of other activities, because through Sir Horace Plunkett he became a worker for the Cooperative movement (the Irish Agricultural Organization Society), and spent much time travelling about Ireland establishing branches of the society. He was also at various times editor of *The Irish Homestead* (from 1905) and its successor, *The Irish Statesman* (from 1910), for which he wrote most of the contributions.

None of these duties ever interfered with the experiences about whose supernatural character he never had the slightest misgiving. "I really see them," he said quite simply of the visions which he was convinced had been his life-long experience. He seems never to have taken any steps to induce them, he never went in for Yeats's kind of the occult, for magic or spiritualism. His visions, he felt, emanated from another world, surrounding this

---

[1] *The Living Torch, A. E.* Edited by Monk Gibbon with an Introductory Essay. New York, 1938.

world, but in every way more beautiful, and inhabited by men and women who were not only more beautiful than human beings, but in every way superior. Since he was an artist as well as a poet he frequently painted pictures of what was vouchsafed to his sight, but to his alone.

What is incontestable about Russell is his greatness of soul, his sheer and unaffected goodness, for his conception of mysticism led him to insistence on the development of character rather than the practice of the occult. He himself credited much of his wisdom, which he would have been the last to call by that name, to Theosophy, although he never uses the word in his published works, and he resigned his membership in the Theosophical Society when its leader, Katherine Tingley, objected to his activities in behalf of the Cooperative movement. In his appreciation of him, Mr. Monk Gibbon remarks that while it was Theosophy which enabled him to endow the figures of Celtic mythology with symbolic meaning and to adapt its terminology to his own literary purpose, it would be wrong to regard Russell as a pagan enemy of Christian values, since he was not a pagan at all.

It is none the less true that in accordance with the spirit of Theosophy he was able to adopt Christian as well as pagan terminology, and in many instances to place the most august Christian mysteries on the same level with the pagan arcana. Still, there was never any deliberate irreverence in this. He was a Theosophist, he said, inasmuch as he recognized a degree of Divine goodness in the Sacred Books of all the world religions, calling what they possessed in common by the name of Divine Wisdom. In consequence of these ideas and practices it is possible to give a Christian interpretation to many of his verses, to read them, that is, in a sense of which Russell had no real knowledge or understanding, although he certainly knew the content of Christian belief.

The verses in his first book, *Homeward: Songs by the Way* (1894), are an expression of his conviction that this life is a pilgrimage toward the Light of Lights. Later volumes are entitled

The Earth Breath (1897); *Voices of the Stones* (1925); *Vale and
Other Poems* (1930). *Song and its Fountains* (1932) is especially
interesting for its analysis of his theories, both "mystical" and
literary, for the simplicity of his explanation that he always had
a sense of a will above his own without which he had no inspiration. His only novel, *The Avatars* (1933), he calls "a futurist fan-
tasy," but the future in which its action is set is obviously part
of the eternal Now.

In what sense is AE an Irish poet? Certainly not in any racial
or historical sense. The fact that his poems abound in the names
of the old pagan gods and the ancient heroes is only of incidental
significance, since they occur side by side with names out of the
Upanishads and the Christian Scriptures. His poetry is melodious,
much more consistently so than that of Yeats, but there is no
evidence of Gaelic influence in its melody or its diction. Although
he declared that composition did not come easy to him, most of
his verse seems to have the fluency which his critical sense condemned, but this facility, which usually indicates lack of thought,
is only apparent in him, because his work is highly symbolic, and
the symbols are the veil of a profound, if somewhat confused,
wisdom. When all is said, he was, as Mr. Gibbon observes, his
own masterpiece, for the testimony to the beauty of his character
is general and unequivocal. "I have known one great soul,"
Katharine Tynan said of him, while of his work as a whole
another Catholic said, "His life unconsciously has cast incense
on the altar of the Unknown God."

As editor of *The Irish Statesman*, the only literary journal then
published in Ireland, he wrote a great deal of prose criticism,
much of it, for its discernment, courage and quiet humour, of an
exceptionally high order. Thus he deplored certain aspects of
Yeats's work, notably his Cabbalistic system, recognized in
Francis Thompson's verse that which would keep his name
among the poets, wished that James Joyce had tried to penetrate
into the palace chambers rather than "into the crypts and cellars
and sewers of the soul."

It is in this phase of his work rather than in his poetry that

Russell's nationalism is manifest, but there is no questioning the *nationalistic effect* of his poetry, with its nobility of tone and its great heroic themes, on high-minded young patriots like Pearse and his associates. Certainly Russell regarded the Easter Rebellion as tantamount to a national resurrection, so that as Mr. Gibbon remarks, it is possible that he contributed the first spark of ignition to a conflagration from which he would have shrunk. Writing after the event, however, he likened Pearse to Cuchulain fighting against a host, and one of his finest poems is a tribute to MacSwiney slowly dying in Brixton prison. Russell's own death came in 1935. His share in the Abbey Theatre movement is treated below.

The influence of Theosophical doctrines on the work of Yeats and Russell having been briefly considered, it remains to deal with the relations between Theosophy and the Irish Renaissance so called, since acceptance of the doctrines obviously affects the right of the movement to be so designated.

Theosophy is a form of Buddhistic pantheism founded in New York in 1875 by the Russian, Madame Blavatsky, and introduced into Ireland by her disciple, Annie Besant, and the writings of A. P. Sinnett. The system presents itself as a religion, although it makes no claim to Divine origin, except for the supposed revelation to Madame Blavatsky, subsequently completely discredited, nor does it teach belief in a Supreme Being. Since it regards all religions as equally true and equally meritorious, the result is a syncretism which finds it possible to combine elements of Oriental religion and philosophy with various pagan forms, as well as certain of the more "picturesque" aspects of Christianity. It is a highly esoteric system, whose adepts claim to have acquired superhuman powers by their mastery of the occult laws of nature, hence the widespread practice of magic among its devotees and the use of the term "mysticism" to describe their ideas.

In Ireland, Theosophy meant the restoration of pagan practices, the ancient gods becoming the object of a worship never accorded them by the pagan Irish. The gods thus reinstated seem to have been the more poetic deities, members of the De Danann race, such as Aengus and Brigit, for to the best of my knowledge Crom Cruach has never been worshipped by the Theosophists, although according to their principles he was equally deserving of divine honours. These same principles accorded room beside the Celtic gods to Isis and Osiris, the gods of Greece and Rome, as well as of the American Indians, but when the Renaissance was being inaugurated the Irish gods and demi-gods, having been more recently discovered, lent themselves more readily to poetic treatment, since strangeness always has a certain literary value.

If it were merely a matter of literature, there could be no more objection to the introduction of beings from the Celtic pantheon than to those from the Greek, since obviously Aengus is as legitimate a subject of poetic treatment as Apollo, Brigit as Athena, but to the Theosophists the gods were not by any means mere poetic symbols; they were actual beings to whom were paid divine honours, in whose honour the ancient festivals were revived and new ceremonials were invented, while all manner of preternatural occurrences were credited to their aid. Christianity was not rejected, but it was subjected to even worse treatment by being placed on an equal footing with paganism and all the nature cults, to which, indeed, it was generally made vastly inferior. As a result, there was every excuse for those who knew no better to get the impression that the Irish had only been waiting for the abrogation of the penal laws and the restoration of their cultural privileges to rekindle the druidic fire which St. Patrick had extinguished and revive the worship of the deities whom they had forsaken under his guidance.

Ireland, it was implied, was a particularly fertile field for such ideas, since the Irish had so long been represented as an ignorant and superstitious people, who believed in ghosts and fairies. Now since the existence of ghosts and fairies is a matter which psychic societies consider worthy of serious study, such a belief is not necessarily an evidence of superstition, as Hamlet realized when he reminded Horatio, fresh from his studies, of the number of things in heaven and earth that were left unexplained by his philosophy. But superstition is always superstition, no matter what admixture of religion there may be in it. Belief in ghosts and fairies is not religion, nor a part of religion nor a substitute for religion, as the most ignorant Irishman, ignorant, that is, of everything save his religion, is well aware. But it is noteworthy that it was not among the Catholic Irish, that is among the reputedly ignorant and superstitious Irish, that Theosophical doctrines spread, but among the Dublin "intellectuals," since by grace of Madame Blavatsky a belief in ghosts and fairies suddenly ceased to be superstition, and became instead a superior sort of wisdom, as the knowledge and the practice of magic became an integral part of the cult.

Pagans the Irish undoubtedly once were, but they foresook paganism with unprecedented haste to embrace the Catholic religion, not in an outburst of emotion, in a kind of race hysteria, but with the clear-eyed sanity which, acted upon by grace, impelled them to cling to it not only during the lightsome Catholic era, but throughout seven dark centuries of unparalleled persecution. For it they relinquished even their cherished native culture, and despite their great love of learning chose poverty and ignorance rather than material well-being and temporal prosperity. That, they considered, was what it meant to be Irish; to an Irishman any other course was unthinkable. Can anyone believe that it was for the sake of their mythology they suffered? Henry VIII and Elizabeth, to give them their due, knew better than that; so did Cromwell and William of Orange, neither of whom would have lifted a finger to interfere with the worship of Manannan. They knew that it was the Mass that mattered, wherefore it was not for communing with "elementals" but for professing and teaching the Catholic religion that the priest was hunted like the wolf, as it was for accepting his teachings that an entire people was reduced to penury, starvation and ignorance. To imply, as did such exponents of the Irish Renaissance as Yeats and Russell, that in the Irish Christianity is merely skin-deep and that the pagan under the skin was awaiting only the enlightenment of Theosophy, to spring into the joyful freedom of nature, is to do a cruel injustice to an already too cruelly treated race.

Strictly speaking, therefore, that is, to the extent that the Irish Renaissance is represented by Theosophy and the Hermetic Society, the term is a misnomer. Inasmuch as it either ignores or attempts to discredit the source of Ireland's greatest culture, the Catholic religion, it is not a renaissance, that is, a restoration, but a mutilation, and any movement which ignores or attempts to discredit more than a thousand years of Irish history is not Irish.

However, apart from that represented by the "Dublin mystics," the Irish literary movement has aspects in the light of which it is seen to be a movement towards the creation of a new literature, new not because it is written by Irishmen, but because it is written by Irishmen in English under the influence of the Gaelic language and the Irish tradition, which means that it is necessarily an expression of the influence of the Catholic religion. Happily, this influence manifested itself from the very beginning, in the work, for instance, of such a man as Lionel Johnson, as it has continued to manifest itself to the present time, even in the midst of many evidences to the contrary.

Johnson, one of the close associates of Yeats's early years, was born in Kent about 1867, of a Sligo family. He was educated at Winchester and Oxford, where he became a disciple of Pater. He made himself a man of the most prodigious learning, a humanist in the highest sense, a devout Platonist, but never a pedant. Having entered the Catholic Church, his literary interests took a profoundly religious turn, his faith finding utterance in some of his finest lyrics, such as *Te Martyrum Candidatus, The Dark Angel* and *Old Silver*. His faith, too, was partly responsible for his interest in Irish affairs, which grew into an ardent love for Ireland and her people, for religion is an integral part of what may be called his Irish poems, and Yeats said that Johnson saw Irish nationality and the Catholic religion as one sacred tradition.[2]

Some of his Irish poems (*Parnell, To Weep Irish, Celtic Speech, St. Columba*) were included in the volume entitled simply *Poems*, published in 1895. Two years later appeared *Ireland and Other Poems* (dedicated to Mrs. Clement Shorter who, as Dora Sigerson, was a poet in her own right), of which the title poem is an

[2] *Trembling of the Veil*, p. 273.

impassioned lament for Ireland's sorrows, its lines aglow with the names of Irish heroes. Together with the pagan sagas, the annals of sanctity are invoked in witness of past greatness; anger flares up into words of malediction at the memory of immitigable anguish, only to be hushed into prayer, a rapturous plea to the Mother of Sorrows, entreating her to set Ireland free. Johnson's love for Ireland made him an active member of the London Irish Literary Society, Yeats bearing witness to the multiplicity of his contributions, and a devoted worker for the Gaelic League.

In his Foreword to her *Collected Poems* (1930) AE calls Katharine Tynan the earliest singer of the Irish Renaissance, a statement which is warranted by the fact that her first volume of poems, entitled *Louise de la Vallière*, was published in 1885. There was little about the volume to indicate that it was the first flowering of a new Irish poetry, for only three of the poems it contains are on Irish subjects (*The Flight of the Wild Geese, The Dead Patriot*, and *Waiting*), the remainder of its contents being in an exceedingly Pre-Raphaelite vein. But in the numerous volumes which followed (and Russell bears witness to her facility, the facility of the born singer) her verse grew increasingly Irish. She came, as a matter of fact, to have a most distinctive style, which, while it is often marred by defects growing out of her facility, is always characterized by charm and grace. It might even be said that it is precisely of her persistent charm that the reader is prone to weary, whereas of any single poem it would be difficult to complain.

She was born in Dublin in 1861, and was educated in part at the Dominican convent at Drogheda, but mostly at home, especially by her own cultivation of literature. Her literary aspirations received every encouragement from her father, whence it followed that she was able to go to London, where she became a member of the Irish literary colony. In 1893 she married Henry Hinkson, who had been a student at TCD and was himself a writer. Thereafter she lived for many years in England, writing much poetry and fiction, but in her later years returned to Ireland to live.

All her poetry is essentially feminine, much of it strongly

maternal, an instinct which impels her to write tenderly not only of her own children, but of the Christ Child, sometimes in terms that are almost too human, of any children in relation to Christ. For her work is predominantly religious and deeply spiritual, which accounts for the generally recognized Franciscan quality of her exquisite nature poetry. In her Autobiography (*Twenty-five Years Reminiscences*, 1913), she describes her father in terms of such simple devotion that it is not surprising to find her writing poignantly of him, especially in his old age and after his death.

Ireland, however, especially under the affectionate title of *The Old Country*, and all things Irish, are her constant theme, sometimes indirectly as when she writes in Irish phraseology on any subject whatever, calling the Blessed Virgin, for instance, by the Irish title *Herself*. While Mrs. Hinkson's form was never directly affected by the Irish forms, it has a lilt that owes nothing to any model save the music in her soul, which had an Irish rhythm. She often affects English archaisms, such as *clomb, sith, St. Luke, his Summer,* which enhance the simplicity of her verse, while at the same time they detract from its spontaneity. But AE was right in maintaining that of all the poets in the early movement she kept closest to the normal.

Irish of the Irish was P. J. McCall, the disarming simplicity of whose verse seems at first sight to link him with the *Nation* poets rather than with those of the Irish Revival. Closer acquaintance, however, shows it to be steeped in Irish lore, especially the native music. McCall was born in Dublin in 1861, and educated at the Catholic University School. However, although he was learned enough to make several translations from the Irish, his verse, published under the titles *Irish Noinins* (1894), *Songs of Erin* (1899), and *Fireside Songs* (1911), deals almost entirely with the peasantry and deliberately avoids literary artifice. Many of the poems, such as *The Yellow Purse, The Dark Slender Boy,* and *If All the Young Maidens,* were written to be sung to traditional airs, but some of his best work is represented by half humorous but never burlesque sketches of peasant character, such as *Herself and Myself.*

In similar vein are the verses of Francis J. Fahy, born at Kinvara, Co. Galway, in 1854, and active in various literary movements, especially the Southwark Literary Society, which preceded the London organization. He may almost be said to have antedated the movement of which he formed a part by the publication in 1887 of his *Irish Songs and Poems,* the best known of his songs being the famous *Ould Plaid Shawl.*

That men like McCall and Fahy should have captured as they did the precise accent of Irish-English speech, should have found words as they did for the utterance of the Irish heart, is not an occasion for wonder, since they came of Gaelic stock, but for Alfred Percival Graves it was a different matter. Born in Dublin in 1846, he was the son of Right Rev. Charles Graves, an Anglican clergyman who became bishop of Limerick. He was educated partly in England, but took his degree at the University of Dublin in 1871.

Graves has been given credit for raising the Irish dialect to the level of a literary language. The critic who made the claim misunderstood, I think, both the nature of that dialect, an understanding of which would involve an understanding both of its development as a dialect, and the purpose of Mr. Graves in using it as a literary vehicle. He was a sincere student of everything Irish, especially Irish music, his knowledge of which enabled him to write such singable verse as *Father O'Flynn.* That song in praise of the *soggarth* is alone sufficient evidence of the extent to which this Protestant ecclesiastic's son had penetrated to the soul of his Catholic compatriots.

Among his published volumes of verse are *Songs of Killarney* (1873) and *Irish Songs and Ballads* (1880). The *Irish Poems* of Alfred Percival Graves, published in 1908, consists of two volumes, of which the first is entitled *Songs of the Gael, A Gaelic Story-Telling,* with a preface by Douglas Hyde, and the second, *Countryside Songs: Songs and Ballads,* with a preface by the author himself, in which he says that if he has been successful in this lyrical field it is partly because he not only had a countryside upbringing and the consequent advantage of constantly hearing the "translation into English of Irish idioms which renders the speech of the Kerry peasant so peculiarly poignant and picturesque." In addition to this he maintains that in Hyde's *Love Songs* and the translations of Edward Walsh, Sir Samuel Ferguson, Sigerson and Mangan, he had the best published examples of the poetry of the Western Gael.

His own poems are not all equally good, but they are all Irish, most of them in the dialect to which he is credited with rendering such great service, many of them in a quizzical popular vein, but a few are lyric bursts of exquisite literary quality, such as *I'd Roam the World Over with You,* or the unforgettable *Little Red Lark,* to have heard which is to have heard the very voice of Ireland uplifted rapturously at dawn.

Mr. Graves edited a number of noteworthy collections of Irish verse and acted as editor-in-chief of *Every Irishman's Library.* His autobiography, *To Return to all That* (Robert Graves, author of *Goodbye to all That,* is the poet's son), appeared in 1930. The close association of Alfred Percival Graves with the Irish Revival is certified by the fact that he served for two terms as president of the Irish Literary Society. Besides his poetry, he is the author of *Irish Literary and Musical Studies* (1913), which include data concerning certain figures in the early movement, based largely on information received from his father, who was Petrie's biographer. Among his translations from the Gaelic is *A Celtic Psaltery* (1917), which consists of close and free translations from Irish, Scotch-Gaelic and Welsh poetry of a religious or serious character, among its most interesting features being a group of *Triads.*

There is a sense in which Jane Barlow and Emily Lawless reveal a certain kinship. It lies in the fact that they were both by birth members of the Ascendancy class, and yet they both contrived, Miss Barlow invariably, Miss Lawless under certain circumstances, to write from the standpoint of the people. Jane Barlow's *Bogland Studies* (1893) do not represent the best of

her work, and yet they are in the same vein. They are poems in
the dialect with which she showed herself so familiar and which
she uses to depict Irish character or to present a situation in strikingly graphic fashion, as in *The Ould Master* and *Walled Out.*
These sketches lack the range of her prose, but it remains nothing
short of amazing to find this daughter of an Anglican clergyman
displaying so complete an understanding of the Catholic attitude
towards the "souper," as she does in *Past Praying For.*

As the eldest daughter of Lord Cloncurry, the Hon. Emily
Lawless (b. 1845; d. 1913), was, on the evidence of her novels,
thoroughly on the side of her class, but she was one of those of
whom it was said that they were rebels when they wrote poetry.
Nothing could be more openly nationalistic than Emily Lawless's
With the Wild Geese (1902), whose preface by Stopford Brooke
stresses her quick response to the "grief and charm" of Ireland,
as shown in her joy at recognizing a bit of bog cotton growing
in the Tyrol. This sentiment is especially evident in the second
of her two poems on *Fontenoy,* of which the scene is given as
"after the battle; early dawn, Clare Coast":

> "*Mary mother, shield us! say what men are ye,*
> *Sweeping past so swiftly on this morning sea?*"
> "Without sails or rowlocks, merrily we glide
> Home to Corca Bascinn on the brimming tide."
>
> "*Jesus save you, gentry! why are ye so white,*
> *Sitting all so straight and still in this misty light?*"
> "Nothing ails us, brother, joyous souls are we
> Sailing home together on the morning sea.
>
> "Cousins, friends and kinsfolk, children of the land,
> Here we come together, a merry, rousing band;
> Sailing home together from the last great fight,
> Home to Clare from Fontenoy in the morning light.
>
> "Men of Corca Bascinn, men of Clare's Brigade,
> Harken, stony hills of Clare, hear the charge we made;
> See us come together, singing from the fight,
> Home to Corca Bascinn in the morning light."

An impassioned love for Ireland is the characteristic note of the work of Ethna Carbery (Anna Johnson, d. 1902), whether in her prose sketches (see above) or in the poems collected under the title *The Four Winds of Erinn*. For some reason she is not included in the Brooke-Rolleston anthology, which is otherwise so comprehensive, and yet many a lesser one might have made way for her, whether she is writing verse of an obviously personal sort, as in *Our Road, The Quest* or *The Heathery Hill,* or lines which catch something of the weirdness of folk superstition without ever misrepresenting the underlying soundness of Christian faith, as in *The Love Talker* or *Haunted.* Her poems are filled with ancient bardic lore, old names of story, *Niamh, Tirnan-og, Fionnuala, Lugh,* gleam across her pages, but she is at her best in the songs which reveal her devotion to Ireland, whether she refers to the land under the old poetic names of *Mairin ni Cullinan* and *Shiela na Gara,* or with tears laments the *Passing of the Gael:*

The whip of hunger scourged them from the glens and quiet moors,
But there's a hunger of the heart that plenty never cures;
And they shall pine to walk again the rough road that is yours.

They are going, going, going, and we cannot bid them stay;
The fields are now the strangers' where the strangers' cattle stray.
O Kathaleen na Houlihan, your way's a thorny way.

If the poet's gift be judged by bulk of production or range of theme, then Moira O'Neill's is of a decidedly minor order, but she has used it for the purpose of giving such exquisite expression to some of the most abiding human emotions that she cannot be overlooked. Even taking both her published volumes, *Songs of the Glens of Antrim* (1900) and *More Songs of the Glens of Antrim* (1921), into consideration does not give us more than a handful of lyrics, but these are so filled with a combination of the tear and the smile, or poignant sadness and dry humour, that they entitle her to a high place among Ireland's poets.

Of Nora Hopper's *Ballads in Prose* (1894) Yeats wrote that they haunted him as few books had ever done. For the most part they contain so much of Yeats's own type of pseudo-paganism that this reaction is scarcely to be wondered at. Written in a highly artificial poetic prose that is by way of being Celtic in flavour, the ballads recount strange, dream-like episodes that are more than half allegory, a mixture of paganism and Christianity which, except in the case of *The Soul of Maurice Dwyer,* are on the side of the old gods. Yet interspersed through these prose ballads are lovely lyrics, such as *Silk of the Kine* and *The Lay Brother* (which is practically identical with Katharine Tynan's *In Iona*), verses that almost range Nora Hopper among the poets of nationalism.

William Larminie, perhaps best known for his prose collection of *West Irish Folk Tales and Romances* (1893), was also the author of several volumes of verse: *Glanlua and Other Poems* (1889) and *Fand and Other Poems* (1892). The poems in *Glanlua,* which include *The Tower of Glass, The Finding of Hy Brasil* and *The Return of the Gods,* are rather conventional in form but expressive of great love for Ireland. As the title poem of the second volume shows, he sought inspiration for its contents chiefly from the Red Branch, but AE considered him a mystic, who read into the old epics a mystical, because an allegorical, significance. This poet, who was born in Mayo and lived most of his life in the vicinity of Dublin, died in 1899.

To some critics it may seem indefensible that the theme of nationalism should loom so large in Irish literature. To them the utterance of the spirit of patriotism to a degree where an anthologist like Brooke is warranted in listing it first among the sources of poetic inspiration may serve merely as an occasion for condemnation, on the ground that such poetry belongs with the literature of propaganda, which is practically to deprive it of all right to be considered literature at all.

But love of country is universally recognized as one of the great human emotions, of which all the literatures of the world contain noble utterances. Most of them, it is true, like John of Gaunt's famous eulogy of England or Vergil's tribute to the Roman race, through the mouth of Anchises, are testimonials to the greatness of national achievement, paeans of victory, songs of exultation

and joy. Ireland's history has afforded her poets few opportunities
for such songs, but if a poet may rejoice in his country's greatness
and glory without being denied the title of poet, then surely the
title cannot be denied to one who bewails his country's sorrows,
—at least it cannot be denied on that score alone.

In happy countries the spirit of nationalism is taken so much
for granted that it is relegated to the background of national life,
leaving the poets free to write of the thousand themes that
clamour at the gates of their imaginations, at least until some
threat to the national life is offered, when they burst into poetic
activity without concern for their literary status. Since for centuries the Irish felt themselves constantly confronted by such a
threat, it was inevitable that nationalism should acquire an importance out of proportion to what it has among other peoples,
that it should become an occasion of perennial controversy, upon
whose merits the entire population was split into two camps. It
thus became an inescapable factor in Irish life and as such a
legitimate subject of literature, especially poetry.

It was also inevitable that religion should be so closely associated with nationalism as generally, and often unfortunately, to
be identified with it. The misfortune lies in the fact that in some
cases the result is a confusion, making for the worst interests of
both. Needless to say, it was chiefly the Catholic religion, especially as tested and tried by the penal laws, described by Hardiman as the "most unjust and ferocious enactments that ever
disgraced the code of any civilised country" (quoted by Denis
Gwynn in his *Life of Edward Martyn*), that kept the spirit of
nationalism alive. Never throughout the centuries had the Gael
been subdued or the conquest completed. The spirit of rebellion
seethed perpetually beneath the surface and from time to time
broke out into open, desperate and violent revolt. The most important of such "risings" were the Desmond rebellion in 1569-
1582; that of the United Irishmen in 1798; Robert Emmet's rebellion in 1803; the Young Ireland rising in 1848; and the Fenian
attempt in 1865, after the violent suppression of which all tendency to revolt was apparently ended.

But unquestionably the language movement and the literary

revival, though this consequence may have been far from the intentions of many of their leaders, helped to fan the spark of nationalism into a flame, a flame which grew stronger and steadier under the influence of new political parties, some of whose most important members were men of no slight literary ability. Eminent among these parties was Sinn Fein, of which Edward Martyn was president for four years and which under the leadership of Arthur Griffith, its founder, spread throughout the entire country somewhat after the manner of the Gaelic League, although the two organizations were completely separate. Indeed it was to avoid even the appearance of identity between them that Dr. Hyde resigned the presidency of the League.

Griffith was born in Dublin in 1872 and was educated by the Christian Brothers. He was one of the co-founders of the Celtic Literary Society in 1889, and ten years later, after a sojourn in South Africa, established the *United Irishman*, the organ in which most of his writings appeared. In 1906 he organized the Sinn Fein movement, whose membership at first included men of widely different types of political opinion, though all nationalist, from Fenians to Parliamentarians.

The outbreak of the first World War, with the controversy over conscription in Ireland, precipitated several crises, the climax coming with the Easter Rebellion of 1916. This is too often described as a Sinn Fein rebellion, the fact that it was not being proved by the non-participation of Griffith. In 1918, during the troubles which followed the Easter Rising, Griffith was arrested, but was later released. In 1918 he was elected a member of Parliament for Cavan, in 1920 became acting president of the Irish Free State, the following year he was again arrested and again released. He was one of the signers of the treaty between the Free State and England in 1921, and in 1922 was elected president of the Dail. He died in the same year.

This outline of this particular phase of the nationalist movement is necessitated by the fact that several of its most important figures were men who would not in the long run be satisfied with anything short of complete separation from England and freedom to establish an independent government, which included the freedom to restore the national culture. This meant that culturally they all stood for the restoration of an Irish Ireland, including the revival of the Gaelic as a spoken tongue, the establishment of a native educational system and the production of a national literature. Consequently they included many men of intellectual power, such as Eoin MacNeill, leader of the Irish Volunteers and vice-president of the Gaelic League, an Irish scholar of much distinction, who then occupied at University College, Dublin, the chair to which O'Curry had been called by Newman forty-eight years before. Among his claims to literary eminence are the following works: *Notes on the Ogham Inscriptions; Early Irish Population Groups; Celtic Religion; Early Irish Laws and Institutions; Phases of Irish History; Celtic Ireland.*

It was natural that the nationalist movement should attract a number of poets, or perhaps it would be more accurate to say that the fiery idealistic souls of poets were necessarily drawn, as such souls have always been drawn, to the side of the beckoning ideal, the apparently lost cause and the bright eyes of danger. In any case, all the poets who immediately follow allied themselves, either by outspoken sympathy or by active participation, with the nationalist groups described collectively, but inaccurately, as Sinn Fein.

Foremost among these is Padraic Colum, a figure of exceptional interest and importance in the history of the Irish Literary Revival, chiefly because he sprang of native Irish stock so that there was no need for any deliberate working up of either language or spirit to qualify him as an Irish writer. As such he has achieved distinction as poet, playwright and prose writer, his poetry amply demonstrating the fact that he is in the direct line of bardic descent.

He was born in 1881 in Co. Longford, a non-Gaelic speaking region, where his father was master of a workhouse, a fact which gives special significance to his play *Thomas Muskerry*. While still a child Colum went to live in Cavan with his grandmother, in whose house his childish imagination was fed, as Walter

Scott's had been under similar circumstances, by scraps of poetry, stories and legends. When he went to Dublin as a young man the Celtic Revival was reaching the period of its first vitality, and it was natural that he should be drawn into it to the extent of becoming one of its most active participants, especially through the writing of poetry, which was first published by Arthur Griffith, and of plays, the first of which was produced when Colum was only twenty.

He was a prominent member of the group which included Yeats and Russell, Lady Gregory and Synge, but he was also a member of the Irish Revolutionary Brotherhood, and in 1911 he founded the *Irish Review* with James Stephens and Thomas MacDonagh. In the following year he married Mary Gunning Maguire, who as Mary Colum has won eminence as a critic, especially in the United States, where she and her husband have been living since 1914.

There are many circumstances that leave Colum's nationalistic convictions in no manner of doubt, poems such as the *Lament for Arthur Griffith*, whom he compares to Odysseus, because he made "the plan that drove the strangers from the house," and the exultant lines on the death of Roger Casement. But in the long run his nationalism has a quality that needs no affirmation of patriotic devotion. It consists in other things than this,—in an unutterable sense of place, an inarticulate, almost an unconscious assertion of race, of blood. It is this blood that speaks in his verses; their metre is the measure of the Irish pulse, intense, eager, restrained, now racing, now reined in.

In the poems contained in *Wild Earth*, which is dedicated to AE, "who fostered me," it is Ireland, not under the guise of the allegorical Dark Rosaleen, but the land itself, the ancient race, that speaks, that sings. Here and elsewhere in his work it is upon the authentic Irish landscape that we look, the furrowed fields, the wet hills, the grassy pastures, and across that scene move the figures of unforgettable men and women: the old woman wandering the roads longing for a house of her own, "a little house," the ploughman looming gigantic against the sunset, the woman beyond the half-door crooning a wisp of song beside the slowing cradle, the "poor scholar" making the characteristic choice of classical learning above the stir of political agitation.

For such poems Mr. Colum has contrived a melodious measure, music such as the harpers fitted to the blackbird's songs, such as bereaved women brought out of their soul's anguish to keen their dead, such as the saints found for the accents of their prayer. Nowhere in it all is there any artificial Celticism, any imitation of archaic forms. There is, as a matter of fact, scarcely any suggestion of a remote bardic influence or of the historic past. Not that Mr. Colum is not familiar with such sources of inspiration, upon which he draws freely when it suits his purpose. For besides the *Collected Poems* (1932), comprising the volumes previously published under the titles *Reminiscences, Dramatic Legends, Dramatic Idylls, Wild Earth, Other Lands and Seas, Creatures, Old Pastures,* Mr. Colum is the author of two poems based upon Irish legendary history, *The Story of Lowry Maen* (1937) and *The Frenzied Prince* (1943), the text of which Middle Irish romance was edited for the Irish Texts Society by J. G. O'Keefe under the title *The Adventure of Suibhne Geilt.*[3] He has recently (1948) edited an *Anthology of Irish Verse.*[4]

As a prose writer Mr. Colum is best known for his *The Road Round Ireland* and *Cross Roads in Ireland,* books which contain an entertaining medley of travel, legend, history and literary criticism. He has earned a considerable reputation as a folk-lorist, of the Irish as well as of other races.

There is a certain, though slight, resemblance between the work of Colum and that of Joseph Campbell, who wrote under the Irish form of his name, *Seosamh Mac Cathmhaoil,* but the

[3] See Myles Dillon's excellent summary of this under the title of *Buile Shuibne (The Frenzy of Suibne),* in his *Cycles of the Kings,* p. 68.
[4] Other recent anthologies of Irish verse are Kathleen Hoagland's *1000 Years of Irish Poetry. The Gaelic and Anglo-Irish Poets from the Earliest Times to the Present* (1947), and a selection from the work of thirty-seven contemporary poets, edited by Devin A. Garrity and entitled *New Irish Poets* (1948).

resemblance is due solely to the existence in their work of certain racial traits, for nothing could be more unlike than their individual talents. Campbell was born at Belfast in 1881, and developed into an artist and a playwright as well as a poet. Leaving Ireland in the 1920's, he became head of the school of Irish Studies at Fordham University, New York City, but eventually returned to Ireland, where he died in 1944.

Most of his work is contained in a small volume entitled *The Mountainy Singer* (1919), which includes the contents of a still smaller one published in 1907 under the title *The Gilly of Christ*. Like Colum's, these poems are filled with the sound, the colour and the fragrance of Ireland. Like his also they express the grief and the anger and the religious faith of the Gael. He contrives to instill into his verse something of the spirit of Christian mysticism, something that is more truly mystical than anything the Dublin mystics ever succeeded in infusing into theirs. It may be that it is not through any genuine mystical sense that he writes of the gilly of Christ, "the mate of Mary's Son," running the Irish roads or sleeping among the Irish hills, that he describes "the White Christ" Himself, dwelling among the same scenes, although there is a very real sense in which Christ travels the roads of all the world, in which he walks upon the water not only of Gennesareth and Thames but of the Erne and the Liffey. Surely it is in conformity with the soundest Christian doctrine that Campbell writes:

> Every shuiler is Christ.
> Then be not hard or cold:
> The bit that goes for Christ
> Will come a hundred fold.

From a religious source, at least from a racial sense as doubtless out of a depth of personal religious conviction and enlightened faith, Campbell derived the power to write with appropriate sublimity of the most sublime Christian mysteries:

> O glorious Childbearer,
> O secret womb,
> O gilded bridechamber, from which hath come
>   the sightly Bridegroom forth,

> O amber veil,
> Thou sittest in heaven, the white love of
> the Gael.
> Thy head is crowned with stars,
> Thy radiant hair
> Shines like a river through the twilight air;
> Thou walkest by trodden ways and
> trackless seas
> Immaculate of man's infirmities.

If Irish poetry in general is characterized by the themes of nationalism, religion and rebellion (which is merely an extreme type of nationalism), then that poetry may be said to reach a kind of climax in the work of three men, Pearse, Plunkett and MacDonagh, scholars and poets, devout Catholics, whose poetry is ablaze with love of their country, rebels who died in the conviction that they were serving both.

Padraic Henry Pearse was born in Dublin in 1879, the eldest of four children, of whom two were girls, his brother, William, sharing his life, his interest, his activities, and dying the same death only a few hours after him. Padraic first attended the school of the Irish Christian Brothers, but he used to say that his early education he owed to his aunt, who told him stories out of the Gaelic past and filled him with enthusiasm for everything Irish. He made unusual progress in Gaelic studies, joined the Gaelic League at an early age, and after receiving his bachelor's degree (1901) at the Royal University (now the National University), and being admitted to the bar, he taught Irish at University College, Dublin, at the same time as MacNeill.

In 1903 he became editor of *An Claidheamh Soluis*, the organ of the Gaelic League, during which period he wrote a series of attacks on the so-called National educational system, which he called the Murder Machine, and undertook those studies of other systems which led to the foundation of his famous school, St. Enda's, which he established on the old Irish custom of fosterage.

The educational theories to which he gave such practical application were merely part of his dream of an Irish Ireland, which began with his activities in the Gaelic League, for whose founder he cherished the profound personal admiration which makes a man a disciple. To this he later bore witness in characteristically vehement language when he said, "I love and honour Douglas Hyde. I have served under him since I was a boy. I am willing to serve until he can lead and I can serve no longer." Never in any real sense, despite Dr. Hyde's averseness to politics, did that time come.

St. Enda's was first established at Rathmines (1908), Dublin, but two years later it was removed to the Hermitage, already distinguished in the history of nationalism and Irish culture as having been the home of William Elliott Hudson. A school for girls under the patronage of St. Ita was established and conducted along the same lines.

As Mr. Desmond Ryan points out,[5] Pearse became the educationalist of the Gaelic League, since in addition to his practical experiments in bilingual education he wrote texts and articles on educational subjects. An orator of exceptional gifts, he was likewise a Gaelic writer of distinction, who combined his academic and literary methods to expound his theory of "the art form against the folk form," a highly desirable attitude if folk-lore is ever to be anything more than the raw material of literature, the source of literary inspiration rather than its fruit.

The dramatic events which had been in the making throughout Padraic Pearse's life moved forward with terrible speed to their catastrophe. Pearse, who had taken the oath of the Irish Revolutionary Brotherhood in 1912 or 1913, had been made head of its secret Military Council. In that capacity he ordered a three-day march and manoeuvers of the Irish Volunteers for Easter, 1916, an action which was really intended to be a rising. Eoin Mac-Neill, as head of the Volunteers, but ignorant of the secret measures of the IRB, countermanded the order, with the result that the Rising, which might in any case have been doomed from the outset, never assumed more than local proportions, and was suppressed within a week, a week which nevertheless changed the course of Irish history. Pearse had been elected presi-

[5] *The Sword of Light*, p. 239.

dent of the Provisional Government, and as such issued a proclamation, signed by a number of his fellow-patriots, establishing the Irish Republic, the Citizen Army flag of the Plough and Stars was flown over several public buildings, including the General Postoffice, where the rebels held out until Friday. On that day, in order to prevent further bloodshed, Pearse surrendered, was placed under arrest, tried by court martial, and, with fifteen others was shot in the yard of Kilmainham, where the bodies of all were buried in quicklime, the first act in a war of retaliation which shocked the civilized world. Is it too fantastic to detect amid the turmoil thus stirred up, an echo of Ferguson's *Lament for Thomas Davis?*

> Oh, brave young men, my love, my pride, my promise,
>   'Tis on you my hopes are set,
> In manliness, in kindliness, in justice,
>   To make Erin a nation yet.

Pearse's published poems are strangely few, twenty-two in number, strangely few because they are so patently the work of a man whose very habits of thought were poetic. They are unmistakably Irish, not only because they are for the most part Irish in theme and in quality, nor even because they are so profoundly spiritual even when their theme is not religious. The tragic pathos of *I am Ireland* and *The Rebel* could find utterance only through one whose soul had become the lodging of the pent-up grief of seven centuries. *The Rann of the Little Playmate* and *Christ's Coming*, written though they are by a man of broad culture, are born of a faith as simple and implicit as that of any peasant woman in his beloved Connacht. Even before it found outlet in his verse, Pearse's faith was expressed in his life, for as one of his biographers says of him, "Pearse was more than a patriot, he was a virtuous man. He possessed all the qualities which go to the making of a saint. . . . Aodh de Blacam has said somewhere that it would not be astonishing if Pearse were canonised some day." It is not to be wondered at, therefore, that few as his poems are, several of them should express an intense personal devotion to Christ, nor that most of his stories should reflect this, the dominant principle of his life.

But what is especially noteworthy about his verses is the extent to which they are charged with a sense of prophecy, an awareness not so much of doom (Pearse would never have called it that), as of high destiny. This is especially evident in *The Mother*, for surely it is the mother who was to lose both her sons in Easter Week who speaks these words:

> I do not grudge them, Lord, I do not grudge
> My two strong sons that I have seen go out
> To break their strength and die, they and a few
> In bloody protest for a glorious thing.
> They shall be spoken of among the people,
> The generations shall remember them,
> And call them blessed;
> But I will speak their names to my own heart
> In the long nights;
> The little names that were familiar once
> Round my dead hearth.
> Lord, Thou art hard on mothers:
> We suffer in their coming and their going;
> And though I grudge them not, I weary, weary
> Of the long sorrow—and yet I have my joy:
> My sons were faithful and they fought.

Thomas MacDonagh was born in Cloughjordan, Co. Tipperary, in 1878. His parents were teachers and he was educated in private schools and at the National University, where he received his M.A., but in order to perfect his Gaelic he spent some time in the Aran Islands and the Irish-speaking districts of Munster. He became a lecturer on English literature at University College, Dublin, and later a member of Pearse's staff at St. Enda's, living in nearby Rathfarnham with his wife, son and daughter. He joined the Irish Volunteers, participated in the Easter Rebellion and affixed his signature to the document proclaiming the Republic. He was seized, tried by court martial and shot at Kilmainham. A witness said at the time, "They all died well, but Mac-Donagh like a prince." Besides his poems, which will here be

briefly considered, he was the author of a play entitled *Pagans*
and of the posthumously published *Literature in Ireland*, a
brilliant critical study of the subject, which lifts many aspects of
it out of the confusion which has hitherto deterred many would-
be students.

Despite the fact that as a poet MacDonagh was more prolific
than Pearse, his poetic output seems slight, except when one
remembers that the author was cut off before he was forty, with
many songs unsung. With Pearse he shared many things, above
all a great love of beauty, through all his praise of which runs a
sense, not so much of its short duration, which sense heightens all
our perception of it, but of the shortness of his own time of en-
joyment. Strangely enough (although perhaps it is not strange)
what most stirs him in nature is its stormy aspects, high winds
and driving rain and winter weather, although he can exult
in "the coming in of Summer."

Whatever its subject, most of his poetry is an outpouring of
rapturous idealistic human love, and its tone, again regardless of
theme, is unmistakably Irish. As might have been expected of so
distinguished an Irish scholar, many of the verses are explicitly
Irish, either because they are translations from the Gaelic, the
most famous of these being his rendering of *Eamonn an Chnuic*
(*Ned of the Hill*), or because they are characteristic sentiments
of an essential Celt. The most typical of these are the verses
collected under the title *The Book of Images*, because of their use
of symbolism. To some readers they may seem reminiscent of
Blake, but they are too unequivocally Christian for the resemblance to be anything but superficial. His comments in the Preface
to the first edition of the book explain both his understanding
of the use of mystical symbolism and the difference between his
conception of the matter and that of Yeats and Russell: "With
regard to my mystical poems. . . . I wish to say simply that I owe
nothing to any other inspiration than the experiences which they
record. I have no theories of mysticism. The images here en-
shrined I have known since childhood as I have known myself,

without any introduction that I am aware of, and without any need of explanation."[6]

The tragic end which makes every line that these men wrote so poignantly meaningful is nowhere more clearly felt than in the work of Joseph Plunkett. The son of Count and Countess Plunkett, he was born in Dublin in 1887, and was educated at Catholic University School and Belvedere College, going at eighteen to Stonyhurst, where for two years he followed the philosophy course, a subject in which he continued to be intensely interested. At the same time he became interested not merely in an academic sense, but as the food for his own piety and his poetic thought, in the writings of the great Catholic mystics, their influence being manifest throughout his work. Of exceptional importance to his life and work was his friendship with MacDonagh, then teaching at St. Enda's, since both young men were ardent nationalists, both were poets of an almost obsolete idealistic type, and each had a high respect for the other's critical judgment.

It was MacDonagh who selected the contents for Plunkett's first book, *The Circle and the Sword*, published in 1911, in which same year Plunkett became associated with MacDonagh, Colum and James Stephens in the editing of the newly founded *Irish Review*, of which in 1913 Plunkett became editor, in succession to Colum. In 1914, with MacDonagh and Edward Martyn he helped to found the Irish Theatre, but later, disagreeing with the group on what he considered a matter of principle, he severed his connection with the undertaking. On the night before his execution he was married to Grace Gifford in his cell.

Like that of Pearse and MacDonagh, Plunkett's poetry is directed to the praise of earthly and heavenly beauty, the earthly always as a reflection of the heavenly:

> For I have seen your body's grace,
> The miracle of the flowering rod,
> And in the beauty of your face
> The beauty of the face of God.

[6] *The Poetical Works of Thomas MacDonagh.* Dublin, The Talbot Press (1916).

Throughout his work, however, the sense of moral struggle, the Pauline law of the members, is more evident, more definitely recognized and more clearly stated, than in theirs. More definitely also, but without any impression of effort, he makes use of symbolism, neither that of the French Parnassians nor the hermetic code of Yeats and Russell, but the immemorial speech of the great mystics from whom he learned directly this language of the spirit. For this reason he too may sometimes suggest Blake, but the influence of that genuine mystical poet, Francis Thompson, is much more recognizable in his work. For the most part he avoids all secondary sources of inspiration and goes directly to the fountain-head of his faith, illumined as his was by theological study. This is impressively instanced in such a poem as *The Worm Joseph* and *I See His Blood Upon the Rose.*

All three of these men, therefore, abundantly illustrate the elements of nationalism and religion listed by Stopford Brooke as characteristic of Anglo-Irish poetry. What at first sight might seem to be absent from their work is an observance of the Irish Mode, described by MacDonagh himself as a conspicuous feature of the poetry of the Revival. It is true that except for the internal rhymes in such poems as Plunkett's *Your Fear* and MacDonagh's translation of *The Yellow Bittern*, there is no attempt to reproduce the intricate metrics of the Gaelic, to transfer to the modern poems any of the archaic traits of Irish verse, but their poetry is intrinsically Irish nonetheless. There is no mistaking the accent, the intonation cited by MacDonagh, "a quality as it were of chanted speech," no escaping the rhythms fashioned under the influence of Irish music. Their poetry is as Irish as though it were written in Gaelic. They have simply utilized the English tongue as an instrument in the communication of their vision, since (as Plunkett says in his essay on *Obscurity and Poetry*) "all art is revelation."

If the story thus far outlined were fiction rather than fact, it might well at this point come to a stop, if not a conclusion, for surely there would be many to agree that "The rest is silence," and regard any further development as in the nature of an anticlimax. But as the whole world knows, the history of Ireland did not stop with the Easter Rebellion, nor did its literature terminate with the Rebels' unfinished business. In the course of the next few years events were enacted upon the Irish scene that did resemble an anticlimax. To many the Treaty and the establishment of a Free State rather than the republic for which the rebels fought and died seemed such a thing. But perhaps it may be left to an Irish poet like James Stephens, himself a Sinn Feiner though not involved in the uprising, and a friend and literary associate of Pearse, Plunkett and MacDonagh (for whose posthumously published *Poems* he wrote the Preface), to testify to the fact of continuance and survival, as he does in *Spring, 1916*.

Born in 1882, Stephens lived in poverty and obscurity until he was discovered by AE working as a stenographer, a craft which he had taught himself, in a Dublin office. He had always been an ardent student of the Gaelic, and became such an authority on Irish music and art as finally to be appointed assistant curator of the Dublin National Gallery. Long associated with the foremost literary men in Ireland, he has won fame chiefly in the field of fiction, although he is not in the strict sense a novelist. But his poetry would demand attention even if he had never written any prose. In appearance he has been described as answering to the popular notion of a leprechaun, and the elfin spirit which pervades both his poetry and his prose would seem to indicate that his mind has imposed its lineaments upon his body, in an atavism which suggests some pre-Celtic descent.

His is a wholly lyric gift, on which point he makes copious commentary in his Preface to his *Collected Poems* (New York, 1933). While it is not true, as someone has said, that his verses are written mostly in words of one syllable, the fact that they abound in monosyllables is an indication of his economy of diction. In the matter of content they are on the whole pagan poems, but on the whole also his is a rather playful paganism without any Theosophical earnestness, which although it may be quick to see centaurs and satyrs in the Irish woods, and to find kind words for the demons, never expects to be taken seriously nor allows the reader to forget that these are Irish satyrs, while there is many an angel to offset the demons and their pseudo-blasphemy. The love poems are robust and forthright, echoes of those salty lays which Dr. Hyde gleaned in Connacht. In every section of the book, but especially in that entitled *Less than Daintily*, there are poems which are undeniably Irish in theme, in spirit and in metre. Most of them are in the vein of the embittered poets of the past, like O'Rahilly and O'Bruadair, who rail against the evil days upon which the poet has fallen who once knew such honourable estate.

Dora Sigerson, daughter of Dr. George Sigerson, was one of the casualties of Easter Week as truly as though she had fallen before the firing squad. She was born in Dublin about 1870, and grew up to be a singularly beautiful woman, whose face, according to Katharine Tynan, had a curious suggestion of the Greek Hermes. Hers was a native poetic gift, and although after her marriage in 1896 to the English critic, Clement Shorter, she lived mostly in England, the absorbing passion of her life was her love of Ireland. To this all her poetry bears witness, notably the verses entitled *The Story without End*, in which she describes how she had reacted through life to the story of her country's wrongs, how she "ran at Kickham's side" and kept vigil outside Kilmainham's bloodstained walls.

She wrote and published a great deal of verse, but she will be best remembered for two small volumes entitled *The Sad Years* (1918) and *Sixteen Dead Men* (published posthumously in 1919). For she died in 1918, literally of grief for her country, especially the events of Easter Week and the "sad years" that followed. Hers are rebel poems of a fiery intensity. They are poems of heartbreak and sorrow, the expression of which is not so much a prolonged wail or keening as a choking sob, well instanced by *The Comforters:*

> When I went down the long hill I cried and
> I cried.

Ireland, especially literary Ireland, has produced many anomalies, perhaps none more typical than Francis Ledwidge, born at Slane, Co. Meath, in 1891. His father was an evicted tenant farmer who became a farm labourer, so that after leaving the national school at the age of twelve Francis worked as a field labourer and a servant. He was eventually apprenticed to a Dublin grocer, but, loathing the job, walked the thirty miles back to his home, although he was afterwards employed at what must have been the equally distasteful tasks of miner and road mender. At an early age he began to try his hand at writing verse, and sent some of his first poems to Lord Dunsany, whose enthusiasm was aroused and who was thenceforth his patron, introducing him to the literary world of Dublin and writing two Introductions for the *Collected Poems* published in 1919. He had joined Dunsany's Battalion of the Royal Inniskilling Fusiliers and was killed in action in Flanders in 1917.

Ledwidge was primarily a poet of nature, especially in his *Songs of the Fields*. Dunsany calls him the poet of the Blackbird, and although he devotes only three lines in his first poem to the blackbird's song, its echo sounds through all his verse. The final edition of his work contains poems, among them a tribute to MacDonagh, which Lord Dunsany described as revealing "strange sympathies," for which he felt constrained to apologize as emanating from a protégé of his, attributing them to a young man's sympathy with a lost cause. But to this Mr. Andrew Malone takes exception, pointing out that nothing was more natural than for Ledwidge to have grieved for MacDonagh and for Ireland, "weeping among her streams." As a matter of fact these "curious sympathies" are not confined to an isolated poem, but are expressed over and over again, whether by his choice of bardic subjects as in *The Death of Ailill, The Sorrow of Findabar*, or *Before the War of Cooley;* or in his longing and love for Irish scenes remembered in distant places (*Crocknaharna, Through Bogac Ban* and *Ireland*).

It is difficult to assign the unruly Muse of Oliver St. John Gogarty to any of the groups so far mentioned, and yet in one way or another he belongs with all of them. He is said to have been practically a disciple of Yeats, although there is no evidence of such discipleship in either the form or the spirit of his work, and Russell has declared that he enjoyed Gogarty's Rabelaisian poetry because it was so unlike his own. He was a member of the Irish Senate from 1922 to 1936, but during the "troubles" which followed the Treaty he was the declared enemy of Sinn Fein. In consequence of this attitude he was kidnapped and shot at by members of the IRA, and his country house was burned down. He then went to England with his family (he had married in 1906) and is at present living in the United States.

Gogarty was educated at Stonyhurst and Trinity College, Dublin, and by profession is a distinguished throat specialist. He has been called "the wildest wit in Ireland," an assertion which is supported by his poetry, which is brilliantly clever and wittily libidinous. It conveys no hint of Celtic influence as far as form is concerned, being rather the work of a mind steeped in the Classics and expressing a frankly pagan attitude. In its clarity and conciseness it somewhat resembles Housman's, but there is more laughter in it, and more soundness. It is an echo of the English eighteenth century, except that it is better than anything which that influence produced in Dublin except the domestic architecture. If Kuno Meyer was right in his contention that to the ancient Gaels the half-said thing was dearest, then Gogarty is not Gaelic, and yet it is impossible not to detect an Irish twinkle in his most impudent lines. There is beauty in his verses too, breath-taking beauty in poems which flash some radiant glimpse before the eye, such as the plum tree in bloom or the face of a lovely woman. Despite his mockery he can dream of Phoenixes, knowing that his is the age-old longing for the unseen, for all that is symbolized by the fabulous bird and by the lost Atlantides. He knows, too, how impossible this would be "unless within me there were wings."

Frank O'Connor and Austin Clarke are among the younger poets who make liberal use of the ancient Gaelic "matters," the first chiefly through direct translation of exceptional raciness of idiom and harmonious form; the second, by creating his own versions of certain Bardic Tales, such as *The Cattle Drive in Connaught*, *The Frenzy of Suibhne* and *The Vengeance of Fionn*. In his Introduction to Clarke's *Collected Poems* (1936) Padraic Colum calls attention to the younger poet's innovation in verse structure by the use of assonance in place of rhyme, the result being a strange and haunting music, the consequence, says Colum, of the union between English and Irish verse forms. Such verse would seem to be the culmination of the experiments which MacDonagh saw under way in what he called the Irish Mode.

Gogarty, O'Connor and Clarke have all felt constrained to have a try at *The Old Woman of Beare*, and that in such fashion that it is difficult to say which of them most violently transgresses the bounds of decorum, the curb of art.

It is both appropriate and singularly gratifying to be able to bring this chapter to a close with a brief appraisal of the work of Robert Farren, because his poetry is representative of all that is best, which means all that is truly Irish, in the Revival. In it are merged the two strains that are the components of the Irish cultural tradition, the pagan, which at times has been so over-emphasized in the literature of the Revival as to falsify the tradition by minimizing or even ignoring the other, and the Christian strain, which not only preserved the pagan culture but kept the heart of Ireland alive to produce a rebirth and a revival.

Robert Farren was born in Dublin in 1909 of a family that could boast of several Dublin generations, and his whole life up to the present has been inextricably connected with that venerable city. The Easter Rebellion occurred on his seventh birthday, an event which helped to foster his interest in the nationalist movement. Besides learning Gaelic in school, he perfected his knowledge of it by visiting the Irish-speaking parts of Kerry. His interest in the literary movement was awakened by reading Ernest Boyd's *The Irish Literary Renaissance*, and strengthened by the personal acquaintance of Yeats, AE, Stephens, Colum, and other members of its first generation. Meanwhile he had become intensely interested in Thomistic philosophy, choosing as the subject of the thesis that he wrote for the Master of Arts degree, which he received from the National University, *Poetic Experience according to the Aesthetic Principles of Aristotle.*

From childhood he had been cultivating the poetic experience on his own account, and although it was not until he was twenty-one that he began in earnest to write poetry, he has continued to do so ever since, despite ten arduous years as a primary school teacher, and the multifarious tasks connected with the directorship of the Abbey Theatre, to which he was appointed in 1940, and with his present office of director of talks at Radio Eirann.

He is associated with Austin Clarke in a movement to foster the speaking of verse, and is the author of two plays which have been successfully produced at the Abbey, one of them a dramatized version of the Assembly at Druim Ceatt, based on that episode in his poem *This Man Was Ireland.* Although his first two volumes of verse contained unmistakable evidence of his poetic ability, there was really no warrant for expecting that his third book would reveal him as a poet of major importance. This was the book-length poem about St. Columba, *The First Exile*, published in the United States (1943) under the title *This Man Was Ireland*, of which Austin Clarke said when he read it in MS, "This is not something that Robert Farren has written: it is something that has happened to Irish literature."

It is truly a great book, first of all because the poet has risen to the height of his magnificent subject, the epic figure of Colmcille, scion of kings, pupil of saints, himself monastic founder, apostle, poet and saint, saint after the glorious Celtic pattern, which consisted as much in drawing heaven down to the familiar ways of men as in drawing human nature heavenward. Here at last, after nearly fifty years of the Irish literary revival, is an indisputable Irish poem, a poem which brings to life an Ireland that has been hidden as completely as the Ireland of the penal times: the land of kings and saints, of bards and *shanachies*, of natural loveliness and of supernatural marvels, such as the angels crowding the oak groves of Derry or gathering "like falls of foam or troops of suns," about the head of Colmcille at prayer.

Realizing the extent to which this noble figure was the embodiment of both the Christian and the pagan culture, the poet utilizes the legend which credits Colmcille with the miracle of recovering the *Tain* from the dead lips of Fergus, when that great epic was lost to bardic memory, thus demonstrating the continuity between the pagan and the Christian tradition. It is because he is master of the whole vast subject that Robert Farren has been able to write such a poem as this, a poem that would have rejoiced the heart of both Oisin and Dallan Forgaill and stirred the blood of both Patrick and Colmcille.

Nor does its greatness consist only in its subject. Its form is overwhelmingly great in a truly Irish way. Not that the author makes the mistake of attempting to imitate in English the inimitable Irish forms, but his metres are not, strictly speaking, English metres. His genius (and the word is most deliberately and advisedly used) has devised an inspired vehicle for his inspiration, a pattern of English words with all the fire and colour, all the vigorous, pulsating life of the Gaelic without remotely suggesting a Gaelic model.

Here indeed is the fulfillment of the poetic promise of a hundred years, here in full measure the harvest of that hope which Stopford Brooke faintly discerned on the Irish poetic scene, here the realization of MacDonagh's dream of an Irish Mode, fashioned by the music of Irish speech as that has been shaped by Irish music.

> Man of words
> may the Word
> was made flesh
> love and bless you.

Chapter XIV. STAGE DIRECTIONS

*A playwright is as surely to be found in his page of
words as Rembrandt in his smallest sketch.*
>   Corkery, *Preface to* King and Hermit

A LITERARY REVIVAL is necessarily something more than a renova-
tion, the restoration of an obsolete language, the refurbishing
of outworn literary forms. The Irish Literary Revival is the recovery of an ancient culture, in all its aspects, but, much more
than that, although this may not be immediately evident, it is the
recovery of the spirit which originally produced that culture, a
rekindling of the fires that once lit the creative genius of the
people, so that in this later and lesser time that genius has been
stirred, not merely to imitation of past greatness, but to fresh
and vigorous achievement. This is especially evident in the field of
drama, for the most important single contribution of the Literary
Revival is the creation of a native drama, this apart from the
extent to which that drama is authentic and representative, a
highly controversial point indeed.

It had to be a new drama, because, as already noted, this was
the one respect in which the literature of ancient Ireland was
wanting. Before the foundation of the Abbey Theatre, everything
that was written either by Irish playwrights or on Irish themes
(and the records go back to the sixteenth century) belongs to
English rather than Irish literature. This is true even of the
voluminous output of the nineteenth century, which consists of
farcical variations on the stage Irishman, or of sentimental melo-
dramas like the phenomenally popular plays of Dion Boucicault,
The Colleen Bawn, or The Brides of Garryowen, based on Griffin's

novel, *The Collegians; The Shaughraun;* and *Arrah-na-Pogue.* And yet, especially throughout the eighteenth and nineteenth centuries, the annals of the English stage record the names of many Irish actors, men and women, whose talents enhanced the glory of that stage, among the most famous actresses being Elizabeth O'Neill, who was called a younger and a better Siddons; George Ann Bellamy, who played with Garrick; Peg Woffington, and, more recently, Ada Rehan, while the men included James Quin, whom Walpole considered superior to Garrick; Charles Macklin and Macready. This abundance of histrionic ability is significant because such ability proved to be as important as literary talent in the development of the Irish theatre.

It is natural that for the average person the Irish Literary Revival should be represented by the Abbey Theatre; equally natural that the Abbey Theatre should be represented by the plays of Yeats and Synge and Lady Gregory. Since the issue is considerably beclouded and since this book is intended for the average person, I shall do my best to show to what extent this impression is warranted. That there should be any confusion on the point is odd, because certainly all those concerned in the original venture have been at great pains to describe the circumstances under which the Abbey Theatre came into existence and to explain their purpose in inaugurating the movement with which it is identified.

The original, if not the only begetter, of the idea was a man whose literary attainments, although not of the first order, deserve more recognition than they have hitherto received. He was Edward Martyn, a Catholic landed proprietor, born in 1857, and already possessed of a considerable literary reputation when Yeats was at the outset of his career. It was Martyn, as a matter of fact, who on a certain day in 1898, paid a visit to Lady Gregory at Coole, bringing with him Yeats, whom she did not know, and in the course of the afternoon's conversation, launched by Martyn's reference to two plays he had written but could not get produced, the suggestion for an Irish theatre was made which developed into the Irish Literary Theatre, out of which grew the Abbey.

Martyn's was a curious personality, the result largely of the cross-currents which met in him by way of heritage and experience. He was said to trace his descent from Sir Oliver Martyn, who had come to Ireland with Strongbow. The family seat, Tulira Castle, was already centuries old when Cromwell's invasion, wrested so many estates from their Catholic owners and turned them over to Protestants. But the seventeenth-century head of the Martyns took no active part against the invaders, and by a special act of indulgence he and his heirs were allowed to keep their lands. As a matter of fact many feudal strongholds beyond the Shannon were similarly unmolested, which accounts for the fact that George Moore was also a West of Ireland Catholic landlord and a neighbour of Martyn's. This would seem to be the only basis for the friendship which developed between them, for no two men could be more unlike in character, temperament and taste.

Martyn attended Belvedere College in Dublin, and Oxford University, a circumstance which accounts to some degree for the trend of his literary taste, as well as for the conflict reflected not only in his work but in his whole career. For Martyn, it can never be too often affirmed, was a convinced and fervent Catholic, but the period of his sojourn at Oxford coincided with one in which many literary experiments were being made, especially in the writing of plays. In his Preface to Martyn's *The Heather Field* and *Maeve* (1909), Moore lists the Free Theatre of Paris and the English Independent Theatre, but above all, the influence of Ibsen, among the forces that helped to shape the founders of the Irish national drama. Martyn was one of those who came under the gloomy spell of Ibsen, and he returned to Ireland prepared to write in the same vein.

To a man like Martyn, however, literature was a matter of minor importance compared with music. This was the absorbing passion of his life; it afforded him the happy opportunity of giving expression to his love both of his religion and of his country. He more than anyone else was responsible for making the *Feis Ceóil* (musical festival) one of the most successful cultural institutions of modern Ireland. Long before Pope Pius X was elected to the papacy Martyn was an advocate of reform in ecclesiastical music and art. In recognition of his achievements in this field, especially through the Palestrina Society of Dublin, of which he was the founder, Dr. Grattan Flood dedicates to him his monumental *History of Irish Music* (1905).

So much of George Moore's literary career lay outside of Ireland, that if it were not for his brief connection with the Abbey Theatre there would be little occasion to mention him here. Moore was a born poseur, who liked to represent himself as a cosmopolite, thoroughly familiar, for example, with the letters and manners of France, a point on which many Frenchmen took issue with him. He had been living abroad for years when he was summoned back to Moore Castle, his ancestral home, by difficulties with the tenantry, and through Martyn discovered the Irish Revival. Whether or not he was enkindled by Martyn's enthusiasm, he decided to participate in the movement, regretting that at his age it was impossible for him to learn Gaelic. He is reported to have said that if he had written in Gaelic, foreigners would be flocking to Ireland in order to learn the language in which his books were written as they flocked to France to learn the language of Molière, a point on which numerous Irishmen disagreed with Moore. His only dramatic effort seems to have been an adaptation of Martyn's novel, *The Tale of a Town*, made with the author's permission and produced under the title of *The Bending of the Bough* at the Irish Literary Theatre in 1900.

Martyn's two plays, *The Heather Field* and *Maeve* are similar in theme and treatment, both reflecting the influence of Ibsen, although the scene and the characters are Irish. In the first, a wealthy idealist who has already courted disaster by his marriage with a woman for whom his sole importance lies in his money, complicates matters further by sinking his fortune in the reclamation of a heather field, in which after long experimentation the heather crops up afresh, leaving him to final disaster: the financial loss which his wife, not without reason, feared; and the loss of sanity, which she seems also not without reason to have anticipated, although that she should have done so is one of the counts against her.

Maeve, which is called a psychological drama, is beautiful but unreal. The central figure, a girl named Maeve O'Heynes, is obsessed by the "Celtic dream-land of ideal beauty," to a point where she lives in expectation of the coming of a mythical lover from that land, although she is on the eve of her marriage to an exceedingly unmythical Englishman. The dénouement includes a visionary scene in which Maeve O'Heynes is visited by Maeve of Connacht and assured that she will be borne away to Tir-na-noge and there discourse with her beloved.

The play is symbolic in several ways, the most important being that Maeve O'Heynes bases her objection to her fiancé on the parallel she draws between her own wedding and the marriage of Diarmuid MacMurrough's daughter, Eva, to Strongbow, "who with the power that was given him subdued and ruined the ancient splendour of Erin." The parallel is far-fetched and the play might well have confirmed the impression, for which there was already considerable warrant, that the Irish literary movement was a thing of mist and twilight.

The Enchanted Sea, a play in four acts, described as "gloomy and mystic," was produced at the Antient Concert Rooms, by the Players Club in 1904, while *The Dream Physician* was first performed at the inauguration of the Irish Theatre (1914), a venture in which Martyn was joined by Thomas MacDonagh and Joseph Plunkett, for a purpose which Martyn seems never to have relinquished, that is, the production of Irish plays other than peasant plays, plays in Irish and foreign masterpieces. Plunkett withdrew from the group a few months before his death because he felt the terms of agreement had not been adhered to. Martyn died in 1923.

Yeats's interest in the drama grew out of his interest in poetry, although his first play was written for a reason not directly connected with literature, that is, in order to provide a vehicle for the talents of Maud Gonne. This was *The Countess Cathleen* (1892) which became the first offering of the Irish Literary Theatre, as the organization which grew out of the conversation at Coole was at first called. It was presented at the Antient Concert Rooms May 8, 1899.

The second play, Martyn's *The Heather Field*, was produced on the following evening and was much better received than Yeats's had been. From the outset there was a manifest difference in the literary theories of these two men, which eventually led to dissension and final rupture between them. The rift was chiefly the result of Martyn's admiration for Ibsen,—for his technique and occasionally for his ideas, though not for his philosophy as a whole.[1] Yeats, on the other hand, contended that an Irish national drama should be based on the country's large store of myth and legend, then coming to be so generally known. His recognition of the magnificent possibilities of this material inspired him with the ambition of getting the whole heroic age into verse.

Now the dramatic theories of Yeats and Martyn were not irreconcilable. There was no reason why they should not have joined forces in the leadership of the literary movement as far as the drama was concerned. The real difficulty probably lay in their temperaments, in the cast of their minds. Martyn's was undoubtedly the keener and more profound intellect, while Yeats's literary gifts were of a higher order.

When the Irish Literary Theatre presented its first plays it was under the necessity of employing English actors. There was already in existence in Dublin another theatrical group, consisting of Irish actors under the leadership of the brothers, W. G. and F. J. Fay. With this group, known at first as the Irish National Theatre, and later as the Irish National Dramatic Company, when Martyn and Moore went their separate ways, Yeats became associated. Under the joint leadership of Yeats and the Fays the first performance of the Irish National Dramatic Company was given

[1] This point is splendidly elucidated by Mr. Ernest Boyd in *Ireland's Literary Renaissance*, pp. 300-305.

on April 2, 1902, the bill consisting of Russell's *Deirdre* and Yeats's *Kathleen ni Houlihan.*

By the following year the group, of which Lady Gregory had been from the start a most important member, had been joined by J. M. Synge and Padraic Colum, represented respectively by *In the Shadow of the Glen* and *Broken Soil.* Invited to London by the Irish Literary Society, the company was so favourably received that Miss A. E. F. Horniman, founder of the Manchester Theatre, granted them an annual subsidy and leased to them, rent-free, for a period of six years, the Abbey Theatre in Dublin, with which they made dramatic history.

The dissension which has marked the whole course of the Irish dramatic movement (and Yeats appropriately entitled his volume on the subject *Plays and Controversies*) dates from the performance in 1899 of Yeats's first play, *The Countess Cathleen*, which tells the story of a noble woman who sells her soul to demons in order to save her people from famine. Taken literally and viewed from a strictly theological standpoint, her conduct is indefensible, and the Irish, as a people only too well acquainted with the horrors of famine and the price they had refused for their own soul, protested against what they regarded as blasphemy. There were some, however, who saw more deeply into the matter, perhaps more deeply than Yeats himself, and one of them, a Catholic priest, defended the Countess's action as exalted charity, comparable to St. Paul's willingness to be anathema for the brethren.

Yeats once more stirred up resentment when in *The Land of Heart's Desire* (1894) he persisted in dealing with sacred things in what can only be called an arbitrary manner. The play is a strange, fantastic thing, hardly to be taken seriously except for the undeniable intention of drawing an unfavourable comparison between religion, as represented by a Catholic priest and several members of his flock, and irreligion, as represented by the fairy child.

Yeats's remaining plays fall into three categories: those in which he endeavoured to carry out his desire to put the heroic age into verse, plays which include *The Shadowy Waters* (1900);

The King's Threshold (1904); *On Baile's Strand* (1904); *The Green Helmet* (1911) and *Deirde* (1911); those which have a kind of folk quality, a core of Irish poetic reality, which include *The Pot of Broth* (1902); *The Hour Glass* (1903); *The Unicorn from the Stars* (1907, originally *Where there is Nothing*); and *Kathleen ni Houlihan* (1902); and those in which the author experiments with new dramatic and stage techniques, mostly under the influence of the Japanese theatre, and these consist of *Four Plays for Dancers.*

In the first group, *Baile's Strand* is an impressive dramatization of the Red Branch episode in which Cuchulain becomes the unwitting slayer of his own son. It is a highly literary and poetic play, which calls for a knowledge not only of the saga from which it is taken, but of the social history which made the situation possible, knowledge of so special a kind that it is difficult to reconcile it with Yeats's reiterated boast that what the Abbey was engaged in creating was a people's theatre, for which the impulse had come from the people themselves. For that matter, it is difficult to reconcile this last statement with Yeats's anger when the people expressed resentment of certain of the Abbey offerings.

Kathleen ni Houlihan is not only Yeats's best play, because it is so directly dramatic; it is also the one great nationalist drama sponsored by the Abbey group, in which Yeats goes to the Aisling poetry of the Hidden Ireland for that figure of a broken, defrauded, stricken queen, disguised as a woman of the roads, revealing herself as still young and beautiful and powerful to allure to her service the youthful and the daring.

In all Yeats's work the element of symbolism, as one of the fundamentals of his literary creed, predominates. As time went on he became more and more preoccupied with its dramatic use, the result being the publication in 1920 of *Four Plays for Dancers*, two of them, *At the Hawk's Well* and *The Only Jealousy of Emer*, based on the Red Branch saga, the first and last plays of a series of four dealing with the life of Cuchulain, but so stylized as scarcely to be recognized as of Irish origin; the other two being

The Dreaming of the Bones, based on the story of Devorgilla, and *Calvary.* None of these were Abbey plays; in fact nothing more un-Irish could be imagined than these artificial fantasies with their use of masks, their symbolic dances, their patterned singing, but by this time artificiality was of the very essence of Yeats's dramatic theory.[2] They were written, of course, under the direct influence of the Noh stage of "aristocratic Japan," but the spirit which breathes through them, even through *Calvary,* is not that of either Japan or Ireland, but of Arabic Buddhism interfused with Yeats's own "system" of lunar philosophy.

It is undeniable that throughout his life Yeats displayed a class consciousness which closely resembles snobbishness. His biographer describes him as "haunted" by the problem of how to bring the aristocratic and Protestant tradition into line with "Gaelic" nationalism; he is quoted as expressing impatience that he should be going through all sorts of trouble for a mob that knew nothing of literature when he might have been elsewhere writing plays for his equals and his betters (and if his, then immeasurably the mob's). As a matter of fact he was not alone among the Abbey group in taking this attitude, for the harshest phrase in Mr. Frank O'Connor's vocabulary is *middle-class mind,* which, as represented by Daniel Corkery, is the type of mind that ventures to disagree with the "ascetic," meaning the Abbey, mind.

In his Notes on *The Four Plays for Dancers* Yeats outdoes himself in asserting his intellectual exclusiveness, which implies a certain degree of social exclusiveness, by emphasizing the fact that these plays were not meant for a public theatre nor a common audience, having first been performed in a drawing room, before an audience of less than fifty of his "friends," persons capable of appreciating the fine points of the performance and incidentally of providing an appropriate theatre. He exults in the pleasurable experience of appealing to such a group after so long sharing the lot of those who must "applaud the common

[2] *Plays and Controversies,* p. 334.

taste or starve."[3] But perhaps the acme of this sense of exclusiveness is not reached until in his Notes on *Calvary* he remarks
that he wrote its songs to please himself, feeling confident that
when the time came for performance, singer and composer would
see to it that an audience, even an elect audience, would not
understand a word.

Lady Gregory has been variously described as godmother of
the Irish dramatic movement and charwoman of the Abbey. Certainly from the day when she participated in that first interview
at Coole out of which the movement grew, she was tirelessly
active in its behalf, first by lending it the support of her encouragement, her purse and her generous hospitality, later by contributing to the repertoire of the Company through the writing
of plays, and at intervals by her readiness to fight for it by word
and pen. The publication in 1947 of Lady Gregory's *Journals*,
splendidly edited by Lennox Robinson, not only throws much
light on the inside story of the Abbey Theatre, but gives us
intimate glimpses of the most important figures associated with
it, such as Yeats, of course, and Martyn, Russell, Synge and
O'Casey. Above all, although certainly this was not her intention,
it throws into strong and sympathetic relief the figure of Lady
Gregory herself, emphasizing her nobility of character, her generosity and kindness of heart, her essential nationalism, and
despite certain inevitable prejudices, her kindly attitude toward
the Catholic Church, her heart, the editor assures us, being with
the "chapel" rather than the Establishment.

The first of her efforts was a one-act play entitled *Twenty-five*,
first played in March, 1903, an offering that is generally forgotten,
as it deserves to be. But in the following year was presented
Spreading the News, the first of the delightful comedies by which
Lady Gregory dissipated the almost unbroken gloom that had
hitherto characterized Irish drama. Other plays in this vein are
Hyacinth Halvey (1906), and *The Rising of the Moon* (1907).
The second of these with Yeats's *Kathleen ni Houlihan* are the
most unequivocally nationalistic plays in the history of the Abbey.

[3] Op. cit., p. 420.

Besides these straight comedies, Lady Gregory wrote two groups of folk history plays, the first described as tragedies, including *Grania, Kincora,* and *Devorgilla;* and the second, called tragic comedies, *The Canavans* (1905), *The White Cockade* (1905) and *The Deliverer.* Her *The Gaol Gate* (1906) is a powerful one-act tragedy, while *The Travelling Man* (1910) is an impressive miracle play in whose technique Lady Gregory shows exceptional skill.

She is the translator of the following plays written in Gaelic by Douglas Hyde: *The Marriage, The Twisting of the Rope* (1910), while in collaboration with him she wrote *The Workhouse Ward, The Lost Saint,* which Dr. Hyde is said to have written in the course of an afternoon at Coole, and *The Nativity,* a miracle play in one scene. In 1913 she published *Our Irish Theatre,* of which the sub-title is *A Chapter of Autobiography,* but which is really a history of the Abbey Theatre to that date and consequently an invaluable bibliographical item.

Padraic Colum, whose purely poetic work was considered in the last chapter, was already an associate of the Fays before the organization of the Abbey group, and under their auspices his first play, *The Saxon Shilling,* was produced at Banba Hall, Dublin, in 1903. His most serious dramatic work, however, is contained in a series of plays written to celebrate the redemption of the soil of Ireland, made possible by the Land Act of 1903. These were *Broken Soil* (revised as *Fiddler's House,* 1907, and produced under the auspices of the Theatre of Ireland), *The Land* (produced at the Abbey in 1905), and *Thomas Muskerry* (produced at the Abbey in 1910). These are powerful plays of a type that Mr. Colum was well fitted to write, since he himself is of peasant stock and thus able to see both characters and background with a clear and "innocent" eye. Furthermore he presented them with a simplicity that is in itself art, a simplicity that is immeasurably more effective, especially in a dramatic sense, than all the picturesque dialogue and fantastic situations of James Millington Synge, who is one of the best known of the Abbey group.

Synge was born at Rathfarnham, Dublin, in 1871, was educated at Trinity College, where he received his degree in 1892, after which he took up his residence in Paris. There, about 1898, he was discovered by Yeats and by him persuaded to return to Ireland, study its racial types and utilize them as the basis of his contribution to the new Irish drama. It seems, however, to have been by his own inclination, rather than at the suggestion of Yeats, that he went to the Aran Islands and the Irish-speaking West, where he lived with the people and came to know them as well as was possible in view of the barrier of race and religion. Mr. Boyd's study of Synge is interesting and illuminating, but it is written from Synge's own standpoint, which was that of the Ascendancy, and the extent to which Synge's interpretation of Irish character is authentic is not considered by Mr. Boyd, at least it is never questioned. This, however, is a point on which the "native" critic is entitled to an opinion. For this reason (and no serious study of Synge can be undertaken which does not take it into account), Mr. Daniel Corkery's dispassionate study of Synge as set forth in *Synge and Anglo-Irish Literature* (1931) demands a hearing. Mr. Corkery's own creative work is sufficient refutation of the charge of "moral jingoism" which Mr. Boyd brings against those who do not whole-heartedly endorse Synge's point of view, while at least a partial refutation of Mr. Frank O'Connor's assertion that Corkery represents the "middle-class mind" would seem to lie in the fact that Mr. O'Connor considers Corkery the greatest artist of his generation.[4]

As a matter of fact, Mr. Corkery's study of Synge is of invaluable assistance in any attempt to grasp the essence of Anglo-Irish literature as a whole, since it presents such a comprehensive, penetrating and profound analysis of the entire subject. The gist of his thesis is that whereas most Ascendancy writers, having "never shared the Irish national memory," were prevented from understanding and therefore from interpreting Irish life, Synge, although "a true child of the Ascendancy," was also an artist, and acting on his artist's instinct, "he, an Ascendancy man, went

[4] Robinson ed., *The Irish Theatre*, p. 52.

into the huts of the people and lived with them." In consequence
he succeeded in many respects where others of his class had
failed, since they "could not even had they wished, come in
contact with the profound and common interests of Irish life. But
even he did not succeed wholly since, although he was free of
the peasant's hut, he was not free of his soul"[5]—and that, with
a race that for seven hundred years had refused to make an
exchange for its soul, amounts to no slight exclusion.

Synge's sincere desire to know the real Irishman is manifest in
his sojourn among the peasants of the Aran Islands, a procedure
in which he was actuated by Yeats's advice to study the peasantry
at close range. His prose account of that experience, published
under the title *The Aran Islands* (1907), is interesting on its own
account, but also for the extent to which it contains in germ the
theme of his plays, as well as for the light it throws on the
"gentleman's" failure to reach the peasant soul, since in characteristic fashion his hosts revealed what was compatible with
hospitality and no more. Not that there was any obvious effort on
their part to be secretive or mysterious. They were probably as
oblivious as was their guest of their failure to meet his needs,
because they had no suspicion that anything of the sort was
expected of them.

Of the plays that were subsequently written and produced
(*The Tinker's Wedding*, 1902; *In the Shadow of the Glen*, 1903;
Riders to the Sea, 1904; *The Well of the Saints*, 1905; *The Playboy of the Western World*, 1907; *Deirdre of the Sorrows*, 1910),
Riders to the Sea is the only one that is admittedly authentic in
the sense of being true to both character and scene. In addition,
it is filled with a grandeur and nobility of spirit that lifts it away
from the merely local and ranges it with works that endure by
reason of their universality.

If the author had gone on from there, or even stopped there,
his work would not have had to depend so much on elements of
the picturesque, not to say the sensational qualities whose pre-
dominance in the *Playboy* made it the occasion of such stormy

[5] Corkery, op. cit., p. 82.

scenes on the occasion of its production by the Abbey Players in Dublin and New York, which have aroused its partisans to acrimonious charges against the mere Irish who objected to this new version of the stage Irishman, a version calculated to make them appear the savage barbarians described by Cambrensis and Spenser. Perhaps their outbrust was not an expression of literary criticism, but they knew the time to be past when they dared not protest against misrepresentation. Even as criticism, however, the violence was not without a certain validity, since it is required of a work of art that it shall be a recognizable portrayal, even though it be intended for caricature, and if Synge did not intend to make his work "representative," he might have written about the Aran Islanders without ever leaving Paris.

Synge's admirers, both then and since, have accused the Irish of manifesting a Puritanical fear of facing the reality of sin, an accusation that could scarcely emanate from anyone who understands the realities that underlie the sacramental system of the Catholic Church, with which the average Irishman is thoroughly familiar. Understanding and compassion for the sinner he has in plenty; that is one reason why he so hotly resented the implication that his normal reaction to crime is the exaltation of the criminal. Cited as an evidence of this "Puritanism" was the report that the *Playboy's* first-night audience objected to the "bad language" used throughout the play on that occasion, but on the witness of Lady Gregory,[6] she and Yeats objected to it, too, and directed that those parts should be deleted before the performance. By an accident this was not done, but after that first production Lady Gregory took out many phrases that were never afterwards spoken on the Abbey stage, although they remain in the printed book. In the long run the arguments against Synge's work are based on those reasons of the heart that no amount of logic can wholly refute, but that are nevertheless part of the very substance out of which literature is made.

There is another aspect of Synge's work that has occasioned extravagant praise, as it has also aroused considerable objection,

[6] *Our Irish Theatre*, pp. 133-134.

and that is the idiom which he puts into the mouths of his characters. This is a point on which Mr. Corkery touches incidentally, according after his impartial habit now praise, now blame. Perhaps it will do no harm to give the last word on the matter to one who made no pretense of impartiality, the dogmatic Dr. Henebry, whose reactions are reported by Professor Stockley, who had persuaded him to read *Riders to the Sea*: "As he returned me Synge Dr. Henebry seemed excited almost to hate; certainly to contempt; and, for once, to wrath, at the suggestion that in the Aran Isles, or on this mainland, any set of people ever used the romantic lingo of those Synge books. 'And I,' Henebry maintained, 'have studied and noted Irish forms of English all over Ireland.' "[7]

It must be remembered that Dr. Henebry objected with similar violence to the Anglo-Irish written by Padraic Pearse.

Whatever the shortcomings of these early exponents of the native Irish drama, their sincerity cannot for an instant be impugned. To what extent Yeats was sincere in his Cabbalism is a matter of opinion, a point on which even his friends differed, but that he was in earnest in his desire to perform a great cultural service for Ireland has never been in any doubt. Lady Gregory was a high-minded, generous woman who had the courage of conviction to an extent which made her willing to fight both the criticism of the "mob" (the Irish people when they did not see eye to eye with the Abbey) and the tyranny of the Castle, on a point that seemed to her a matter of principle. As for Synge, he was throughout the whole stormy period a suffering, dying man. No one who reads Lady Gregory's description of his efforts to write between operations and attacks of pain can fail to be filled with compassion for him. That the demonstration against the *Playboy* shortened his life was the conviction of Lady Gregory. Doubtless if the Irish had known they would have refrained from that expression of their displeasure, but would their attitude on such grounds have been any more soundly critical?

Deirdre of the Sorrows, which Synge did not live to finish, is

[7] W. F. P. Stockley, *Essays in Irish Biography* (1933), p. 174.

charged with much of the pathos of its author's last days, but its beauty is its own, that is, its tragic quality does not depend upon the reader's knowledge of Synge's tragedy.

The plays of T. C. Murray, while stamped with his individual style, resemble those of Colum in the unmistakable veracity of their characterization and background, a natural consequence of the fact that like Colum, Murray is writing about his own people out of the fulness of his personal knowledge of them. His work as a whole is marked by that stark simplicity which is the very essence of art, the unadorned directness of his method leaving one stirred and shaken. Mr. Murray was born in Co. Cork in 1873, and in 1891 was graduated from St. Patrick's Training College for Teachers, a profession in which he rose to be headmaster of the Inchicore Model Schools, Dublin. The first of his plays to be produced at the Abbey Theatre was the powerful peasant play, *Birthright*, first acted in 1910, and used as the piece with which the Abbey Players opened their first American tour. If there was no outcry from "moral jingoists" against its tragic dénouement, in which Shane Morrissey kills his elder brother, Hugh, it must have been because the Irish were only too well aware of its terrible plausibility and did not interpret it as in any sense a misrepresentation.

Anyone who had the privilege of witnessing that other heartbreaking and mercifully short drama, *Maurice Harte*, must have agreed with the *New Witness* critic, who emphatically pronounced it great. The play itself, however, has a slightly sensational quality, of which the unforgettable *Autumn Fire* is quite devoid. To realize the intrinsic "Irishry" of this play, one has only to speculate briefly as to what the situation, which involves the marriage of an elderly man with a young woman, with whom his son falls in love, as she does with him, might have become in the hands of another author, say Ibsen or Chekhov or even Synge. There is nothing Puritanical or sentimental about the talent which had the courage to depict the young people as parting after a single kiss, which is witnessed by the old man and naturally misunderstood, so that the curtain falls on a crushed figure sitting in a darkened room and murmuring, "They've broken me . . . son . . . wife . . . daughter . . . I've no one now but the Son o' God."

Mr. Murray is likewise the author of *Spring* and *The Briery Gap*.

Seumas O'Kelly (1881-1918) was the author of several plays produced at the Abbey, *The Matchmakers,* presented in 1907, and *The Flame on the Hearth,* 1908. *The Homecoming* was presented by the Theatre of Ireland at Molesworth Hall in 1910. But the best of his plays is *The Shuiler's Child,* which the Theatre of Ireland produced at the Rotunda in 1909. It is described as a tragedy, and certainly there is a terrible pathos in the two scenes which unfold the story of the beggar woman whose wandering has brought her to the house where the child she abandoned is being cared for by foster parents, and show how her attempt to prevent the child's removal from that kindly shelter by an officious inspector leaves her facing arrest for that desertion. The pathos, however, is so submerged by the grandeur of her soul that we feel something akin to joy as she prepares to face the humiliation of imprisonment, applying to herself the words of the oracular Tim O'Halloran: "When a woman leaves her pride behind her she loses her step in the march of the angels." One almost sees the angels getting into step with Moll Woods.

Lennox Robinson, born in Douglas, Co. Cork in 1886, the son of a Protestant clergyman, was educated at Bandon Grammar School and became a member of the Irish National Theatre early in its history. In 1910 he became manager of the Abbey, which since 1903 had been supported by Miss Horniman's subsidy. There had been occasional clashes between patroness and management, rifts which Yeats was able to patch up until at the time of King Edward VII's death, Robinson persisted in keeping the Abbey open, although all the other theatres in the kingdom were darkened in token of respect. That was the final outrage, and Miss Horniman permanently withdrew her support. In 1923 Robinson became producer for the Abbey, but throughout his career his major contribution to the Irish drama has consisted of plays, mostly comedies, written by himself.

The first of these, *The Clancy Name,* was presented at the

Abbey in 1908. This is a predominantly serious play, as is *The Cross Roads* (1908), which has been called the most dramatically powerful of all the Abbey offerings. But inspired by an almost uncanny insight into human nature, especially in its weaker aspects, broad, delightful humour irradiates *The White-Headed Boy* (1920) and *The Far-off Hills* (1929). This knowledge is manifested to an almost depressing degree in *The Harvest* (1910), while the fact that the author is an Irishman at least once removed comes out in *The Big House* (1928), in which Kate Alcock, with the same breath with which she declares that she and her people have been wrong in pretending not to be different from "every Pat and Mick in the village," maintains that "Ireland is no more theirs than ours."

Other Robinson plays, all produced at the Abbey, are: *Patriots* (1912), *The Dreamers* (1915), *The Lost Leader* (1918), *The Round Table* (1924), *Crabbed Youth and Age* (1924), *The White Blackbird* (1928), *Ever the Twain* (1929), *Is Life Worth Living?* (1933), *Church Street* (1935).

Among the most interesting of the early Abbey playwrights were William Boyle and George Fitzmaurice, whose plays made Abbey history. Boyle was born at Dromiskin, Co. Louth, in 1853. His first play, *Shane the Proud*, was never produced, owing to its excessive stage requirements. *The Building Fund*, produced at the Abbey in 1905, depends for its comedy on the miserly characters of a mother and son and the manner in which the building fund profits from their efforts to avoid contributing to it. *The Eloquent Dempsey* (1906) portrays the struggle of a small-town publican, caught in a political dilemma, to adhere to the principle which he puts so trenchantly: "A man must twist a little in order to please both sides." In addition to these, his most successful plays, Boyle wrote *The Mineral Workers* (produced 1906), and *The Family Failing* (1912), a kind of *Cherry Orchard* in reverse. It is generally conceded that this author never fulfilled the promise of *The Building Fund*.

Fitzmaurice's *The Country Dressmaker* (produced at the Abbey in 1907) presents some excellent character studies in unfolding the story of a girl who lives in the dream of an absent lover, only to lose the dream on his return, but to awaken in him a truer love and in herself more common sense. Although given a realistic setting, both *The Piedish* (1908) and *The Dandy Dolls* (1915) are in most respects grotesquely unreal, nowhere more flagrantly than in the priest's pronouncement, "He's damned," when the old maker of the piedish dies without the rites of the Church.

A. E. Waldon, who wrote under the pseudonym of "Brinsley MacNamara," first became famous as the author of satirical novels, of which *The Clanking of Chains* is typical. His most popular play was the comedy, *Look at the Heffernans*. His other plays *The Master* and *Margaret Gillan,* are dramas of disillusionment and disaster, the second a dire tragedy.

The plays of St. John G. Ervine, born in Belfast in 1883, are set against the background of the Protestant North, and deal with character and outlook stamped with the spirit engendered by that background, especially that of religious controversy. The best known are *Mixed Marriage* (1911) and *John Ferguson* (1915).

The 1911 season at the Abbey Theatre was signalized by the production of Padraic Pearse's *Passion Play*, spoken in Irish, and presented by the students of St. Enda's and St. Ita's colleges, its final scene having been described by a competent critic as "the most profoundly impressive and touching I ever beheld." The Easter season of five years later saw the author engaged in that venture which cost his life, but won for his country some measure of that freedom for which he and his associates strove.

But Pearse was the author of a number of dramatic compositions in English, which are important for the extent to which they are representative both of Pearse himself and of certain habits of Irish thought which up to that point had been practically ignored by the Revival. These works are not in any technical sense of the word *plays*, but they are dramatic, that is they are pervaded by that sense of the eternal significance of things of which action is the natural expression. For while action is by its very nature temporal and transitory, it is capable of being endued with a quality which seems to arrest its flight by signalizing its enduring import. This was the quality with which Pearse abundantly endowed his handful of plays, *The Singer, The Master, The King, Iosagan*, a quality which time and subsequent events have enhanced by demonstrating their startlingly prophetic character.

For without intending to do anything of the sort it is himself that Padraic Pearse has dramatized. Who can doubt that Mac-Dara in *The Singer*, the poet who becomes the leader of his people, is Pearse himself? Words that his own mother might have uttered he puts into the mouth of Maire: "Men of this mountain, my son, MacDara, is the Singer that has quickened the dead years and all the quiet dust! Let the horsemen that sleep in Aileach rise up and follow him into the war!" Who save Pearse might have spoken the words with which MacDara leaves his mother's house: "One man can free a people as one man redeemed the world. I will take no pike. I will go into battle with bare hands. I will stand up before the Gall as Christ hung naked before men on the tree." And surely it is Pearse who in the guise of Ciaran in *The Master* has sought truth so relentlessly that Michael, Captain of the Host of God, comes at his summoning. In *The King*, Pearse makes himself the Child who triumphs in the battle from which the King has been driven in defeat, but who pays with his life for the victory.

These may not be plays in the fullest sense of the word, but they are filled not only with a dramatic beauty of language, but a greater and more flaming beauty of spirit, which lifts the action out of the merely practical and allies it with the heroic folly that is so characteristically Irish, especially as it is expressed in the interchange between Diarmuid, who objects, "We thought it a foolish thing for four score to go into battle against four thousand," to which MacDara replies, "And so it is a foolish thing. Do you want us to be wise?" The extent to which Pearse had mastered the wisdom of this divine folly is most clearly shown in *Iosagan* in which old Matthias is saved because he had remained so childlike in spirit that it was "among the children" that he found Christ, Who went Himself, "a mannerly little boy," to summon the priest to his deathbed.

Obviously Pearse was too great a man to have written deliberately of himself. For that matter it was not merely of himself he wrote, but of Ireland, that Ireland which even when it was pagan was so filled with that high heroic spirit that it readily recognized in Christianity the fulfillment of all its dreams of glory, in sanctity the pattern of all its ideals, in Christ the Hero and the Champion to Whom Cuchulain and Conchobar would willingly have paid homage, for Whom they would gladly have died.

The extent to which this was a matter of literal fact is illustrated by those Christian centuries during which every pagan dream was brought to fullness and fruition, as it was illustrated no less by the subsequent centuries during which all the ancient glories perished and only the Irish faith remained. The story of the Irish Renaissance, even when so briefly surveyed as it has been in these pages, must necessarily have made it clear that, however laudable its efforts had been, they had resulted in an incomplete and one-sided picture, carrying the implication that the Irish were greatest when they were pagan and that any cultural restoration meant a revival of paganism. Such occasional glimpses as were afforded of their later degenerate condition either did not account for the condition at all or at least carried no hint that as a race the Irish were still animated by the same spirit, a spirit which so instinctively expresses itself in dramatic deed and speech that it caused Cuchulain to lash himself to the pillar stone, impelled Columba to cover his eyes when he returned to the Ireland which he had vowed never to see again, gave to Robert Emmet on the scaffold words which matched his death, and filled Pearse himself with foresight of the death he was to die.

Except for his speeches, Pearse's literary work is fragmentary, but those fragments were written at intervals in a life that was itself articulate of that spirit, for which by his dramatic pieces especially he challenged a place in the Literary Revival, which it had hitherto, although perhaps unconsciously, been denied.

Sean O'Casey's work brings the Irish drama well past another milestone in its history, especially by reason of the fact that he has made controversial use of a phase of current history which a sounder aesthetic sense would have taught him was too recent to be seen in perspective. This is illustrated specifically by *The Plough and the Stars*, with its disillusioned and embittered portrayal of the Easter Rebellion of 1916. Also filled with a bitterness that spills over even into the scenes of authentic comedy and comic characterization are *Shadow of a Gunman, Juno and the Paycock, The Silver Tassie, Oak Leaves and Lavender* and *Red Roses for Me*.

In order to understand not only O'Casey's plays, but his treatment of his dramatic material, it is necessary at least to be acquainted with the circumstances of the author's life, the best sources for which are his *I Knock at the Door* and *Pictures in the Hallway, Drums under the Windows* and *Inishfallen, Fare Thee Well*, which constitute not so much a biographical narrative as a series of vivid scenes. Against the background of a depressing Dublin slum, and a still more depressing religious creed, moves the figure of a pathetic, suffering child, stricken with ulcers of the eye and terribly impoverished, groping in physical and spiritual purblindness, while always close by hovers the figure of his mother, cowed by poverty until this helpless one of her children is threatened, when she assumes heroic dimensions. The later chapters deal with his mature life, his literary experiences, his political opinions, which finally settled down into the radicalism towards which they had been tending from the first. After a break with the management of the Abbey Theatre, he left Ireland and now resides in England. The narrative is lighted here and there by gleams of beauty, but it is so stripped of the decencies, so filled with brutalities and blasphemies, that one senses the irremediable hurt to a sensitive spirit wrought at some period of that frustrated life, and finding outlet in plays that resemble the shrieks of pain to which he was so often driven by the agony in his eyes. In many pages of the autobiographical volumes the style closely resembles that of James Joyce.

While the Abbey Theatre represents the most considerable dramatic venture in Ireland, it has not by any means been the only centre of dramatic activity, the Dublin Gate Theatre for the production of unorthodox literary plays having been founded in 1928.

Other large towns, such as Belfast, with the Ulster Literary Theatre, whose most prolific playwright was Rutherford Mayne (*The Turn of the Road*, 1906; *Blackmouth*, 1908; *The Captain of the Hosts*, 1910), and Cork with the Cork National Theatre and the Dun Theatre, have afforded opportunities for Irish playwrights, notably Daniel Corkery, and the talents of native players. Of these, only Mayne and Corkery reached the Abbey, the former in 1911, with *Red Turf*, the latter in 1918 with *The Labour Leader*. Excellent as this play is, it is far from being Corkery at his best. As a matter of fact, Professor Corkery is so versatile that it is difficult to say in which literary form he most excels. He has creative gifts of a high order, which naturally reveal themselves even in his critical writing, but which seem to reach their height in his fiction. Next to the novel and the short story, which become almost a new art in his hands, the drama, especially the one-act play is his most successful vehicle. The whole difference between the colonial or Ascendancy and the native Irish point of view is demonstrated (although that is not their purpose) in *King and Hermit* and *Clan Falvey*, both produced in 1909 by the Cork Dramatic Society at the Dun, Cork; and *The Yellow Bittern*, first performed by the Munster Players, in Father Mathew's Hall, Cork, in 1917.

Of these *Clan Falvey* is the finest, crowding as it does the whole of a stormy, blood-stained, agonized era, the whole of a racial consciousness and tradition, within the compass of a single act. The time element is lengthened incredibly by the transitions of mood through which the soul of Sean O'Falvey passes, as his eyes scrutinize "the poem book of his fathers" for the vindication of his rights and the warranty of his hopes. Also, the scene seems to be widened beyond the narrow confines of the peasant's hut by the variety of characters, despite their fewness, a variety which is accentuated by the contrast between Sean, clinging to his dream of the greatness of the O'Falveys, and his son, Hugh, struggling between the instincts of his class and the harsh duty of wresting a living from the unwilling soil, uttering words of bitter irony in the midst of the final disaster when the last few acres of that soil are confiscated, even as the rising river floods the fields: "Ring! Ring! The dykes are down. We are broken. Ring the O'Falveys from Lissnagaun! Father, rise up now. Rise up to us. We are free of all Desmond and of Corkaguiney too. Great days are come to us. Our book will tell us its grand stories —may they have no end. Rise, father, and be glad."[8]

[8] Under the title *The Story of the Abbey Theatre* Peter Kavanagh has published (1950) a lively, diverting and informative book, which brings the history of the institution to the year 1949. It is filled with forthright expressions of the author's conviction that the death of Yeats and the government subsidy brought the venture to artistic bankruptcy. As I have sought briefly to show, the terms *Irish drama* and *Abbey Theatre* are not synonymous, and unquestionably there have been later manifestations of both than I have attempted to record. The reason why I have not pursued the subject further is because the drama is of all literary forms the most current, the most fluid, the most difficult to set down as history until Time has rung in its evidence that a given playwright is something more than the success or failure of a season, has verified such promise as his work held of permanence.

Chapter XV. *THE STORY-TELLERS*

One thing the Irish shanachie could do supremely well, and that was tell a story.

Publications, Irish Texts Society, Vol. V, p. xxix

DURING THE CENTURY in which the English novel reached such a high degree of technical excellence, Gaelic Ireland was writhing under the penal laws, dragging out a stricken cultural life behind the hedge. There, however, together with that of the poet, the art of the *shanachie* still flourished, although it was untouched by the literary developments of the rest of Europe. It is therefore useless to speculate concerning the form the novel might have assumed in Gaelic if it had been suffered to develop naturally out of saga and folk tale under the impulsion of racial genius, but one fact lies beyond speculation: If the novel as such was unknown to Gaelic Ireland, it was not for lack of that narrative ability which is so essential to the novelist's equipment.

While Miss Edgeworth, Lover, Lever, and even Carleton are often regarded as constituting the first generation of Irish novelists, they belong in reality to the second generation of English novelists, their work being merely a branch of English literature and therefore not in the least representative of Irish Ireland. These earliest so-called Irish novels were actually English novels, written about Ireland from what Professor Corkery calls the colonial point of view, even when their authors were of Celtic stock as were Carleton, the Banims and Griffin. However, despite the fact that these men wrote for an English public, their possession of the *shanachies'* gift is indisputable, especially in the case of Michael Banim who composed his tales during the day, while engaged in the task of serving customers in his father's shop, and put the result on paper during the night. It is only when we come to Kickham that we have a genuinely Irish novelist, the very defects in whose work are probably to be accounted for by the fact that he was essentially a *shanachie* and hence not completely the master of form, at least as far as plot was concerned. This would explain his lack of success in the organization of his material in accordance with the demands of what is known as the standard novel.

That even during the penal times the *shanachie's* art continued to be plied is evident from the numerous collections of folk tales produced during the nineteenth century, above all, those published by Dr. Hyde under the title *Beside the Fire*. For the art of the Irish story-teller is essentially a fireside art, and it was only to be expected that so native an art should in some way impose itself upon the novel as it developed under Irish auspices. We are warranted, therefore, in looking for some evidence of this in the later Irish novels, whose authors, whatever their descent, profess to be representative of Irish-Ireland. We are certainly warranted in expecting that later Irish fiction should exhibit, as Irish poetry and drama have exhibited, unmistakable signs of their origin, that they should be written about the Irish for the Irish as the French novel, e.g., is written about the French for the French. We are warranted in scrutinizing the Irish novel for the veracity of its presentation of character, its reproduction of idiom, but above all for its portrayal not only of the external facts of Irish life but of the innermost depths of the Irish soul. In consideration of all the history that has been enacted in Ireland, all the water that has flowed through the Boyne and the Liffey, the scene that confronts the modern Irish novelist is one of the utmost complexity, from which it follows that an Irish novel can never be a replica of an English novel, even though it be written in English. The difference is not merely a matter of background and characterization, but of racial heritage and historical experience, which add immeasurably to the difficulty of the novelist's task and make the writing of an authentic Irish novel an exceedingly rare achievement, although novels about Ireland are common enough. The Irish novelist therefore, is confronted by the problem of singing the songs of Sion in the language of Babylon, in the full recognition of which fact the Irish novel will be discussed in these pages.

Oddly enough, the name which in the light of these facts first challenges attention is that of Jane Barlow, who presents a curious anomaly, inasmuch as she was sprung not only from the Ascendancy class, but from its most Protestant centre, and yet she was filled with the deepest love and understanding of the Irish peasant, especially his devotion to his religion. The eldest daughter of Rev. James Wilson Barlow, fellow of Trinity, where he became professor of history, she was born at Clontarf in 1857. In the strict sense she is not a novelist, since she is at her best in the short sketch, a type of story which demonstrates her kinship with the *shanachie*, as represented by *Irish Idylls* (1892), *Strangers at Lisconnell* (1895), *A Creel of Irish Stories* (1897). Such full-length narratives as *Kerrigan's Quality* (1893) and *The Founding of Fortunes* (1902) are less successful, although even these contain fine bits of dialogue.

Jane Barlow is a realist, pitiless when she is depicting the extremes of Irish poverty, but her realism is tempered by a pathos which the salt of humour preserves from sentimentality, while the humour itself never verges on farce. Among the most memorable of her sketches, particularly for the extent to which it exemplifies the enduring Irish love of learning, is *Mr. Polymathers*, a phrase on which Carleton throws light in his comment on the hedge schoolmaster's ambition to write the title *Philomath* after his name. Having witnessed the terrible scenes of the famine, Miss Barlow was only too well equipped to depict Irish poverty, which she does both as the habitual condition of life in Lisconnell, and in the starkness of rending tragedy in particular instances, as in the story of the homesick child who returns to his cabin to find all the members of the beloved family, whom he has forsaken comfort to rejoin, lying or sitting about the room, stark in death—from starvation. This is also the theme of the

verse monologue, *Past Praying For*. Like both Carleton and Kickham, Miss Barlow possesses to an extraordinary degree the ability
to reproduce Irish speech without resorting to extravagance or
burlesque.

The desiderata of the Irish novel seem for the first time to be
realized in the work of Canon Sheehan, whose first novel, *Geoffrey Austin, Student,* was published in 1908. Patrick Augustine
Sheehan was born at Mallow, Co. Cork, in 1852, and was educated
at St. Colman's College and Maynooth. Ordained in 1875, he was
sent on the English mission, where he served for two years, being
attached after his return to Ireland to the staff of the cathedral at
Queenstown, and in 1895 appointed parish priest at Doneraile,
where he remained until his death in 1913, having been made a
Canon in 1903.

Canon Sheehan was a man of exceptional learning, widely read
in both classical and modern literatures. In his boyhood he had
thrilled to the exploits of the Fenians, of several of whom he had
personal recollections, and unquestionably he cherished a deep
and abiding love for his own people, a love that was not a whit
abated by the fact that residence out of Ireland and his non-Irish
cultural training placed him in a position to see them in perspective. Politically he was a supporter of Home Rule, as Padraic
Pearse was for a time to be, but where the priest saw no hope for
his country save in some form of conciliation, to Pearse, Home
Rule meant merely payment on account.

Canon Sheehan was an admirer of German educational
methods, of which he had made a close study and which formed
the basis of his criticism of the Irish National School system. He
supported the Wyndham (Land Purchase) Act in 1903, and
assisted in every way to carry out its measures within the limits
of his own parish, where he was known as an exemplary rector
and dearly loved shepherd, the humblest of whose flock was
unabashed by the intellectual power and literary renown of the
Canon, probably because completely unaware of either.

It goes without saying that all Canon Sheehan's novels are
Catholic novels, in the broad sense of being imbued with the
Catholic spirit, as well as in the narrower sense of faithfully

depicting Catholic, especially clerical, life, from behind the scenes. It seems strange that his first book was not an immediate success, since it was indisputably something new in the way of a Catholic novel, a portrayal of the Catholic scene in terms which do not imply that it is necessarily all sweetness and light. Both *Geoffrey Austin* and its sequel, *The Triumph of Failure* (1899), should, one would have thought, have had an almost sensational success, but despite the fact that their literary merits were generally recognized, it was not until *My New Curate* appeared within the same year that there seemed to be warrant for the claim that the great Irish novel had at last been written. Here was a first-hand portrayal of Irish life and character, running over with humour in which there is nothing of burlesque (although an Irish critic reproached the author with being too hard on "our poor people"), filled with a pathos that never becomes sloppy, and presenting a plentiful variety of characters, all of them memorable.

There has never been any attempt to disguise the fact that much of the material in *My New Curate* is autobiographical, an observation which is true to an even greater extent of Canon Sheehan's next book, *Luke Delmege* (1901), a really powerful study of temperament and environment. It has elicited unfavourable criticism on the ground that its hero, a Catholic priest, seems to die with the questions which have harried him throughout life unanswered, but there is never the slightest intimation that the Catholic faith and the priesthood did not constitute for him an answer in the light of which he was content to leave the rest to God.

Canon Sheehan's grasp of the facts and implications of Irish history is illustrated in *Glenanaar* (1905) and *Lisheen* (1901), but above all in the posthumously published (1915) *Graves of Kilmorna*, in which he seems to regard the outlook for Ireland, when viewed in the light of the Fenian ideal, as gloomy in the extreme, and yet in the year following the publication of that book sixteen men were to die before a firing squad for the cause for which the Fenians fought.

But successful as Canon Sheehan was in so many respects, he

was not entirely successful as a novelist. This was because his intellectual and philosophical habits of thought made the essay a fitter medium than the novel for his unquestionable literary gifts. His narrative is too frequently interrupted by a tendency to philosophize, an inclination which found fuller and happier vent in the volumes entitled *Under the Cedars and the Stars* and *Parerga.* Canon Sheehan was a typical Irish scholar in the sense of possessing a superior and well-trained mind and wide-ranging intellectual interests, and of sharing the racial heritage, including the profound and simple faith of the mass of the Irish people, but he was not, strictly speaking, representative of the Literary Revival, although his admiration for Yeats's earliest work was expressed in a most practical fashion, and he could write to a friend: "Think what Ireland would be today if the stream of genius that has come forth from her schools and universities had been diverted towards the needs and wants of Ireland instead of being utilized by other and even hostile nations."[1]

The course of Irish history has so often taken the form of an attempt to ignore the fact that the majority of the Irish people are Catholic, that it is not strange that the attempt should so often have been transferred to literature, where it generally takes the form of misrepresentation. That is why any true Irish literature must not only take cognizance of the fact, but of all its implications, which Canon Sheehan's novels assuredly do. What gives its almost paradoxical character to Jane Barlow's work is her ability to do just this, to understand and depict the Irish peasant in the light of his religion.

On the other hand, the complexities of life in Ireland are increased by the fact that many of the Irish are Protestant, although the situation is simplified by the circumstance that most of the Protestant population is rather densely congregated in one section, the North, although even there they do not constitute a majority. This region, in which two races and two religions are thus brought into contact, and sometimes into conflict, provides an exceptional opportunity, of which novelists have not been as

[1] Herman Heuser, *Canon Sheehan of Doneraile* (New York, 1917).

quick to avail themselves as might have been expected. Among those who have done so with generally fortunate results to literature is Shane F. Bullock, born in 1865 in Co. Fermanagh, the son of a Protestant landowner on Loch Erne, the region which supplied Bullock with his literary material. *The Squireen* (1903), *Dan the Dollar* (1908) and *Hetty* (1911), are his most representative novels, but his characteristic traits are best shown in stories such as those contained in *Ring o' Rushes* (1896) and *Irish Pastorals* (1901).

It is not only by incidental touches such as a reference to the picture of William of Orange hanging on a cottage wall that one is made aware of the background of the Black North, but by the prevalence of a certain dourness of temperament, an absence of the humour which so often tempers the starkness of Southern poverty. It is chiefly in the handling of character that Bullock displays the sincerity of the artist, the understanding and the power of sympathetic portrayal that fills his slightest sketch with an unforgettable poignancy. This is well exemplified in *They that Mourn*, the story (*Ring o' Rushes*) of an old couple who go to town with a few hoarded pennies for the purchase of some needed "bits o' groceries," and who on their arrival find awaiting them a letter from America which informs them of the death of their son. Neither of North or South is the heartbreak which trembles in the old father's voice as he falters, " 'I can read no more. It's too dark. I can read no more,' " but heartbreak beyond tears is in their decision to forego the groceries and use their money for "bits of crape."

Relentless veracity amounting almost to cruelty pervades *Her Soger Boy*, as it is again manifest in several of the *Irish Pastorals*, which are bucolic, but never merely earthly, not to say animal. Many passages in these *Pastorals* are devoted to the beauty of the landscape against which the events are enacted; the grace and glory of the changing seasons are faithfully observed and recorded, but the human lot depicted consists for the most part of terrible drudgery, a drudgery that is powerless against blight. The consequence is an almost habitual discouragement, which, however, never becomes despair, as the appalling and incessant toil seems never to make for degeneracy and decay.

Indeed in his portrayal of the poverty which is too often the portion of those whose stories he relates the author is exceptionally successful. "No time is there for the decencies of civilization, no chance of its luxuries, no white cloth on a well-scrubbed table with knives and forks, plates and spoons, and smoking dishes for which to render unto God due thanks. No, no. These things— mercies, we call them—are not for Judy Brady and her kind. A full quiver, a two-roomed cabin, somewhere to sleep, and a little to eat: such year in, year out is the portion of life doled out to the Bradys. There are not three knives in the house, not two forks; there is no cloth, no meat, only a rickety table, a few stools and chairs, a tin or two, a pot or two, and of the earth's good increase, potatoes and salt, tea and buttermilk, a handful of Indian meal and a cake of soda bread" (*The Reapers*). If a note of impatience is discernible in such descriptions, it emanates from Bullock, not from the Bradys nor the others of whom he writes. Indeed it would be difficult to conceive of forebearance of such sublime proportions as that shown by Henry in *The Herd*. Its quality could never be mistaken for weakness or cowardice or anything but an assertion of the majesty of his soul.

While, as indicated above, it is possible to describe Emily Lawless as a rebel when she writes poetry, her novels range her unmistakably with the Ascendancy. In *Hurrish* (1886), admittedly the best of them, she undertakes to study the "wild Irish" with disastrous results, at least as far as Hurrish's mother, the blood-thirsty Mrs. O'Brien, is concerned, and she is presented as typical of her race and class.

The story itself, however, is powerfully written, its sincerity and good will are unquestionable, and even in the act of misstating it Miss Lawless did so far succeed in delineating the Irish issue as to have brought its reality home to Gladstone himself. But it is above all in the character of Hurrish O'Brien that the novelist approaches greatness. This was, as it were, forced upon her by the greatness in the character of Hurrish himself. This is manifested especially on his deathbed, to which he has been brought by the deliberately aimed bullet of a friend, to whom with his dying breath he is able to send his blessing and the assurance that he always said he would be "a Gran' man." This is the passage in which, at least from the standpoint of the Ascendancy, the whole situation is summed up: "Poor Hurrish! he was a martyr, too, after a fashion, though he knew it not. A martyr to a not very glorious cause, one that was certainly not very much worth dying for. A martyr to a long and ugly past—a past in which he, not having been born, had at least no share of the blame. He was dying because Hate of the Law is the birthright and the dearest possession of every native son of Ireland. He was dying because, for many a weary year, that country had been as ill-governed a morsel of earth as was to be found under the wide-seeing eye of God. The old long-repented sin of the stronger country was the culprit as surely as if it had pointed the gun at his breast."

Emily Lawless's novels include the following titles: *With Essex in Ireland* (1890); *Grania* (1892); *Maelcho* (1895) and *The Race of Castlebar* (1914), in which last she had the collaboration of Mr. Bullock.

The Big House made a somewhat belated reappearance in Irish literature through the work of Somerville and Ross, whose first novel was published in 1889, although their reputation rests chiefly on *Some Experiences of an Irish R.M.*, published ten years later, and *Further Experiences of an Irish R.M.*, which appeared in 1908.

The true names of this famous pair of collaborators, who were second cousins, were Edith Oenone Somerville and Violet Florence Martin, Violet having been born at Ross House, Ross, Co. Galway, in 1862, of a family whose ancestors had come to Ireland with Strongbow, while Edith was born in 1858 at Corfu, where her father was quartered with his regiment. Both girls were reared in Ireland in typical Big Houses, although they did not become personally acquainted with each other until 1886. Almost immediately, however, they inaugurated the joint literary career which was interrupted only by the death of "Martin Ross" in 1915. In 1932 both authors were awarded an honorary Litt. D. degree by Trinity College, Dublin, at which time an earlier novel entitled *The Real Charlotte* was made the basis of the award, jointly with the more famous *Experiences*.

It should be explained that the initials R. M. in the title of this book stand for Resident Magistrate, an office that has ceased to exist in Ireland, but which at the time of the narrative provided its incumbent, Major Sinclair Yeates, a bewildered Englishman whom Fate has thrust into a society of fox-hunting squireens, with a series of incredible but hilariously funny experiences.

The volume is packed with humorous scenes and diverting characters, the laughter being provoked not only by such successors to Handy Andy as Slipper, Mrs. Cadogan and John Kane, who, as native Irish, would naturally be expected to provide amusement, but by such specimens of the squireen class as Flurry Knox and his prodigious grandmother. It is difficult to decide which of the absurd situations in which the book abounds is most enjoyably ridiculous, but most readers would agree that *The House of Fahy* could scarcely be surpassed. As far as the native Irish are concerned the attitude is invariably that of the Big House. An occasional tribute is paid to a figure such as that of old O'Reilly, who boasts that his hounds have been in his family "seed and breed, this hundred years or more," or to a racial characteristic, such as the instinct for hospitality, an art which, according to the narrator, can be studied in its perfection "under the smoky rafters of Irish cabins." However, the words with which this tribute is qualified suggest some of the reasons why the distance between the Big House and the cabin was so hard to bridge: "If it is insincere it is equally to be respected; it is often amiable to be insincere." In this book, for obvious reasons, the distance is never bridged.

It is hard to understand why the reputation of this gifted pair of collaborators should be sustained chiefly by the *Reminiscences* when *The Real Charlotte* is not only their best work but a novel with many of the marks of a masterpiece. It can scarcely be the humour of the first book that causes it to be preferred, because *The Real Charlotte* is not only written in a style so brilliantly witty that every page scintillates, but it is packed with laughable situations and characters, from Norry the Boat to the amazing Charlotte Mullen herself, who is correctly described as sometimes vulgar but never dull.

But the book is serious too, in fact it is tragic, a profound commentary on the wages of sin (the sin in this case being, for a change, not sexual love, although that provides the underlying motive, but the passions of envy, ambition and hatred). It is a marvel of understatement in which the moral is never stressed, presenting an array of characters who hold the attention throughout the swift-moving narrative. There is nothing commonplace about either story or characters, the characterization providing numerous opportunities for psychological astuteness, as when it is remarked of Francie Fitzpatrick: "Her sense of her misdoings was like a dog's, entirely shaped by other people's opinions, and depended in no way upon her own conscience."

Long out of print, *The Real Charlotte* has recently (1948) been reissued and is now available for the increased number of readers it deserves to have.

The Protestant North is the scene of St. John Ervine's novels, as it is of his plays, especially *Mrs. Martin's Man* (1915), which is really the story of Mrs. Martin herself. She is the kind of person who would always have had a story, although it would have been quite different if her man had not proved so worthless, leaving her to support herself and their two children, which she does most competently. After sixteen years her man returns to her for "a rest," utterly oblivious of the situation he created when he became her sister's lover before he beat a cowardly retreat. To all of this, even to her sister's disillusionment and her son's bewilderment, Mrs. Martin, with her quiet strength and the wisdom born of colossal patience, is more than equal. This book, with its unusual but far from sensational developments, its exceptional handling of character and its humour, is the basis of the author's well-deserved reputation as a novelist, a reputation which has been further sustained by *Changing Winds* (1914), *The Foolish Lovers* (1920), and *The Wayward Man* (1927).

The folk-lore atmosphere, which is characteristic of both Ethna Carbery's poetry and her adaptations of the bardic tales (*In the Celtic Past*), is present in *The Passionate Hearts* (1903), although perhaps to a lesser extent. These are stories of a primitive but deeply spiritual people, who for all their outward calm and kindly ways, feel with a terrible intensity. The title story might have lost all its beauty if the action had been transferred to another environment or time, an observation which is equally true of the tale which explains why on Tory Island it is only the women who lift their voices in song. Ethna Carbery's style is a perfect medium for her stories, so much does it possess of Gaelic flavour and inflection, without for a moment suggesting dialect.

Considering the slightness of Padraic Pearse's literary achievement—and it consists of a handful of verses, four short plays and ten compositions that are difficult to classify, but which are listed among his writings as stories—the importance of that achievement can only be explained in terms of his personality, which was so forcibly impressed not only upon everything that he wrote but upon all that he did. That personality endows his memory with gigantic proportions as the embodiment of an exalted ideal which in the course of time has acquired all the significance of a symbol. It is not, therefore, too extravagant to maintain that most of the Irish literature written since his time bears his imprint upon it as truly as though he had set the pattern and fashioned the mould.

His "stories," like his plays and his poems, are highly symbolic. Their symbolism is not obvious, but neither is it esoteric, because it relies for its interpretation upon either a common experience or a half-forgotten knowledge. For an understanding of his stories, which have been called those of a patriot aware of his country's danger, Pearse was appealing, and this is particularly true of *The Dearg-Daol, Brigid of the Songs,* and *The Keening Woman,* to the long racial memory of his readers, to that spiritual insight which was theirs almost before they knew Christ, to the

valorous visionary soul which made it so impossible for them as
a race to accept slavery or apostasy. Out of the depths of his
Irish soul he spoke to the soul of his people, confident that in
time, although perhaps not in his time, he would be understood.
That even in his own time his meaning was clear to many, that
many who then did not grasp his meaning have since, and by the
very force of his message, been given ears to hear, is clear from
the subsequent course of Irish history, which has necessarily had
an effect on Irish literature. Of the value of his work as a whole
the claim may be made that has been made specifically for *The
Singer*, that it "is to the new Irish-Ireland English speech what
the works of Villon, Marie de France and Rabelais are to the
French and those of Chaucer to the English."[2] His stories, like his
poems and his plays, are pervaded by an almost terrifying spirit
of prophecy, a sense, not of doom, but of high destiny.

If ever any writer possessed the gift of the *shanachie* in its
fulness it is James Stephens. His first published novel, *The Charwoman's Daughter* (1912; published in New York as *Mary, Mary*)
won wide recognition, but it was *The Crock of Gold* (1912) that
established his reputation, the manner of its telling signalizing
the advent of a new talent of the first order. What this talent
consisted in did not immediately become apparent, although
his readers had no difficulty in accepting him as the leprechaun
of the Irish movement. Through all his work, but particularly
through this book, which it would be absurd to call a novel, runs
the undercurrent of mocking fairy laughter that was to be heard
again and again, especially in *Here are Ladies* (1913) and *The
Demi-Gods* (1914).

It is next to impossible to appraise Stephens's work—it is so
various, so charged with unexpectedness, so packed with what
might be called the author's philosophy except that it is too
delightfully contradictory to constitute a system. *The Crock of
Gold* is a strange mixture of Irish mythology and folk-lore, with
a dash of the cult of Pan, the whole apparently amounting to a
glorification of naturalism and a repudiation of the moral code,

[2] Le Roux, *Patrick H. Pearse,* p. 201.

except that it is probably no more than a bit of foolery such as only an Irishman could perpetrate. In its way, this phase of Stephens's work confirms the impression made by that of the "Dublin mystics," that the Irish Literary Revival was a pagan revival, with this difference, that Stephens does not treat the subject in the tone of high seriousness adopted by the professed mystics.

In 1923 he published a version of *Deirdre* in the English prose of a Gaelic-speaking Irishman, which won high praise from AE, and in 1924 the same prose was made the effective medium for a volume entitled *In the Land of Youth*, a re-telling of the stories of Nera and Etain, of Hy Brasil and the Lands of Faery and the Introduction to the *Tain*.

But Stephens's work is far from consisting merely of foolery and folk-lore, imbued with a pagan spirit, for although *Etched in Moonlight* (1928) contains several sketches in fantastic vein, similar to those in *Here are Ladies*, it includes others that are grim and tragic, such as *Darling* and *Hunger*. Hunger has been so common, so almost commonplace a fact of Irish experience, that numerous writers have inevitably attempted to use it as a literary theme. In fact an anthology of such attempts would make a book of no small dimensions, yet in all its bulk there would be nothing to equal the thirty pages into which James Stephens crowds so much terrible, silent, bloodless tragedy, a story of starvation which is a masterpiece of the restraint and understatement that are so much more impressive and convincing than any amount of piled-up agony.

It would have been odd if, at the turn of the century, when so many strange winds of doctrine were blowing through the literatures of the world, the literature of Ireland should have been left unruffled by their breath; if the naturalistic theories and practices of Zola, the realism of Ibsen, the relativism of the neo-philosophies which constitute such a frontal attack on absolute values, especially in morals, the abnormal psychologies which stem from Freud and reduce all human experience to terms of sex, did not find some echo and reflection in Irish fiction. As a matter of fact, it is in the novel more than in any other form that the dualism which has almost come to be the distinguishing mark of contemporary Irish literature finds its clearest expression. Here especially the paganism that has already been noted in poetry and the drama is revived. Indeed, it may almost be said to be accentuated by the circumstance that in the novel it is shown against a Christian background. The contrast is heightened by the fact that the new paganism asserts itself in a country that is steeped in the Catholic tradition, among a people whose habits of thought and behaviour are Catholic, not merely by instinct but by discipline and in consequence of the long ordeal of suffering through which they have brought their convictions.

Under date of May 20, 1923, Lady Gregory records in her *Journal* that Mr. George Bernard Shaw had recently remarked to her how "curious" it was that the most indecent writers at that time should be three Irishmen, Harris, Moore and Joyce. Lady Gregory gave it as her opinion that the explanation lay in a reaction from Catholic teaching. Other things apart, the attitude of both speakers clearly shows their recognition of the extent to which the Church stands with St. Paul on this point. They realized that in indecency there is something definitely un-Catholic, and yet in recent years Ireland has produced a considerable crop of indecent fiction whose authors are all Catholic, at least in origin and by education. In some cases their books are likewise vehicles for the expression of their hatred for the Catholic Church, its teaching and its clergy. Of the three men mentioned by Shaw, Joyce is the only one whose reputation is identified with Ireland, although he eventually expatriated himself and included his fatherland with the other objects of his detestation (his home and his Church).

James Joyce was born in Rathgar, a suburb of Dublin, February 2, 1882. No account of him would be complete that failed to emphasize the importance of his father's influence on his life and character, not because this implied conformity with a paternal ideal, but because the elder Joyce was typically bibulous, impecunious and garrulous, especially on political themes. The talented boy therefore grew up in an atmosphere in which he could not but have felt humiliation, despite his father's extravagant pride in his precocity and his own confidence in his gifts.

His education was of the intermittent sort that might have been expected under the circumstances, including three years at the Jesuit school at Clongowes Wood, and when that became a financial impossibility, attendance at Belvedere College, where he remained from his eleventh to his sixteenth year, during which period he concentrated his attention on philosophy and languages, exclusive of the Gaelic, which he refused to learn.

He has written of these years as no one else could write in his *Portrait of the Artist as a Young Man*, to my way of thinking his best because his most rational book, which at the same time is one of the most heartbreaking books ever to come out of Ireland. Perhaps I may be permitted to quote in explanation of this what I have written of it elsewhere: "The book is in a sense a Catholic novel, the story of a soul which has exercised its terrible prerogative of saying NO to the urgency of grace. Only a Catholic could have conceived it, perhaps only an Irish Catholic could have set down this record of a great refusal, this repudiation of a spiritual inheritance. His fashion of recording it, but above all the influence he has exercised through it, and more especially through *Ulysses*, makes it imperative to acknowledge James Joyce as one of the most important factors in the development of the modern novel."[3]

To write thus, however, is to anticipate the events of Joyce's life and career. Already in his college years he had felt the impact of Ibsen, having learned Norwegian in order to read him in the original, and publishing an essay on the subject in 1900. In the following year, under the title of *The Day of Rabblement*, he denounced the National Theatre of Ireland, and shortly thereafter left for Paris with the intention of studying medicine, but was compelled to abandon the idea for lack of funds. He was on the verge of starvation when he was recalled to his home by his mother's last illness, which imposed on him four months of vigil

[3] Kelly, *The Well of English*, p. 323.

beside her bed, during which period he refused her dying request to kneel there and pray. The self-torment he endured in consequence of his refusal is poignantly treated in *Ulysses*.

In 1904 he left home to become a teacher at Dalkey and in the same year he married Nora Joseph Barnacle, by whom he had two children. After several disappointments he secured a post as teacher in the Berlitz school at Trieste, where he remained until 1918, when he went to Zurich in the same capacity.

Meanwhile he had made several ventures into publishing, a slim volume of poems entitled *Chamber Music* having been printed in 1907. The frail and exquisite verses are completely within the romantic and idealistic convention of love poetry, with some direct borrowings from the *Canticle of Canticles*.

In his Introduction to the collection of short stories entitled *Dubliners* (Modern Library edition), Padraic Colum points out that at the period when they were being written Joyce had just left University College, Dublin, which as a Catholic college had affinities with the great Catholic universities of the Continent, this by way of emphasizing Joyce's Catholic cultural background. The book was completed about 1905, and almost at once Joyce began to experience the difficulties he was thenceforth to have with publishers who had a wholesome fear of the statutes against obscenity, although in this case it was not so much on the score of indecency as of politics. The dialogue in these stories is excellent, and in such a sketch as *The Sisters* he foreshadows the skill later Irish writers were to display in the handling of a single situation.

In 1912, after a fruitless brief visit to Dublin in an attempt to procure the publication there of this book, Joyce left Ireland never to return. His *Portrait of the Artist* was published serially in *The Egoist*, through the good offices of Ezra Pound, but when it came to publication in book form English printers refused to set the type. It was published in Trieste in 1914 and in America in 1916. His one play, *Exiles*, was published in 1918.

Joyce had now withdrawn with his wife and two children to Zurich. He was in desperate financial straits and suffering from a serious eye condition which necessitated numerous operations. At this juncture Pound was instrumental in procuring for him, through Prime Minister Asquith, a sum of money from the King's Privy Purse, which brought some relief and enabled him to continue his work on *Ulysses*, which he finished in 1921.

When parts of this book were serialized in American magazines the editors were fined, which darkened the prospect of publication until Miss Sylvia Beach, owner of the Shakespeare Bookshop in Paris, undertook to bring it out under that imprint. Joyce received the first copy on his fortieth birthday, but five hundred copies that had been smuggled into the United States were burned by order of the postal authorities, and the work acquired high value as contraband. A controversy as to its literary value and moral turpitude raged until 1933, when the ban was removed by decision of U. S. Judge J. M. Woolsey, who declared that it was not obscene in the legal sense of the word, "somewhat emetic, but nowhere aphrodisiac."

Ulysses, as the reading world knows, is the novel in which James Joyce devotes 767 pages to the portrayal of twenty-four hours in the life of Stephen Dedalus (hero of the *Portrait*) and incidentally of Leopold Bloom, an Irish Jew, and Molly, his wife, with incidental glimpses of other characters whose paths cross and re-cross theirs, especially Stephen's friend, Buck Mulligan (commonly identified with Dr. Oliver Gogarty, then a medical student). It is concerned with sensual and sexual experiences detailed with an extreme naturalism which finds words for subjects which many a robust mind would shrink from admitting to its thought or imagination, and it is written in a style that many readers regard as a cataclysm in English speech. It is an inundation of verbiage which sweeps away most of the forms and usages of conventional composition, but let no one who has not read it imagine that it is unintelligible for it is appallingly lucid. Moreover, it contains passages that read like parodies of noble Early and Middle English prose, and others that are examples of sheer beauty of form.

As to the question of its indecency, Judge Woolsey seems to have taken a rather artless view of human concupiscence when he exonerated this book on the basis of a legal definition of obscenity, "a tendency to stir sex impulses or to lead to sexually impure and lustful thoughts," especially when he adds, jocularly, "It must always be remembered that his locale was Celtic and his season was Spring." This is to give the book an idyllic character which Joyce would be the first to repudiate. Indeed it is no madrigal of love inspired by the natural tendency of a young man's fancy in the Spring. It is not concerned with love at all, but rather with a frenetic hatred which is the perversion of love, a hatred that condemns the body and all its functions while seeming to exalt them.

But even if the learned judge were right in clearing the book of the charge of indecency, it is filled with something worse, and that is blasphemy. Again, as in the *Portrait*, Joyce utters such irreverences as only one reared in the Catholic tradition, steeped in the perennial philosophy, penetrated through and through with a sense of the meaning of the liturgy and his own share in it, could commit. Something of this is indicated when, in the midst of Buck Mulligan's travesty of the Mass, he recalls his days at Clongowes and remembers: "So I carried the boat of incense there."

After the publication of *Ulysses* Joyce worked on the novel known in general as *Work in Progress*, parts of which appeared at intervals in the magazine *tradition* under the titles *Haveth Childers Everywhere* (1931); *Anna Livia Plurabella* (1932); *Tales of Shem and Shaun* (1932); and *The Mime of Mick, Nick and Maggie* (1934). The completed book was published in 1939 under the title of *Finnegan's Wake*.

This proved to be if anything a more terrific literary bombshell than *Ulysses* had been. The difference between them is said to lie in the fact that *Ulysses* records the workings of the conscious mind and therefore represents what is known as the stream of consciousness, while *Finnegan's Wake* is an attempt to record the experience of the sleeping mind, the phenomena of the world of dreams. Certainly it is to some extent reminiscent of *Alice in Wonderland*.

On being confronted with *Finnegan's Wake* the average reader had difficulty in grasping the fact that he could not read, much less understand, a clearly printed book of 628 pages of words that at first sight he has every reason to suppose are English, but such a reader soon realized that the resemblance was superficial, that these words had been so manhandled and telescoped that even those that were arranged in what was recognizably a natural order remained unintelligible. Hence the interpretation and appreciation of *Finnegan's Wake* have been taken out of the hands of the average reader to become the undisputed province of the intellectuals.

Among them they have produced numerous commentaries and keys to the significance of the book, to none of which I have had recourse, since I regard it as one of the indisputable functions of a writer to convey his meaning to a mind that not only is not imbecile, but is able to understand Plato and Aristotle and even grasp the greater profundities of Aquinas without the use of keys or crowbars.

It is not that *Finnegan's Wake* is utterly incomprehensible. Parts of it, in spite of a jumble of languages that would daunt a Cardinal Mezzofanti (the illustrious polyglot being one of the persons mentioned with typical irrelevance in the course of the book), a smashing of words on a par with the treatment of the atom, and a massacre of orthography, the meaning of a passage or a page is inescapable, is only too painfully clear. Too often it is quite obviously revoltingly coarse, childishly indecent or cheaply irreverent.

But, it may be objected, it is not fair to judge the book on the basis of such piecemeal interpretation. Surely the book itself is profound, is of enduring value, or it would not have received such acclaim. As to the meaning of the book as a whole, frankly I haven't the stiver of an idea, though I realize that to make such an admission is to be expelled into the outer darkness of Philistinism. Even so, I must make it and find such consolation as I can in the example of the little boy in the fairy tale who refused to praise the Emperor's new clothes when the evidence of his eyes assured him that the monarch was wearing no clothes at all.

As it happens, I have recently found further comfort in a commentary on Joyce that seems to me exceptionally deserving of respect. Under the title of *They Think They Know Joyce* it was written by Dr. Oliver St. John Gogarty (who, it will be remembered, was the original of Buck Mulligan in *Ulysses*), and contributed to the *Saturday Review of Literature* under date of March 18, 1950. It expresses the opinion of one whose intimacy with Joyce enables him to throw light on his idiosyncrasies without blinding him to their origin and meaning. Dr. Gogarty's knowledge of the novelist and his background enables him to describe Joyce's two major works as deliberate hoaxes, "one of the most enormous leg pulls in history." His critical acumen and common sense lead him to dismiss Joyce's eccentricities of style as infantilism, a form of Mairsy Doates, while his sanity impels him to deplore in Joyce the manifestations of the persecution mania as well as the failure of all the bright promise with which his life had begun, so that his final achievement was "a triumph of ugliness and chaos and ineffectuality." Dr. Gogarty goes further and applies to his one-time friend a terrible phrase; he calls him "the most pre-damned soul I have ever encountered."

The later years of Joyce's life were spent in Paris with his wife and his son and grandson. His daughter, Lucia, having developed a nervous disorder, was confined to a sanatorium, where she had to be left when, after the fall of Paris in 1940, Joyce and his family were forced to seek refuge in Switzerland. There on January 31, 1941, he succumbed to an illness from which he had been suffering for ten years.

Today, apart from Joyce's literary achievements, however their value may be appraised, his importance is twofold. It consists in the extent to which he reflects the literary fashions of his time, already enumerated at least in part, and in the extent of his influence on other writers, those of his own generation and the next.

In the case of Francis Stuart, however, one of the most prolific of Irish novelists, the chief influence is not so much that of Joyce as of the pseudo-mysticism which stemmed from Yeats. His work as a whole reflects many of the strange cross-currents that have met in his own life. Born in Australia in 1902, the son of Irish parents, he was educated at Rugby, and in 1920 was married to Yseult Gonne, the daughter of Maud Gonne MacBride. At twenty-one he published his first book, a volume of poems, but he is primarily a novelist.

The subtitle of *Things to Live For* (1935) is *Notes for an Autobiography*, but the acquisition of biographical data from its pages is a matter of gleaning them from a collection of inconsecutive comments and opinions, which boil down to the implication that the things which have made Stuart's life worth living are horse racing, fishing, women, travel and Lourdes, items which have been repeatedly utilized against a more or less remote Irish background, as the theme of his novels, of which the most representative are: *Women and God* (1931); *Pigeon Irish* (1932); *The Coloured Dome* (1933); and *Try the Sky* (1933).

The chief characteristic of Mr. Stuart's work is its symbolism, the symbolism being obviously regarded as belonging to the mystical order, and the mystical experience signifying, as it so often does for D. H. Lawrence and Yeats, the sexual experience, with the difference that Mr. Stuart is apparently a Catholic, and as such might have been expected to display at least an awareness of another plane of experience.

As was to have been expected, one of the results of the Easter Rebellion has been the appearance in fiction of persons whose lives have been in some degree affected by that event. This is exemplified in Mr. Stuart's *Pigeon Irish* and *The Coloured Dome*. In the second of these books, for example, Garry Delea and Tulloolagh MacCoolagh, she a rebel leader and he somewhat inexplicably involved in the final stages of the movement, give themselves up as hostages on the understanding that they are to be shot while two other prisoners are released. Garry and the girl, who is dressed as a man, are placed in the same cell for the night, where the girl, despite her raiment, shows herself a very woman and a weak one at that. When, as the result of a slight error and by way of anticlimax, they are released and the others shot, she agrees to marry Garry, but he, apparently out of a conviction of sin, instead of keeping his appointment with her, returns to the prison, why, it must be confessed, one scarcely knows.

Women and God is an incredible farrago, written to the text of *The Chinese Nightingale* and combining most of Mr. Stuart's usual ingredients, including Lourdes, an invalid girl who is miraculously cured, and immediately thereafter drives all night across France in a racing car with the hero, with whom she is in love, despite the impediment of his wife, who has remained in Ireland to manage their poultry farm. To this ménage the hero returns with another woman for whom he professes what must be a symbolic love, since he likewise protests that he loves only his wife.

Try the Sky is the story of an even more symbolic affair between Carlotta, an Austrian girl, and an Irishman unaccountably named José, who, in the course of a journey which they take on the spur of the moment with two strangers, one of them a North American Indian princess, engage in quite casual though highly mystical relations, which José regards as preliminary to inevitable marriage. To this, however, Carlotta, obviously the more mystical of the two, demurs, objecting that the Church "does not understand about lovers," and that she wants just to be his love before she is his wife. When in an ecstatic frame of mind in which there is not a little of the maudlin, José exclaims, "O Ireland! O Carlotta! O Love!," it is with difficulty one refrains from adding, "O Fiddlesticks! If this be mysticism, give me Caliban."

There is nothing particularly Irish about Mr. Stuart's mysticism, in fact there is nothing particularly mystical about it, for all the novelist's devotion to St. John of the Cross, to which Yeats refers. It is a result of a confusion in thought which is so typical of contemporary life that it could not but be reflected in Irish literature, as it was especially in the earlier stages of the movement. Because many mystics, among them St. John of the Cross, have recognized in the nuptial relation a symbol and sign of that great reality of the spiritual order, the relation between God and the human soul, the modern symbolist, aware only of phenomena on the

material, especially the physical, plane, has reduced all reality
to the sexual experience. As a consequence, such symbolism is
purely arbitrary and esoteric, implying no resemblance between
itself and the thing symbolized. Hence, despite the frequent
use of realistic methods, the general impression is one of un-
reality. There seems no other way of accounting for Mr. Stuart's
failure to convince us that his fleshly mystics are not actually
creatures of flesh and blood.

The Irish novelists who follow fall roughly but definitely into
two classes: the naturalists, who for the most part ignore the
spiritual element in man or, if they recognize it, subject it to the
same realistic treatment which they accord to the physical; and
those who not only recognize a higher reality than the material,
but handle every phase of their theme with the restraint that is
not only characteristically Irish but the final evidence of the
artist's mastery over his material.

The novels of Liam O'Flaherty present a type of realism which
at first sight would seem to be the direct result of Joyce's example,
except that too many other factors enter into it to make such
a derivation tenable. Born in the Aran Islands in 1897 of a Gaelic-
speaking and intensely nationalistic family, he was educated at
Rockwell College, Blackrock, and University College, Dublin,
at first with the intention of entering the priesthood. During
World War I he outraged his family's principles by joining the
British army, but since this act was inspired by the plea of the
Catholic bishops in behalf of Catholic Belgium, it should have
enlisted their sympathies.

Having been shell-shocked, he returned to Ireland, where he
participated in the Easter Rebellion. In August, 1918, as he relates
himself (*Two Years*, 1930), he left home to visit his sister in
Tyrone, but went instead to London, where he worked at menial
jobs until he shipped as a stoker on a steamer bound for Brazil,
eventually landing in Canada. There he worked in lumber camps,
thence slipping across the border into Maine, and finally arriving
at his brother's flat in Roxbury, Massachusetts. It was his brother

who persuaded him that he should write fiction, but his first attempts were completely unsuccessful.

Somewhere along the way, under circumstances which as far as I have been able to discover he does not describe, he had lost his Catholic faith, so that he is able to record with a cold detachment that is almost worse than anger, his "dislike" of "the character and teaching of Jesus Christ." In *I Went to Russia* (1931) he "thanks Heaven" that Bolshevism means no more to him than Lord Beaverbrook's Empire Crusade or the Roman Catholic Religion. Eventually he began to be successful in his literary ventures and is now recognized as an outstanding Irish novelist. The following is a complete list of his works: *Thy Neighbour's Wife; The Black Soul; Spring Sowing* (short stories); *The Informer* (1925); *Mr. Gilhooley* (1926); *The Assassin* (1928); *The Mountain Tavern and Other Short Stories* (1929); *The Puritan* (1932); *Land* (1936); *Famine* (1937); *Two Lovely Beasts* (1948); *Insurrection* (1950).

As might be expected, O'Flaherty's novels and short stories are pervaded by his hatred of all religion, especially the Catholic, by his anti-clericalism, and a moral attitude deriving from his rejection of the Christian code. There is a gross kind of animalism in his treatment of sex, not only in the sordid *Mr. Gilhooley*, the story of an elderly bachelor who is seduced by a girl for her own purposes and who, on discovering her treachery, strangles her, but in such a story as *The Water Hen*, in which his delineation of the sexual relation in water fowl bears a close resemblance to his portrayal of the same experience in human beings.

If Mr. O'Flaherty was unsuccessful in his first literary ventures, however, it was not because he could not write. His style has a kind of stark simplicity which rises in such works as *The Informer*, *Land, Famine*, and *Insurrection*, as well as in some of his short stories, to something approaching grandeur. His writings on the whole are nationalistic, a point on which he differs from Joyce, who came to hate Ireland, but it is certainly part of his intention to show the Church as unsympathetic to nationalism. He writes of the Irish people, mostly the peasantry, from the standpoint of

one who knows their life intimately, and with the technique of
the naturalist who assembles the facts unflinchingly, so that we
are spared nothing of the poverty, the dirt, the squalor which
so often constitute their physical environment. It is never his
intention to depict the spiritual background of those lives, but
occasionally, almost unwillingly, he does it, as in the short stories
Life and *The Old Woman,* in *The Informer,* but above all throughout the terrible chronicle of *Famine.*

O'Flaherty is not the best-qualified person to interpret the
Catholic religion, but he is artist enough, or perhaps Irishman
enough, to realize that the Irish cannot be truly represented
without emphasis on the extent to which that religion is part of
the very texture of their lives, as demonstrated in *The Informer,*
the action of which develops from the fact that the one unfor-
givable crime in Irish eyes is the betrayal of a fellow-Irishman
to the law, its heinousness being partly due to the fact that so
often it had meant the betrayal of the innocent. The consequence
was a sacred unwritten code which protected even the guilty, so
that any violation of the tradition carried with it a terrible stigma,
which caused later generations to endeavour to conceal the fact
that they were of the breed of an informer.

O'Flaherty's book unfolds the terrible, swift-moving story of
Gypo Nolan, offspring of the Dublin slums, driven by hunger to
claim the reward offered by the police for the apprehension of
his friend and fellow-unfortunate, Frankie MacPhillip, wanted
for murder. Both Nolan and MacPhillip have been members of a
group striving pathetically to be Communists and atheists, but
unable, through force of age-long habits of faith, to "leave God
alone." It is a sordid, brutal tale, out of whose very blackness
the compassion which O'Flaherty feels for the physical and
spiritual wrecks who move through its pages gleams resplendently.
Its action, crowded into the hours of a single night, moves with
the relentlessness of a Greek tragedy from scene to scene,—the
horrible lodging house, the filthy streets, the brothel, the cellar
in which Gypo is tried by the "Organization," and from which he
escapes, to the running to ground and shooting of the informer

in the early hours of the morning when the faithful, including Frankie's mother, are at Mass in the church across the road. Out of all that "lowness" emerges a scene which bears comparison with the high peaks of literature, the final scene in which the dying Gypo drags himself to the kneeling figure of Frankie's mother, to fall in a sprawled heap beside her, where he confesses his crime against her, begs her forgiveness and hears her whispered answer, "I forgive ye. Ye didn't know what ye were doin'."

This, and indeed all the concluding passages of the book, could only be the product of a racial consciousness which has clung for centuries to a clearly envisioned spiritual truth and all its consequences. This does not mean that the writer shares that vision, since obviously he does not, but he must at some time have done so or he could not recognize it as so inseparable from the race of which he writes. This book is written for the most part in an appropriately unadorned, almost repellent style, that nevertheless rises at times to heights of beauty and pathos, its tragic occurrences being handled uniformly with the restraint that has come to be characteristic of the typical Irish novelist.

Famine is a book so steeped in agony and horror that one shrinks from the recollection of it as from a ghastly and inhuman reality, despite one's realization that for all its realism it does no more (who could do more?) than adumbrate the truth. The truth is first of all historical fact, although neither this book, nor *Land*, which is concerned with the land agitation of the 'seventies, makes any pretence at being an historical novel, but against the facts of the Black '47 it depicts the heights of patience, heroic self-sacrifice and spiritual splendour to which the Irish people rose.

Related in terms of the Kilmartins, a family of small farmers, already impoverished when the blight strikes the potatoes, it is less melodramatic than *The Informer*, but immeasurably more dramatic, for the swiftness of the action, the beauty of the dialogue, which often enough is the language of people whose poetry of thought is stamped on their English speech, but especially for the stark tragedy of its most memorable episodes. These include the behaviour of Thomsy in dragging himself out to die alone of starvation rather than deprive Mary and her child of the few remnants of food; the utter horror of the scene in which Mary discovers that crazed Sally O'Hanlon has killed her starving children, pleading that she was always a good mother and is still looking after what God sent her; the unutterable pathos of old Brian Kilmartin's farewell to his daughter-in-law when she is about to rejoin her "wanted" husband on the way to America: "When he was going out the door the old man gave her a piece of mortar which he had taken from the wall over the fireplace. 'Give that to Martin,' he said. Then he drew his calloused hands across the child's face."

Although *Insurrection* is concerned with the bloody events of Easter Week, 1916, it is not in any sense an historical novel, much less a political tract. The fact that it is a study of human conduct under the impact of battle may suggest a comparison with *The Red Badge of Courage*, but to pursue such a comparison would be to do a gross injustice to O'Flaherty's masterpiece, which is so much wider in scope and deeper in insight than the American classic.

The theme of *Insurrection* is the portrayal of fear and valour, of courage and cowardice, as reflected in the behaviour of a handful of men involved in the Rising, as well as in the reactions of those who for one reason or another remain uninvolved. In consequence we are afforded glimpses of human nature at its most craven and despicable as well as at the loftiest height of its capacity for greatness. This is especially true of Kinsella, who has had to conquer his own fear in order to become the dauntless personification of an ideal under whose leadership men are eager to die. Although it is not an historical novel, one senses the authenticity with which the events of those terrible days are unfolded, the author's artistry being unforgettably demonstrated in the poignantly brief passage through which Pearse and his companions move to surrender and their doom.

Grim though the chronicle is, it is shot through with gleams of humour unusual in O'Flaherty's work, especially in some of the scenes which portray Mrs. Colgan, the book's supreme achievement in characterization. Its most important figure, however, is Madden, the man from Connemara, "drafted" by Mrs. Colgan for the sole purpose of protecting her son, Tommy, but whom the heroic example of Kinsella awakens to "the exultant satisfaction of the slave who has freed himself from resentment by taking up arms and going forth to do battle for the Idea of freedom." It requires no exceptional astuteness to detect in the memorable conversation between Kinsella and his friend, Stapleton, the dilettante turned rebel, echoes of a remembered knowledge of high spirituality acquired in some early period of the author's life as a Catholic.

The novels of Austin Clarke (*The Bright Temptation* [1932]; *The Singing Men at Cashel* [1936]) resemble his poems in their choice of subjects from the past rather than from the contemporary scene, an extreme naturalism and a poetic style that often becomes entrancingly beautiful. Mr. Clarke, who was born in Dublin in 1896 and educated at Belvedere College and University College, Dublin, is filled with antipathy to the Catholic religion, which inevitably influences his attitude toward morals. In *The Bright Temptation*, for instance, he writes with something like rage of the teaching of the Church on the marital relation, as though the moral law were an invention of the Irish priests. For all its learning and for all its realistic intention, this book is a most unconvincing picture of life in any age and is rightly subtitled "A Romance."

Sean O'Faolain, who was born in Cork, February 22, 1900, and educated at the National University of Ireland, has, for an Irish author, the probably unique distinction of holding a Master's degree from Harvard University, where, according to him, it was earned "mostly by good conversation." He has lectured on English literary subjects at Boston College and at St. Mary's College, Strawberry Hill, near London. He is the author of the following works of fiction: *Midsummer Night Madness* (1932); *A Nest of Simple Folk* (1933); *Bird Alone* (1936); *A Purse of Coppers* (1937); and *The Man Who Invented Sin* (1948).

Cork and its environs provide the background for Mr. O'Faolain's stories, in utilizing which material he displays exceptional skill, although this is a gift which he shares with most Irish novelists, for while there is a wide variety in the locale of their works, they all manifest exceptional sensitiveness in this respect. The result is something far removed from what is known as local colour and must be recognized as singular ability to capture the spirit of place.

The special merit of Mr. O'Faolain's fiction seems to lie here, in his successful re-creation of the background, the atmosphere in the midst of which his characters live out their lives whether in the full-length portrayal of *Bird Alone* or in the swiftly drawn sketches of the short stories for which he is best known. Woven in and out of these lives, as the chief element in that background and atmosphere, is the Catholic religion, although it cannot be said that in his handling of this factor the author is always demonstrably Catholic. He is never irreverent, in the manner of Joyce and O'Flaherty, but he comes close to it, and his attitude on moral questions is, to say the least, casual. Despite the fact that many misconceptions concerning the Church and its practices might well be sustained by some of the situations he depicts, he can, on occasion achieve genuine poignancy by his understanding treatment of the Catholic faith as a factor in Irish life, as when the hero of *Bird Alone* attends Tenebrae, or when in the concluding chapter of that book the same man looks back over his life and realizes that the type of freedom for which he has striven leaves him "free among the dead."

Considerable light is shed on Mr. O'Faolain's treatment of religion as a factor in human life by his diverting travel book, *A Summer in Italy* (1950), in which he describes his own return to the sacrament of Penance after an absence of some years. The joy which is felt in heaven over the return of the prodigal must on this occasion have included no slight degree of amusement over the religious naïveté which impelled him to the step,—the discovery that it is possible for a Catholic to be interesting.

It is true, as Cardinal Newman once said, that you cannot have a sinless literature of sinful men. It is therefore inevitable that the

subject of sinful man should engage the attention of Irish novelists, but since it is equally true that you cannot have great
literature where the subject is treated with a sneer and a shrug,
as it so commonly is by Frank O'Connor (pseudonym of Michael
O'Donovan), one is warranted in entertaining some misgivings
concerning the permanence of his fame. For he enjoys not only
fame but popularity, especially for his short stories, which are
more widely read in the United States than those of some of his
contemporaries who have a deeper understanding of the complexities of human nature. For him these are over-simplified by
being sublimated in the sexual urge.

That, at any rate, is the significance of the title and the contents
of *The Common Chord* (1948), but even when the matter is not
put so bluntly, it is the prevailing tone of his work, so that his
publishers are warranted in describing his characters as "licker-
ish." Besides *The Common Chord* his works include the following
volumes: *The Saint and Mary Kate* (1932); *The Wild Bird's Nest*
(1932); *Bones of Contention* (1936); *Crab Apple Jelly* (1944),
and *Traveller's Samples* (1951). The author, who was born in
Cork in 1903, was educated by the Christian Brothers. He lives
in Dublin, where he follows the profession of librarian.

Besides his skill in handling the technique of the short story,
this author's special gifts include his ability to use dialogue as a
means of keeping the action moving, although his stories are not
on that account dramatic. What he portrays, or professes to portray, is Irish life and character, and his cynical attitude towards
virtue (judging by the article Mr. O'Connor contributed some
months ago to an American travel magazine, he has little faith in
the chastity of Irish women) is, if anything, heightened by the
extent to which his naturalism is mixed with religion, as in the
case of the widower who persuades a "good" girl (one who is
always making novenas) to have the honeymoon first and the
marriage after (*The Holy Door*), and the priest who continues
to make love to a married woman even after the word *Adultery*
has forced him to hear "the loud double knock of the old post-
man conscience" (*The Frying Pan*). What he can achieve when

he turns to other aspects of life and experience is illustrated by *The Long Road to Ummera* (*Crab Apple Jelly*).

From the standpoint of technique, as far as this connotes the essential elements of the novel, Kate O'Brien ranks foremost among contemporary Irish novelists. Born at Boru House, Limerick, in 1898, she was educated at Laurel Hill Convent and University College, Dublin. She now lives in England.

The list of her novels to date is not lengthy, but not one of them is negligible. They were published in the following order: *Without My Cloak* (1931); *The Ante-Room* (1934); *Mary Lavelle* (1936); *The Land of Spices* (1941); *The Last of Summer* (1944); *That Lady* (1946), published in America as *For One Sweet Grape*, the original title having been restored to the dramatic version of the book which was presented on the Broadway stage in 1949.

Miss O'Brien's technical skill is shown first of all in her ability to construct a plot along the lines which have become a literary principle in the English novel, hers being more organic than most Irish novelists devise, or perhaps even attempt to devise, a certain looseness in this matter being in the Irish *shanachie* tradition. Her books are chiefly concerned with the Irish scene, with the portrayal of various types of Irish character whose authenticity seems beyond dispute. She is more than ordinarily successful in reproducing the features of that scene, as she does when Angèle Maury (*The Last of Summer*) stands drinking in all the beauty of the countryside which was her father's birthplace.

She is little concerned, however, with rural Ireland, or its peasantry, although she has achieved some masterly bits of characterization among them. Her attention is centered on members of the prosperous middle class and is therefore generally directed to the comfortable and often luxurious interiors of their homes. Indeed it may come as a surprise to readers of Jane Barlow and the Banims, O'Flaherty and McLaverty, who had no choice but to depict the poverty which was the common Irish lot, to discover that there were people like the Considines and the Kernahans, who enjoyed an abundance of material ease and might have enjoyed intellectual pleasures if their tastes had run to them.

It goes without saying that the Irish of whom she writes are
Catholics, and she writes understandingly, if not always sympa-
thetically, of the part which religion played in their lives. Her
priests and nuns, although sincere and faithful, are somewhat
cloddish, devoid of spiritual light and fire, the one exception
being the English nun, Mother Helen Archer, heroine of *The
Land of Spices*. This, apart from the repulsive episode of her discovery of her father's perversion, is a superb book, and although
it never convinces us that Helen had a religious vocation, at least
it does not imply that all nuns are victims of sexual frustration.

In her scrutiny of the human heart Miss O'Brien displays profound intuition. Above all she understands the passion of love and
is unsurpassed in her portrayal of what are known as love scenes,
as in the interviews between Agnes and Vincent in *The Ante-Room*,
and Ana de Mendoza and Antonio Perez in *That Lady*, illicit
love in both cases. The author fully understands the moral issues
involved in such situations, but her tone is completely detached,
and it cannot be said that conscience and the moral law are de-
ciding factors in either, because, although Agnes has been to
confession and received spiritual direction, the only reason why
she does not elope with her sister's husband is because she does
not want to hurt her sister's feelings, while Ana's liaison has been
forcibly broken off by the king.

A close study of Miss O'Brien's novels convinces us that, unlike
most naturalists, she has a spiritual sense, but it likewise forces us
to the paradoxical conclusion that despite this spiritual outlook
she lacks a sense of the supernatural. Certainly she practically
ignores it. She recognizes the spiritual element in man, even
when he is a sinner, but she does not, except in one instance, and
that almost incidentally, recognize sin for what it is, an offense
against the majesty of God. This is so common a reaction among
Irish Catholics that some explicit recognition of it would not
seem to be forcing the issue.

Miss O'Brien may be the greatest of Irish novelists, and yet her
greatest novel is not Irish in the sense of dealing with an Irish
theme. It is the book (*That Lady*) in which she tells the story,
wholly fictitious although set against an historical background,

of the beautiful Ana de Mendoza, Princess of Eboli, who in St. Teresa's account of her assumes such formidable proportions. This episode precedes the opening of the story and St. Teresa does not appear in it at all, although Miss O'Brien had already shown her fitness to deal with this subject by her book of memorable travel sketches, *Farewell, Spain* (1937), in which she pays such understanding tribute to the great Spanish mystic, whom she calls "a genius of the large and immeasurable kind of which there have been very few, and only one of them a woman," even though at the same time she gives it as her opinion that Teresa would have been on the side of the Loyalists in the Civil War.[4]

In the novel, the Princess is still formidable for her beauty, pride and self-will, and she deliberately enters upon a passionate love affair with the King's secretary of State, a protege of her dead husband and a married man. When Philip II discovers the intrigue he visits both of them with his anger, her punishment consisting in life-long imprisonment which finally becomes solitary confinement. At first she is persuaded that sin is something invented by the theologians, "nervous old men" like the King's confessor, but at last, although she continues to love Antonio, her "long-trained conscience" fights against her and she is able to say to her lover, "My soul has no place in your arms." Even then she is still a long way from moral victory and serenity of spirit, but at last, in the course of a marvellous interview with Cardinal de Quiroga, who visits her in her imprisonment, she reveals the anguish of her soul and her clear-eyed perception of her guilt: "I have not sinned," she says, "without all my wits about me."

On the other hand, the Cardinal tells her that in her foolish sinful life he has sometimes seemed to catch intimations of "what

[4] As this book goes to press Miss O'Brien has published under the title of *Teresa of Avila* a brief but brilliant study of the great Carmelite as a woman of genius. She ranks Teresa with Sappho and Emily Brontë as "the only female geniuses of our recorded knowledge in history," but although she necessarily recognizes sanctity as an element of Teresa's genius, she protests that she is not writing of her as a saint, which seems to substantiate what I have said above concerning the paradoxical character of Miss O'Brien's attitude towards the supernatural.

I apprehend by God's love." The book ends on a triumphant note
when Ana confides to her daughter that she now realizes the
greatness of her indebtedness to Philip who, she is convinced, has
saved her soul.

Among the writers whose work demonstrates the artistic possibilities of understatement is Seumas O'Kelly, already mentioned
as attracting favourable attention as a playwright with *The
Shuiler's Child*. Born at Loughrea in 1881, O'Kelly, who died in
1918, was educated at St. Brendan's College in his native town,
and after engaging in newspaper work, went to Dublin, where he
participated in the theatre movement. His narrative writing,
which is similar in theme to his plays, consists for the most part
of tales or short stories, represented by volumes entitled *Way-
siders, Stories of Connacht* (1917), *The Hillsiders* (1921), por-
traying the same background, and *The Golden Barque*, with
which is included *The Weaver's Grave* (1919). O'Kelly's work is
not symbolic, except in the sense that what he says fills the reader
with an unutterable realization of what he has not said, because
he achieves the artistic paradox of seeing life at close range, yet
depicting it in perspective. His plots are negligible, his characterization almost impressionistic, but with what seems like a
minimum of effort he achieves an incalculable effect, which is
nothing less than the interpretation of life as overwhelmingly
though ineffectually beautiful. This is particularly well exemplified in *The Golden Barque*, the story of the love that blossoms
but never blooms between Michael, a hand on a canal boat, the
"golden barque," and Mary, a dweller beside the canal upon
which it passes. Recognizing no portent of disaster, she is touched
when Michael confides to her, "The wide ocean is lovely. I always
think of the wide ocean going over the bog." Mary waits one day
for the passing of the barque, only to discover that Michael is no
longer aboard, since he has answered the call of the "wide ocean"
and gone voyaging. The barque passes, leaving the girl standing
at the lock: "She stayed there until a pale moon was shining
below her, turning over a little trinket in her fingers. At last she

dropped it into the water. It made a little splash and the vision of the crescent was broken."

The marvellous dialogue between the two old men engaged in the search for the weaver's grave at Cloon na Morav helps to accentuate in that story the sense of remote antiquity and almost prehistoric custom that is of the very essence of life in Ireland, while the scene between the weaver's widow and the young grave-digger is a reminder of the extent to which everywhere in the midst of death we are in life.

Daniel Corkery, professor at the University of Cork, is a writer of unusual versatility and distinction who has already been repeatedly referred to in these pages. His work, for all its distinctive individuality, bears unmistakably upon it the mark of Padraic Pearse, which is a character of which he would probably be the first to boast, because of course it is a mark that does not to the very slightest extent consist in imitation.

He is the author of *Hy Bhreasil* (1921), a book of lyrics upon whose rhythms the influence of the Gaelic is plainly discernible, although he is equally successful in the use of English metres. His scholarship is unostentatiously demonstrated in *The Hidden Ireland* (1925), a masterly study of the Gaelic poets during the penal times, which is indispensable to the student and a delight to the general reader, both for the interest of its contents and its felicities of style, as when he writes of the hedge poets, "The charms of natural things, so intimately a part of the consciousness of the ancient Gaels, were hidden from them as in a mist of sorrow." Learning is likewise everywhere evident in *Synge and Anglo-Irish Literature* (1931), a penetrating and temperate study of an exceedingly vexed question. In all these books the proof of professor Corkery's artistry is indisputable, but it is especially in his creative work, in his one novel and his short stories, that its essence is truly revealed.

The Threshold of Quiet (1917) is written to the text of Thoreau's statement that "The mass of men lead lives of quiet desperation," words to which, it need scarcely be said, Corkery attaches a meaning far beyond any conception of Thoreau's. For in the phrase, "quiet desperation," what Corkery stresses is the quiet, first the quiet of Cork city, especially of its hillsides, where one encounters "the very fruitage of the spirit of contemplation." It is this quiet which constitutes the soul of Corkery's art, the half-said thing of the ancient Gaels, whether we become aware of it in the lives of "the handful of wayfaring souls," so elusively presented in the novel, or in the figures whom we glimpse in the sketches of *A Munster Twilight* (1916); *The Hounds of Banba* (1920); *Earth out of Earth* (1939); *The Stormy Hills*. Corkery's is the very antithesis of the so-called realistic method, which labours under the delusion that to accumulate all the external data concerning a man is to present the living man himself. Virginia Woolf reasoned more soundly when, in criticism of the method as employed by Arnold Bennett, she pointed out how much of the real man eludes such efforts, but the only improvement she could suggest was the addition of fresh data, of another sort, it is true, but assembled in the same scientific spirit, whereas Corkery and those who share his conception of reality realize that no man is ever truly known except to God. For the most part life is a matter of half-words and broken glimpses, glimpses of souls, which perhaps gaze from eyes too familiar to us to be perceived, which sound in a voice heard in a crowd of strangers, are watched wonderingly or perhaps noted not at all, because they are masks, in habits that have been formed upon our own. It is this sense, a sense of the sacredness and inscrutability of human life which he shares with Virgil, that constitutes the greatness of Daniel Corkery. It is a greatness that may never be universally recognized and acclaimed, because it is not flagrant, nor sensational, nor hot upon the tongue, but unquestionably it will endure.

Until the publication of his most recent book, *The Fire in the Dust* (1951), one would have accorded to Francis MacManus a foremost place among the masters of restraint, those who with the ancient Irish relished "the half-said thing," which is surely what Dante meant by "the curb of art."

The Hidden Ireland as expressed in the life of the Munster

poet and "luckless fellow," Donnacha Ruadh Mac Conmara, is the subject of his trilogy, *Stand and Give Challenge* (1935); *Candle for the Proud* (1936); and *Men Withering* (1940), of which the last is perhaps the most powerful. That is because the others stand to it in the relation of first and second acts of a tragedy, a tragedy of waste and frustration whose descending action moves to a dénouement which is not tragic but triumphant.

The story opens with Donnacha's return to Ireland after dismissal from a seminary in Rome in which he has demonstrated his complete unfitness for the priesthood. The Ireland to which he returns is that of the penal times whose hardships he is exceptionally unfitted to endure, because his clear mind shows them to him in all their injustice and that injustice in all its heinousness, thus engendering resentment in his fiery nature, so that he is in constant rebellion against "the insults that come after the evil deeds." His violence is somewhat subdued by the love of Maire, who becomes his wife only to enable her death, as a consequence of poverty, to become for him a fresh disaster.

Candle for the Proud resumes the story at a point twenty years after Maire's death, by which time Donnacha's struggle is not only with the penal laws, in consequence of which he is reduced to beggary, but with the powers of darkness, in consequence of which he is reduced to temporary apostasy. How little this is of mind or heart is shown in the scenes in which, with all his natural powers aroused and his faith aflame, he struggles to rescue the priest from hanging.

The third volume brings Donnacha through the humiliation of weakness, blindness and decline to the last anointing and a death in which there is something of exaltation: "This, he thought, is no hosting for Charon, no mobbing of souls in a frenzy of fear and longing, but the ample, compassionate companionship of the dead coming for one of their own, and he began to pray, gathering up his powers to a pin-point as a man musters up his strength and bunches his muscles to crash from the ring of his enemies."

The earlier MacManus novels include *This House was Mine,* a study of avarice which is no mere sermon; *The Wild Garden,* the story of a gifted child's terrible encounter with a cruelty that amounts to madness; *Flow On, Lovely River,* which portrays a schoolmaster's love for a girl whose ineligibility is recognized by all his world; and *Water Gate,* in which an enterprising Irish woman returned from America undertakes to set her family's house in order, succeeding in one of the strangest struggles between woman and woman, only to find that getting what she wanted constitutes an even bigger problem. *Pedlar's Pack* is a Miscellany of this author's work, which includes a handful of poems and several tales, these in the manner which is becoming so typical of the Irish school of fiction.

These qualities are so magnificently combined in his *The Greatest of These,* as to constitute it his greatest novel. It would be difficult to deal adequately with this book. The bald statement that it is the story of a bishop and a silenced priest does not do it anything like justice, especially if the element of the sensational, which is unquestionably there, is seized upon as indicative of its character. For there is nothing sensational or even exciting about it.

It was through the good offices of the priest, then in the first flush of characteristic zeal, that the bishop was led in boyhood to the priestly vocation, and it is through the bishop, elderly and ailing, that the aged priest is restored to his forfeited priestly estate. This is not a book to be evaluated by the standards of Hollywood, with its tendency to deal in external incident, its partiality for sound and fury and colossal size, because the events with which it deals occur within the arena of the spirit. When St. Paul asked "What man knoweth the things of a man but the spirit of man that is in him?" it was because he realized how unutterable such things are, how inscrutable is the human soul. Out of a kindred wisdom Francis MacManus deals here with the things of a man, God's man, a priest, veiling his own scrutiny before that soul, and yet revealing its greatness and its littleness, its amplitude and its narrowness, not in the merciless light of so-called realism, but in such gleams and glimpses as those in which it shows itself, even to itself. And throughout this process, the same restraint, the same persistent muting prevails that we have seen to be characteristic of those of the later Irish novelists who are most essentially Irish.

The pattern of *The Greatest of These* suggests a musical composition; despite its brevity it might be compared to a symphony, opening as it does with the chiming of all the church bells of the city, in a way which not only sets the theme of the book, but becomes the tempo of its action. The marvel is that although that action is concerned with the soul's innermost arcanum, the author does not rush into that sanctuary, but, kneeling, makes way for God.

After this, it is disappointing to have to record that *The Fire in the Dust* is decidedly inferior to its predecessors among MacManus's novels. The "fire" emanates from the Golden family, consisting of the much-travelled, philandering father, Mark, his daughter, Maria, her illegitimate child, Joannie, and his young son, Stevie, a boy of considerable force of character, intelligence and charm, mature and sophisticated beyond his years. The "dust" is provided by the people of a small Irish town in which the Goldens take up their residence.

The story, which is related by Larry Hackett, a contemporary of Stevie's who becomes his friend, brings into conflict two views of life, the hedonism of the Goldens as typified by Botticelli's *Birth of Venus,* and the narrow moralistic views of the townspeople. It is not a naturalistic novel, but it is a plea for naturalism as preferable to the morbid preoccupation with sex as typified by the town boys, and especially by the perverted piety of Miss Dreelin, a specimen of Freudian frustration who sets her affections, not without encouragement from him, on Mr. Golden, and brings stark tragedy crashing into all their lives.

It is not only that the story is confused and the characters, with the exception of "dumpy, waddling, benign, God-loving Katie," are dimly realized. Where the book fails in artistry is in the fact that it is a piece of special pleading whose thesis is that the attitude towards sex which is characteristic of the townspeople, especially Miss Dreelin, is the result of their upbringing as Catholics. It is an attitude which, as Stevie confides to the school-master, is unhealthy and hateful. But Stevie was too young to realize what Mr. MacManus must know perfectly well, that "Miss Dreelin and other people like her," do not represent the Catholic teaching on sex.

Between the work of Corkery and that of Michael McLaverty there is a certain affinity, although Corkery depicts the South with which he is familiar, and McLaverty the North where he was born, especially the vicinity of Belfast, where he received his education, at St. Malachy's College and Queen's University, from which last he was graduated in 1933. The passage which he quotes from an anonymous source as the text of *The Three Brothers* might well serve the same purpose for everything he has written: "Sorrow and suffering and joy are three strands in the tether of God; sorrow and suffering strengthen fervour and joy strengthens hope. Without fervour and without hope the spirit breaks loose, and when the spirit breaks loose from the tethering Man roams like an animal without a home."

It is in the light of that great realization that Michael McLav-erty sees life, sees man, and it is because he sees them so that he is able to portray them as he does, with such economy of means, so unforgettably and without one syllable of moralizing or sen-timentality. This is his procedure in *Call My Brother Back* (1939), the story of the way in which the boyhood hopes of Colum Mac-Neill were brought to a tragic end by the shooting down of his elder brother in the horrible religious warfare that in Belfast was a preliminary to the partitioning of Ireland; in *Lost Fields* (1941), the pathetic chronicle of a family compelled by poverty to bring the old grandmother from her cottage in the country to share their life in the city because of the assistance her meagre pension will bring to them; *In This Thy Day* (1947), the tale of a pair of lovers whose love is kept from fruition by the cross-grained character of the young man's mother, who finds her ultimate vic-tory turned to dust and ashes in her mouth; *The Three Brothers* (1948), a study of the assorted temperaments that make up a single family in a small town in County Antrim. These traits are, if anything, accentuated in the short stories published under the title *The Game Cock and Other Stories* (1947). A first or a casual reading of these books might convey the impression that they are marked by a certain sombreness, but apart from the fact that they are not devoid of humour, as in the figure of the "Curate" in *This Thy Day*, so called because the priest's outworn garments are his only wear, and an abundance of salt in the dialogue, they contain not the slightest intimation of anything remotely resembling despair. Their theme is not only sorrow and suffering, but the joy that results from understanding we are not as they that have no hope.

For the title of his most recent novel, *Truth in the Night* (1951), Mr. McLaverty has gone to a sublime source, the poem in which the Psalmist exclaims "It is good. . . . to show forth Thy mercy in the morning and Thy truth in the Night." It tells the story of a self-centered, self-willed woman who comes to the wisdom of self-knowledge in the course of a single night, a night so packed with suffering, mostly of her own making, that it is impossible not to be struck by the resemblance between her experience and the dark night of the soul, although the author never intimates such a thing, nor perhaps, for all the profound spiritual insight revealed in his book, did he even intend it.

The scene of its action is an island in the region which Mr. McLaverty knows so intimately and understands so well, Northern Ireland. It is peopled by characters whom he draws to the life, men and women who are not angels, but whose human faults and weaknesses are lifted out of the muck of animalism by the breath of the supernatural with which the religion they so simply profess suffuses their nostrils. They are all vividly and memorably portrayed, but it is not so much the younger folk, interesting though they are, with their loves and their jealousies, their gayety and their quarrels, who cling to the memory, as the noble figure of the aging Mrs. Reilly, striving so pathetically to win a meed of happiness for her beloved son's forgetful widow. She is unforgettable.

A word must be said here of the style in which Mr. McLaverty's artistry is chiefly but unobtrusively shown. Of this style he is now complete master, making it serve all the purposes of his creative will, and they are various and high. By this means he breathes life into his characters, evoking at the same time the details of their background, in this book the smallness of the island which they inhabit and the vastness of the sea with which they contend. By it he fashions a dialogue so picturesque yet so authentic that we cannot but wonder whether this is not what Synge was aiming at in the speech which he puts into the mouths of his Aran Islanders.

Like McLaverty, Bernard Kiely, already mentioned in these pages as the author of a discerning Life of Carleton, is a native of the North of Ireland, where he was born in the County Tyrone in 1919. A graduate of the National University of Ireland, he has engaged in various literary and journalistic ventures, but he is primarily a novelist and a distinguished one.

His novels include *Land without Stars, In a Harbour Green* (1950) and *Call for a Miracle* (1951). In the handling of his material he is much more concerned with the physical aspects of sex than is McLaverty, but his books are none the less filled with a profound sense of spiritual values, an awareness of the importance of moral issues. More than most of his contemporaries he seems conscious of the "tears in things," the extent to which they are the result of man's moral failure, the sadness which attaches to the experience of seeing "the end of all perfection."

His *Modern Irish Fiction* (1950), a critical survey of the subject since 1918, should be in the hands of every serious student of contemporary literature. It is authoritative, spirited and sound. This does not imply complete agreement with all his opinions, but certainly they deserve respect.

Like most Irishmen, especially the novelists, Mr. Kiely writes the English language with a combination of power and magic charm that unquestionably derive from a racial heritage, a fact which gives special significance to a passage in *Call for a Miracle,* in which the hero, Brian Flood, recalling Pearse's expectation of a miracle that would make Ireland Gaelic and make it free, comments, "Miracles don't happen any more, for Ireland is not Gaelic and no one is free."

There is no disputing the truth of this statement, since Ireland is not wholly Gaelic and it is not completely free, but surely there is an element of the miraculous in the fact that the Voice of the Irish is once more making itself heard through the medium of literature. After centuries during which it was stifled in a throttled throat, reduced to a whisper behind the hedge, used only for the expression of resentment or of woe ("All mourners of the world weep Irish"), and hushed at last into ignominious silence, the Voice of the Irish is once more audible, not only in Ireland but throughout the cultivated world. Compelled to the use of an alien tongue, it has woven the syllables of that tongue into another harmony, the harmony of a beautiful and virile prose. Surely the people who have fashioned this noble instrument will not put it to debased or ignoble use, but employ it for the utterance of things to which the world will eagerly listen, as St. Patrick listened more than fifteen hundred years ago. After all, the Voice is still the Voice of the Irish, and the Irish above all people have learned Truth in the Night.

INDEX

Abbey Theatre, 185 sqq., 202, 253
255, 256-277, 278n.
Absentee, the, novel, 112
Absenteeism, 84
Acaill, Book of, 25
Acta Sanctorum Hiberniae; Colgan,
74
Actors, Irish, 260
Adamnan, St., Abbot of Iona, 39,
175, 180
Adventure of Suibhne Geilt; Colum,
239
Adventures of a Luckless Fellow, 176
AE; see Russell, George
Aebhinn, fairy, 197
Aeneid, Irish translation, 46
Aengus, god of youth, 11, 214, 225
Aengus the Culdee, 39
Aisling, poem, 98, 99, 262
Albanach, O'Daly, 56
Alcala, Irish college, 67
Alcuin, at Clonmacnoise, 39
Allingham, William, poet, 170-171
Alphabetical Hymn, early Irish, 175
Amergin, legendary figure, 2, 4, 11,
15
Ana, Goddess; see Dana, 11
Anann, war goddess, 11
An Chraobhin Aoibhin, 165, 190, 213
Ancient Irish Music; Bunting, 127
Ancient Irish Poetry; Meyer, 180
Ancient Legends of Ireland; Wilde,
183
Ancient Music of Ireland; Petrie, 138
Anglo-Normans, invasion of Ireland,
52
Anima Mundi, Yeats's theory, 215
Anna Livia Plurabella; Joyce, 297

Annals, of Flann of Monasterboice,
49
Annals of Ireland, 43, 71
Annals of the Four Masters; see
Four Masters
Annals of the Kingdom of Ireland;
see Four Masters
Annual Register, periodical, 133
Anspach, Professor, anthologist, 61n.
Ante-Room, The, novel, 310, 311
Anthologia Hibernica, 72
Anthology of Irish Verse; Colum,
239
Anthropology, and Irish Studies, 179,
182
Antient Concert Rooms, Dublin, 259
Aran Islands, 266, 267
Aran Mor, island, 38
Arbois de Jubainville, Henri d', 2n.
6n., 16, 180
Archaeological Society, Irish, 173
Ardagh Chalice, 44
Arduchar, 197
Armada, Spanish, 73
Armagh, 38, 174
Arrah-na-Pogue, play, 256
Aryan Origins of the Irish Race;
Bourke, 182, 183
Ascendancy, The, 82-93, 220
Assaroe, 197
Assassin, The, novel; O'Flaherty, 303
Atkinson, Robert, scholar, 76
At the Hawk's Well; Yeats, 262
Automatic writing; see Yeats's work,
216
Autumn Fire, drama, 270
Avatars, The; Russell, 223
Avenging and Bright, poem, 131
Axel's Castle; Wilson, 215, 220

321